Table of Contents

Section 1

1. Foundations of Youth Ministry
   by Dennis Miller 8
2. A Philosophy of Youth Ministry
   by Dennis Miller 12
3. Principles of Youth Ministry
   by Dennis Miller 17
4. Youth Work—a Network of Relationships
   by Ray Willey with Randy Sykes 22
5. The Intern Program
   by Bill Stewart 24
6. Recruiting Youth Sponsors
   by Phil D. Kennemer 27
7. Equipping Leaders
   by Joseph C. Aldrich 30

Section 2

8. The Care and Feeding of the Volunteer
   Youth Worker
   by Gary Downing 34
9. The Support Team
   by Chris Renzelman 37
10. Developing a Team Ministry
    by Tim Kimmel 39
11. Student Leadership
    by Jana Sundene with Dan Webster 43
12. Leading and Motivating Students
    by Chuck Klein 45
13. The Parent Factor
    by John Miller 48

Section 3

14. Discipleship
    by Barry St. Clair 52
15. Discipling—a Holistic Ministry
    by Chuck Miller 57
16. Evangelism
    by Mark Gold 60
17. Training Youth for Evangelism
    by John Musselman 62
18. Full-cycle Evangelism
    by Don Cousins 65
19. Youth Trends (An Analysis of Youth in the Church)
    by Pat Hurley 68
20. The American Student—Misery in the "Me" Generation
    by Dawson McAllister 74

21. State of the Youth
      by Dan Maltby 77
22. Campus Ministry
      by Keith Braley 79
23. Access to the Public Campus (Knowing Your Legal Rights)
      by John Whitehead 83

Section 4

24. Financing the Youth Program
      by Leland A. Hamby, Jr. 88
25. Publicizing Youth Activities
      by Mark Zier 91
26. Reaching Youth through Music
      by John Bowers 93
27. Music or Missions?
      by Keith Green 96
28. Involving Youth in Missions
      by Mel Bittner 98
29. Designing a Christian Camp Program
      by Richard McFarland 100

Section 5

30. The Youth Worker and the Church
      by James Borror 104
31. Youth Ministry and Christian Education
      by George Hreha 107
32. The Interdenominational Youth Organization (A Resource for Reaching
      the World's Youth)
      by Paul Fleischmann 109
33. The Youth Worker and the Christian College
      by Catherine J. Foote 116

Section 6

34. The Imperative of Bible Study
      by John MacArthur 122
35. Informal Youth Bible Study
      by Larry Richards 124
36. Preparing Messages That Meet Needs
      by Bill Perkins 129
37. Discouragement and the Youth Worker
      by Alan Hlavka 132
38. Prayer and the Youth Worker
      by Curtis Mitchell 135
39. Trusting God for the Impossible
      by Bill Perkins 139

Foreword

Developing spiritually mature young people is not an easy task in today's pressurized world. Young people face pressures that undermine the very bases of Christian convictions. And church youth programs face intense competition from the media, entertainment, and school programs. These problems are compounded by the fact that, often, pastors and youth workers are trained theologically, but lack experience in the non-theological, or methodological, aspects of youth ministry.

In my extensive traveling, I have had the privilege of observing a wide variety of effective youth ministries. I am a more effective Christian and youth speaker as a result of my personal acquaintance with the ministries of many of the leaders involved in writing this handbook. And I have long felt that the vision and effectiveness of pastors and youth workers would be increased, as has mine, by exposure to the ministries of these key leaders. Of course, it is impossible for most youth workers to visit these ministries and talk with all these leaders. Therefore, *Working with Youth* provides the next best thing—it brings these people and their ministry insights to the youth worker.

Contributors to this comprehensive youth ministry handbook have been selectively chosen to write in the area of their expertise. They have been chosen because of the variety of their ministry experiences, educations, and church affiliations, and because they are committed to a biblical model of youth ministry. Many of these leaders I have known personally through the years. I have been impressed not only by their effective, God-honoring ministries, but also by their personal walks with Jesus Christ.

Set forth in *Working with Youth* are the basic principles pertaining to youth ministry. These principles are presented in such a practical form, reinforced by personal experience, that you will find this handbook to be a valuable enrichment to your own ministry with youth. This work will be an asset, not only to the pastor and youth director, but also to the Sunday School teacher, youth sponsor, and lay volunteer.

—Josh McDowell

Preface

The idea of putting together a handbook for youth workers started with a personal need. I had often looked for materials to help me as a youth worker—and found that few were available. Seeing the need for such a tool, I eventually decided to compile *Working with Youth*. As I began contacting potential writers, I communicated to them my idea of assembling a resource that would help *volunteer* and *professional* youth workers—anyone who ministers to youth. I also began to form some additional objectives. I wanted the book to be . . .

▶ **COMPREHENSIVE** *Working with Youth* is the work of 38 contributors from local church and parachurch ministries, each writing in his particular area of expertise.

▶ **THOROUGH** Each chapter builds on the preceding one. Beginning chapters deal with foundational areas. Subsequent chapters "fan out" to cover the gamut of youth ministry concerns.

▶ **PRACTICAL** Though the chapters compliment each other, each can be profitably read alone. *Working with Youth* is the kind of resource you'll want to keep and refer to again and again as particular needs arise.

My thanks go to those Christian men and women whose support, financial and otherwise, made this project possible—especially Charlie and Ann Bowles, John and Doris Crain, David and Mary Dean, Bill and Connie Brown, Alane LeGrand, and Bill McKee.

—Ray Willey

Section 1

"A relational thinker relates all programs and activities to the ultimate objective—the development of discipled students."

—D. Miller

1 Foundations of Youth Ministry

by Dennis Miller

Dennis Miller is founder and president of Church Youth Development, Inc., an organization that assists the local church in developing effective ministries to youth. Before starting this consultant ministry, Dennis served for 16 years on the staff of Campus Crusade for Christ, International. His responsibilities there included stints as national director of Church Youth Development and as high school coordinator of Here's Life America. He is author of Youth Worker's Notebook and Youth Director's Notebook. For information about Church Youth Development, Inc., contact: Church Youth Development, P.O. Box 652, Brentwood, TN 37027.

The siren song of youth ministry today is: "I do it *this* way. You do it this way too, and you'll be successful like I am."

Such a claim rarely holds up because every church, every youth ministry, is different. Each ministry has its "fingerprint," its uniqueness.

The leadership style of the youth worker is unique. The students being served are unique. The culture of the area is unique. The style of the senior pastor is unique. The movement of God's Spirit in a particular church is unique. As a result, every youth ministry must be developed through a unique application of ministry principles.

If youth ministries are all so different, how can a youth worker find a model of ministry that he can follow? Are model ministries even important? Of course they are. It's helpful to see how the Holy Spirit at work through a particular youth ministry has made it successful. But in evaluating any ministry, it's important to look for the underlying *principles*, not at the *program* and its activities. Principles of ministry are universally applicable. Programs are not.

When a youth worker realizes that individual ministries are unique like fingerprints, he stops seeking the perfect program—the program that he may have hoped would make his youth ministry look successful like some other ministry he knows about. Instead, he begins to look to the Lord and ask, "Father, what do You want done in *my* church with its unique needs and characteristics?"

So, a foundational truth of youth ministry is: *Every youth ministry is unique.*

Youth-centered Ministry

Another foundational truth of youth ministry is: *Youth ministry exists to serve youth.* As a youth worker consultant, I've seen ministries preoccupied with events, activities, youth choirs, projects—ministries preoccupied with nearly everything except the students. I spend most of my time helping youth workers understand how the activities of their programs can relate to the development of their students.

Too many youth workers have never asked these basic questions: Who is serving whom? Does a youth ministry exist for the youth worker's growth and development? Are the students his servants? Do they exist to make him successful in his life and ministry? Or does the youth worker exist to help students be successful in their lives and ministries?

The following cartoon illustrates what happens when youth ministries do not exist to serve youth.

Now answer these questions: What is the youth worker doing? What are the students doing? What's happening to the ship? What reason does the youth worker have for directing this activity?

Youth ministries often fall prey to the problem depicted in this cartoon. Their leaders have little or no idea *why* they are doing what they do. They are involved in *activities for activities' sake*.

A discouraged youth worker in north Florida explained to me how he'd had Bible study till his kids lost interest. Then he had tried nearly every program and activity imaginable till his kids would no longer attend any activity, "not even miniature golf."

We made a list of the activities he had directed during the year. Then I asked him to look at each activity and answer, "Who is this activity for? Is it for the youth, or for you?"

For each activity, he answered, "the youth."

Than I asked, "How did you intend the youth to benefit from each of these activities?"

"That I don't know," he admitted. He'd fallen into the trap of directing *activities for activities' sake*.

Youth ministry does not exist to provide a career for anyone. Rather, its existence makes it possible for a youth worker to join with the Holy Spirit in the process of developing discipled students.

Goal-directed Programming

A third building block in the foundation of every youth ministry should be: *It's not what we do that's important, but how we use what we do.* It can be humbling to realize it, but what we do in ministry is not the focus or even the means of blessing in that ministry. We and our activities are, at best, instruments for God's use in the lives of youth. The importance of any activity should be based on *how the*

activity can facilitate the growth and development of students.

How many activities have you directed this month? How many of those activities were planned to accomplish specific goals in the lives of your students?

Developing a Personal Vision

A fourth foundational truth is: *Every youth worker needs a vision*.

The word *vision* has several meanings. But here's a working definition of the word as it pertains to ministry. Developing a personal *vision* is *discerning specific Scriptures and experiences used by God in your life to help develop convictions concerning your ministry*.

The key word translated *vision* in the Old Testament comes from the Hebrew word *chazah*. It means "to gaze at, to mentally perceive, to con-

template."[1] God has placed His desires in you through the Scriptures, through experiences, and through the testimony of people. You develop a personal vision as you "gaze at" and "contemplate" what God has communicated to you of His desires. So developing a personal vision is coming to know God's desires for your life and ministry.

The Personal Vision Worksheet at the end of this chapter can help you develop vision in three dimensions: past, present, and future.

The *past* dimension relates, of course, to things that God has done in the past that have helped form the desires of your heart: for example, the desire to work with youth or to be in

full-time ministry.

Developing vision in the *present* dimension involves developing confidence in God's calling to your present place of ministry. Ask yourself: How did God convince me that this is where I should be? Was it through Scripture: Was it through the testimony of the deacons? Why am I here?

It's also important to develop a personal vision of what God may be designing for the *future* of your ministry.

The past, present, and future then are all involved in developing a personal vision. But how can having a personal vision benefit you?

For one thing, it can give a direction and focus to your youth ministry that will affect the lives of students. Secondly, it can give you confidence in your calling. The average stay of a full-time youth pastor in America in only about one year. In some denominations, the average stay is only nine months. Some youth workers go into other types of ministry, but the most common reason for leaving is an un-

certainty concerning their callings. Knowing that you are called by God to serve in your present ministry (whether you're a professional or a lay youth worker) can give you confidence in working with staff, parents, and students.

Developing a Transferable Vision

A fifth foundational truth is: *A youth worker's vision should be transferable.*

The following illustration depicts a syndrome which is all too prevalent in youth ministry. Please observe it carefully.

> *"The importance of any activity should be based on how it can facilitate the growth and development of students."*

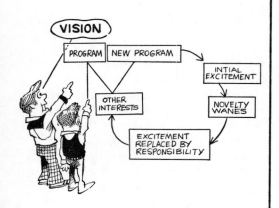

Now answer these questions: To what is the youth worker most passionately committed—program or vision? To what is the student committed?

Let's assume the unusual, that the youth worker has a clearly defined vision. Let's also assume for the sake of illustration that this youth worker began the program in order to fulfill his vision—his understanding of God's desires for the ministry he is leading. With these assumptions in mind, think about and answer the following questions: How does the youth worker view the program? How does the student view the program?

I've often been surprised and disappointed when a student who appeared to be deeply committed to a program suddenly dropped out. But God has used those disappointments

to point out an important principle: *When a person is asked to be committed to a program alone, his involvement only lasts till his excitement wanes.*

Consider an example which is probably familiar to most youth workers: Joe, the youth leader, starts a choir that he thinks will help fulfill his vision of developing ministry-minded students. Bob, the student, sees the choir only as a program. He doesn't have the slightest idea of Joe's vision. After a while, Bob begins to get tired of all the practice. The novelty wears off, and he just isn't motivated or interested in attending choir anymore. Soon Bob joins a skydiving club that meets during choir rehearsal.

Joe is left scratching his head. After a few more people drop out, he begins to look for a new program and settles on a series of inter-church socials. He calls Bob and shares the exciting new program. Bob gets excited again and agrees to drop his skydiving. The cycle begins again. This cycle can happen over and over, from pro-

gram to program, till the activities no longer relate to the vision at all.

Can you imagine students agreeing to the standards of a program without a vision? Stop and think about what is expected of Christian students today. They are told, "All your money belongs to Christ. Your relationships with the opposite sex belong to Him.

"When a student is asked to be committed to a program alone, his involvement only lasts till his excitement wanes."

You should share the Gospel with your peers." Such demands require commitment to a compelling vision, not primarily to programs.

Besides developing a personal vision for ministry (based on the unique needs and abilities of his students), a youth worker should be able to share that vision with his students and challenge them with commitment to it. Vision should be transferable. □

[1]*Strong's Lexicon* quote from *Hebrew & Chaldean Dictionary* (McLean, Virginia. MacDonald Publishing Co.), p. 38.

Personal Vision Worksheet
Perceiving God's Desires for the Past, Present, and Future

EXPERIENCES IN THE PAST

> NOTE: Try to remember specific circumstances and Bible passages that God used in the past to reveal His desires for your life. Doing this can assure you that your involvement in youth ministry is *by God's design, not just coincidence.* Identifying specific experiences will remind you that your confidence is in the *fact* that God has led you.

Questions to ask yourself:

...What specific circumstances and Scriptures has God used in the past to conform my desires to His?

...What happened in my life that made me want to work with students?

...Did any one person show me a need in the youth culture or motivate me to work with students?

...Did any Scriptures influence me to become a youth worker?

CALLING FOR THE PRESENT

The present refers to the time you have been in your present position. Many people talk about being called to their present place of work. The question is, "How did you know that God wanted you to take this position?"

> NOTE: Think through specific reasons why you accepted the invitation to serve in your present position. If you remember Scriptures and circumstances with which God led you, you can know you are ministering where God wants you. You can be confident that you're in God's will. You can have faith to believe God for meeting your present needs.

EXPECTATIONS AND DREAMS FOR THE FUTURE

> NOTE: Your faith will be fresh and growing when you have a dream for the future and keep it before you. Your faith will excite and increase your students' faith.

The future dimension could be called "dreaming in the Spirit," allowing the Holy Spirit to expand your thoughts about the future. Not everything you daydream about will come true, but it's important that you dream!

> KEY POINT: Allow God to sharpen those dreams which are according to His will. A person with no hopes beyond his present situation can easily lose sight of his purpose in life and become program-centered.

When you have fulfilled God's call to minister to students in your present ministry, what do you visualize having happened through that ministry?

How much of this visualization are you willing to trust God for in the coming year?

2 A Philosophy of Youth Ministry

by Dennis Miller

Dennis Miller

The primary objective of youth ministry is to *develop discipled students*—students brought to maturity in Jesus Christ. Therefore, it would seem that every youth worker should have a clear mental picture of a discipled student. Unfortunately, the words "disciple" and "discipleship" have been used and misused till their meanings have become vague to many people.

Youth workers talk about discipleship; they even use "discipleship materials." Buy many can't describe a discipled student. Ask yourself these questions: If I saw a discipled student, would I recognize him? What would he look like? (The Discipled Student Worksheet at the end of this chapter can help you develop a profile of such a student.)

The remainder of this chapter expresses a philosophy of youth ministry. The five traits examined are characteristic of the youth worker who is an effective *discipler* of young people.

Relational Thinking

An effective youth worker thinks relationally.

Most youth workers are either *terminal* thinkers or *relational* thinkers. A terminal thinker doesn't relate programs or activities to a clearly defined objective. Example:

I have a social scheduled next weekend.

Why are you having a social?
Because we need one.
Why do you need it?

I don't know. The kids just seem restless.

That's terminal thinking—terminal because it doesn't relate to the ultimate objective of discipling students.

A relational thinker, on the other hand, relates all programs and activities to the ultimate objective. Example:

We're having a social.
Really? Why are you having it?
To help develop our students as disciples.

How are you going to use a social to do that?

We're having the social to provide a place for our more mature students to evangelize.

A relational thinker evaluates all ministry activities by asking, "How will this activity help develop a discipled student?" He considers such factors as: How can I help my students understand how to use the activity? How can I structure the activity so its purposes are achieved? How am I going to evaluate whether these purposes were achieved?

With the objective clearly in mind, the relational thinker determines which programs are effective and which ones should be eliminated.

Modeling

An effective youth worker models spiritual truth.

People remember far more of what they see and hear than of what they simply hear. Unfortunately, most of the training young people receive is hearing training. Youth leaders *tell* them what qualities they should possess and what the Scriptures teach on specific issues. But youth leaders rarely *show* these qualities in a way students can relate to.

This problem is typified in an individual known as "The Phantom." The Phantom is a youth worker who always smiles. He is never depressed. He never exposes a sin in his life. He always witnesses to everyone he meets, no matter where he is or how embarrassing or difficult the situation. He never makes a mistake in judgment. He never gets discouraged. He never argues with his spouse. He *always* knows what to do. The Phantom is a "perfect" Christian. In fact, by comparison, the peons he serves are mere mortals.

Many youth workers would be surprised to know that their students view them as Phantoms. So often leaders hide behind an image they think they must project. They pretend they're never depressed and that there is no sin in their lives. Why? Because they're afraid that revealing what they're really like would cause their students to stumble. The truth is that students stumble not because they see imperfections in their leaders, but because they don't believe the Christian life is livable. Most of them have never seen anyone deal with Christianity in *real-life* terms.

Ask yourself this question: When I was growing up, how many adults did I see deal openly with a sin?

People can *talk* about dealing with sin all they want. They can explain confession and forgiveness doctrinally. They can quote Scripture. But *seeing* someone deal with sin leaves a far more lasting impression.

Don't make the mistake of being a Phantom to your students. They may become discouraged in trying to live the Christian life because they despair of attaining the kind of perfection they think they see in you. God uses *transparent* people—people who aren't afraid to model the Christian life by revealing their failures as well as their successes; their weaknesses as well as their strengths.

Modeling is particularly important in youth ministry today—when so many young people are growing up in homes where Christian principles are poorly modeled, if at all. Many young people come from homes that lack the basic elements of healthy family relationships: love, discipline, affirmation. As a result, these young people find it hard to relate to such basic Christian concepts as the fatherhood of God.

To effectively model spiritual truth to this generation, then, may require going beyond transparency. It may, for example, involve using skits to demonstrate various aspects of Christian living. It may involve consciously *demonstrating* discipleship skills— *showing* students how to schedule a "quiet time," how to conduct personal Bible study, how to share their faith.

But as modeling becomes more of a conscious demonstration, as opposed to the spontaneous sharing of life, the youth worker must beware of falling into the trap depicted in the following cartoon:

This student needs help in learning how to share his faith. Unfortunately, he's relating to a youth worker whose ministry philosophy appears to be "do what I say, not what I do." An effective youth worker is one whose life *models* the Christian life in action.

Learning Together

An effective youth worker leads as a co-learner.

> ## "A youth worker should be a resource person, not an all-knowing answer man."

Observe carefully the following cartoon:

Now ask yourself: Who ultimately produces spiritual growth in a young person? If you answered, "The Holy Spirit," you're correct (2 Cor. 3:18; 1 Cor. 3:6). What part does the youth worker play in discipling a student? If you answered, "He creates a suitable environment for the Holy Spirit to use," you're right.

A youth worker should be a resource person, not an all-knowing answer man. He and his students are co-learners in the Holy Spirit's school of discipleship. And often the Holy Spirit uses a student to teach the youth worker.

One night after I had spoken to a youth group, a student who had been a leader in my ministry for some time approached me and asked, "Dennis, did you study for that teaching session?"

I stammered, "Well, Ron, no; I didn't."

"Why not?" Ron asked.

I said, "Well, Ron, you see God exercises the gift of prophecy through me; and sometimes I don't need to study as much as some other folks."

Ron wasn't buying. He asked, "Dennis, if you don't study and know the mind of God for this ministry, how do you expect us to walk with God in our ministries?" I felt like I had been shot in the chest with a howitzer.

During the rest of that week, God wouldn't let me forget the incident. He reminded me that Ron, a high school student, was His instrument to show me that I had to deal with pride. The next week I found Ron, apologized, and told him that God's Spirit had been speaking to me through him but I had been too proud to listen. I was learning that the Holy Spirit is the great Discipler, and that youth workers and students are co-learners.

What are the benefits of leading as a co-learner?

First, it develops disciples who depend on God. When a youth worker tries to be the all-knowing, all-seeing, and all-guiding force in students' lives, those students become dependent on the youth worker. But when a youth worker demonstrates dependence on the Holy Spirit and points students to the Holy Spirit for guidance, they become dependent on *Him.* Young people who become dependent on a youth worker seldom develop the spiritual fortitude they'll need once they're outside the youth worker's sphere of influence.

A second benefit of leading as a co-learner is that it gives room for young Christians to disciple their peers. Have you ever known a high school student who was a relatively young Christian and yet had a contagious zeal and excitement for Jesus Christ? Perhaps you wished you could put him in front of a group, but you feared for him since

he was so young in the faith. Seeing that discipling is essentially cooperation with the Holy Spirit frees a leader to trust the Spirit's ministry through others—even young believers. While it's important to be cautious in giving leadership responsibility to young

Christians (1 Tim. 3:6), a person's youth should not disqualify him from the tasks of evangelizing and discipling (1 Tim. 4:12).

Evangelism

An effective youth worker is involved in aggressive evangelism.

Like it or not, the church is not a big draw among most high school students today. An effective youth worker cannot afford to sit back and wait for students to flock to his church. He must be aggressive in communicating the Good News of Jesus Christ to students in a culturally relevant way. Aggressive evangelism doesn't mean "pushy" evangelism. But it does mean going where kids are, not waiting for them to come to you:

Youth groups need the freshness new converts bring. Discipleship without evangelism leads to stagnation. To allow the same group of students to grind on year after year robs the group of the vitality and the joy of new believers. It also robs our min-

istries of a growing pool of believers from which new leadership can emerge.

Multiplication

An effective youth worker is committed to a multiplication ministry.

Multiplication is fundamentally different from addition. The same two numbers will generally increase in value at a greater rate when they are multiplied than when they are added. For example: $10 + 10 = 20$, but $10 \times 10 = 100$.

When one speaks of multiplying students, he is talking about increasing their fruitfulness for the Lord Jesus Christ many times over. A multiplying student is one who passes on to others those things that he has learned from his discipleship training, so that these others "will be able to teach others also" (2 Tim. 2:2).

Consider the following example. If one person disciples just one person a year, who in turn disciples one person a year, how long would it take to reach the world?

Years	Disciples
1	1
4	81
5	243
6	729
7	2,187

8	6,581
9	19,683
10	59,049
11	177,147
12	531,441
13	1,594,323
14	4,782,969
15	14,782,969
16	43,046,721
17	129,140,163
18	387,420,489
19	1,162,261,467
20	3,486,784,401
21	10,460,353,203

"Discipleship without evangelism leads to stagnation."

Now answer this question: If one person led 1,000 people to Christ a day, how many years would it take to disciple the world? The answer: It couldn't be done in a span of a hundred lifetimes. Multiplication is the most effective way to reach the world. It is also the most effective way to reach high school campuses for Jesus Christ.

In review: A youth worker who is an effective discipler of young people is (1) a *relational* rather than a terminal thinker; (2) a transparent *model* of the Christian life; (3) a *co-learner* with his young people in the Holy Spirit's school of discipleship; (4) a participant in *aggressive evangelism*; (5) a practitioner of the *multiplication ministry*. These five emphases express a philosophy of youth ministry whose primary objective is the development of discipled students. ☐

Cartoons © 1977 by J. Dennis Miller. Used by permission.

The Discipled Student Worksheet

A. Keep in mind the following concepts as you complete section B:
  1. Your main objective as a youth worker is to disciple individuals who will walk with the Lord and multiply spiritually for the rest of their lives.
  2. The development of discipled individuals is the ultimate objective of the youth program.
  3. You are the servant, the programs are the methods, and the student is the object.

B. As you answer these questions think about this hypothetical situation: Let's say you've been working in a youth group for four years. You met Jim as a freshman and he prayed with you to receive Christ. You followed up Jim and he grew in his relationship with Christ and gradually became the ideal mature discipled student. Now Jim is graduating from high school. What does Jim look like in the following areas?

  1. He should be committed to these life goals:

  _____

  _____

  2. He should be able to make wise decisions in the following areas of his life: Example: personal (finances, career, home, etc.), spiritual, social (dating, friendships), physical (exercise, nutrition, etc.).

  _____

  _____

3. His spiritual life should reflect these characteristics:

_____

_____

4. He should apply these ministry skills effectively:

_____

_____

5. He should develop and sustain these types of relationships:

_____

_____

6. He should know these principles about beginning and sustaining his own ministry:

_____

_____

7. Read the following passages and note whether your answers in questions 1 to 6 have included these scriptural principles: 1 Timothy 3:2; 1 Peter 5:1-7; Acts 6:3, 5; Titus 1:7-9. If you've left anything out of your profile that you see in these Scriptures, include it in your profile.

_____

_____

8. Using a concordance and your Bible, identify one passage for each of the six major points on the worksheet. Then write it in the space provided.

_____

_____

Principles of Youth Ministry

3

by Dennis Miller

Chapter 1 examined some foundational truths of youth ministry. Chapter 2 presented five characteristics of a youth ministry whose primary objective is the development of discipled students. This chapter offers some principles for *implementing* a youth ministry of discipleship. The cartoons in this chapter are intended to help you think through the ministry concepts presented.

Student-led Ministry

Look at the Graphics Company illustration. Ask yourself the following questions: Who is doing the developing? What is the staff member's job in this cartoon? What ministry principle is being represented in this cartoon?

The principle illustrated in this cartoon might be stated as follows: *A primary purpose of the youth worker and staff is to help each student develop his own evangelism and discipleship ministry.* The following cartoon further clarifies this principle:

Who is doing the acting? What is the staff director's role? This cartoon illustrates the fact that effective youth ministry is _____ led and _____ directed.

Students have a natural ability to influence and lead other students. What they often lack is maturity and direction. For a youth worker to assist students in developing their own evangelism/discipleship ministries, he must strive for a ministry that is *student* led and *staff* directed. By giving students responsibility and by helping them develop their own ministry skills, a student-led ministry takes aim at the youth worker's primary objective—to produce discipled students.

Dennis Miller

> *"Students have a natural ability to influence and lead other students."*

Building on Relationships

DIVORCE COURT
PLEASE HAVE A SEAT

DISCIPLER GROUP MEMBER

DISCIPLER GROUP LEADER

Carefully observe the divorce court illustration. Then ask yourself these questions: Who is mad at whom? Is this youth worker's ministry based more on relationships or on standards of conduct?

Leading by Influence

In this cartoon, what seems to be most important: the welfare of the chicken or the number of eggs she can produce? The chicken seems to be under

1000 EGGS OR BUST!

XEROX

DANGER HIGH YOKAGE

considerable pressure to perform. And the result is—a tired chicken.

"CHICKENS ARE OUR BUSINESS"

The two cartoons represent two different styles of leadership: an *authoritarian* style and an *influence* style. The ministry principle illustrated by the two cartoons is this: *An effective youth worker leads by influence.*

What then is the focus of an authoritarian style of leadership? It's on producing numbers and results. It's on making the program work at almost any cost.

What is the focus of an influence style of leadership? The focus is on developing people. It's on meeting the needs of people so they can minister.

What is the authoritarian leader's method?

It is applying pressure to produce. He makes a practice of externally motivating people; that is, motivating them with external things, standards—an occasional carrot here and there.

What is the influencing leader's method? It's developing an environment of encouragement. He specializes in motivating people internally, so their motivation flows from their own personal convictions.

What are the results of an authoritarian style of leadership? The authoritarian leader turns out students who produce because the program demands it. He has a tendency to turn out dependent students who are conditioned to please people rather than God.

The influence leader develops students who obey God and disciple others because they want to. He de-

---

> ## *"Effective youth ministry is built primarily on relationships, not standards."*

The ministry principle illustrated in this cartoon is: *Effective youth ministry is built primarily on relationships, not standards.*

Effective youth ministry is not based on rules and regulations, but on loving and caring for people. Rules and regulations are important for growth and development, but they should never be a ministry's primary focus. If a youth worker's purpose is to help students develop their own evangelism and discipleship ministries, the youth worker must develop a strong relationship with those students.

Too often, youth workers get confused about what they should emphasize. They forget that the students themselves are more important than any *results* they might produce. Youth workers, in their efforts to help students develop evangelism/discipleship skills, must beware of a performance orientation. It only produces tired chickens.

Now consider the following cartoon. What differences do you see between the methods of production represented in this cartoon and the methods represented in the previous illustration?

velops students who obey God of their own will.

Ask yourself this question: Which style of leadership do I use most of the time? Think of some personal examples that illustrate your style of leadership.

Excited about What?

What do you think about the compliment the youth worker gave the student? If the youth worker were mainly interested in the student's *performance* how might he have complimented him? If the youth worker were mainly interested in the *program*, how might he have complimented the student?

A fourth ministry principle is: *An effective youth worker gets excited about the right things.* Too often, people get excited about the peripheral issues in youth ministry. Numerical growth can be exciting. A good program can be exciting. But the most exciting aspect of youth ministry should be to see a student becoming a disciple—someone who is willing to be conformed to the image of Jesus Christ.

How and in what areas the youth worker shows enthusiasm determines the priorities he communicates to his students. Ask yourself this question: What should I be excited about if I am going to encourage a student to develop as a disciple? Look back at the cartoon. The youth worker could have been excited that the student led the Bible study. The youth worker could have been excited that

there was a tremendous response or that there were a lot of people at the meeting. But what was he excited about? He was excited about the student's personal development, about the student's desire to apply biblical principles.

Salting Students

TRAINING   HIS MINISTRY

In this cartoon, what is making the horse thirsty? What is the natural result of his being thirsty?

Youth workers often try to teach students without motivating them to want to learn. The cartoon illustrates how a little "salt" can be used to make students thirsty for the truth. So, the fifth ministry principle is: *A student's involvement in ministry determines the training he needs and wants.*

A youth worker shouldn't hesitate to thrust a student into ministry as soon as he's willing. But the youth worker should be very careful not to push a student beyond a level to which that student can willingly commit himself. To do so breeds frustration, disappointment, and resentment.

For example: Training an entire youth group in evangelism, then "strong-arming" everyone into the streets to share their faith may benefit some students. But others may turn away from Christ because they aren't ready to accept such a commitment.

To handle this situation in a positive way, *encourage* students to get involved in evangelism. Then make training available to those students who have been "salted"—whose attempts to evangelize have shown them their need for evangelism training.

Creating an Environment

What kind of environment has this youth worker created for the plant? Does he make the plant grow?

This cartoon illustrates a sixth ministry principle: *An effective youth worker creates an environment in which the Holy Spirit is free to help students grow at individualized rates.*

The first element in this principle reminds us that developing a youth program involves creating an environment. And the type of environment, in a large sense, determines how students develop spiritually. The environment includes the soil and water for the Holy Spirit to use in helping people grow.

The second element, ". . . in which the Holy Spirit is free to help students grow at individualized rates," reminds us that people develop at different rates. Some young people grow very slowly, others quite rapidly. Trying to deal with students as if they were all at the same level of commitment is an exercise in frustration.

An environment is needed that will meet each student at his level of commitment, minister to him there, and encourage him to move on to a deeper commitment to the Lord.

Such an environment accommodates a wide variety of students. Some students come to youth group simply for social contact. Others attend because of parental pressure. Some students come because they want to grow spiritually.

The dilemma is this: At which group should the youth worker aim?

itual interest and may not even be Christians. Some are Christians but have neglected their relationships with God and need to be renewed in Christ. At the pool of humanity level, activity is designed specifically to salt students, making them thirsty for the things of God.

Evangelism is not salt. Evangelism is the water that quenches the thirst. So this is not basically a level on which to conduct evangelism.

The only commitment required of young people at this level is that they show up. Activities at this level of commitment might include concerts, plays, sporting contests—activities to which Christians can go and make

take part in Bible study and group discussions.

How might a youth worker challenge a student to the growth level of commitment? At an outreach level activity, the youth worker might announce: "Many of you have expressed an interest in knowing more about what the Bible says on certain topics. This week we have an activity starting that will last three weeks. It's a study on 'getting along with your parents.' How many of you have had trouble getting along with your folks? Those of you who want to learn what the Bible says about getting along with parents, please come. We would like to see you there. But please don't come unless this is a study you're willing to commit some time and attention to." Such an appeal challenges students to make their own decisions about their willingness to grow and develop spiritually. Students who choose to come to a growth activity have part ownership in it—it's something they are doing because they want to, not because they have to.

> ## *"At the* pool of humanity *level, activity is designed specifically to make students thirsty for the things of God."*

If he aims at the students with the highest level of commitment, the students below them will probably feel overchallenged and lose interest. If the youth worker builds a program around students at the lowest level of commitment, the highly motivated students will lose interest. The solution? It's not either-or. It's both-and. The diagram below illustrates an environment designed to accomodate several different levels of commitment.

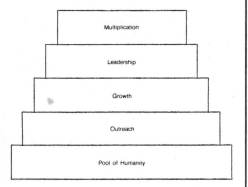

The lowest level of commitment, the *pool of humanity*, refers to a cross section of students: some have no spir-

people thirsty to know more about Jesus Christ.

The second level of the environment is called the *outreach* level. Activities at this level are designed to present the claims of Christ and to allow people to respond. The commitment assumed of students who come to an outreach-level activity is that they *come* and *listen* to what is being said about the Gospel. Activities at this level of commitment might include evangelistic Bible studies (on the campus or at church), topical studies, sports clinics, Sunday School.

All that is asked of students at this level is to come and listen—no more, no less. When they come, they come of their own free will to hear the Gospel of Christ.

The third level of environment, the *growth* level, helps students learn and apply basic spiritual truths to their lives. To be involved in growth-level activities, students should be committed to growing spiritually. They should agree to some minimal standards such as to come to every session, listen, take notes, and actively

What about the students who say no? The youth worker should continue to involve them in outreach activities till they are ready to make such a decision. When they are forced into growth-level activities, students are often disruptive. Even if they hear all the content, they rarely apply it to their lives because they have no desire to do so.

At the next level of commitment, the *leadership* level, activities help students develop their personal walks with God and equip them to minister to and lead other students. At this level, students should be exposed to a variety of situations where ministry skills such as leading a Bible study, teaching Sunday School, and discipling other students are taught and demonstrated.

To be involved at this level of activity, a student commits himself to being discipled for spiritual leadership. At the growth level his commitment was to a class, to a subject matter, to a group. At this level, his commitment is to the youth worker or to some other adult leader. He is committing himself to allow someone to help him become a leader. He is also committing himself to develop a personal vision for helping fulfill the Great Commission in his high school community.

Activities at the leadership level might include: small group interaction to help leadership-level students work through personal needs and problems; training in how to use small group dynamics, possibly by a teacher from a nearby school; a seminar on how to effectively share the faith with non-Christian students; a seminar on time management.

The leadership level is usually entered only on being issued a personal, one-on-one challenge, such as: "Joe, I will do anything I can to help you grow and develop as a leader. Are you willing to let me help?"

At the fifth level of commitment, the *multiplication* level, activities are aimed at equipping students to disciple other student leaders. Activities might include planning and preparing for vocational ministry, training in how to do personal counseling, etc.

Few students ever reach this level of commitment. The standards are high. Students are making almost the same degree of commitment to youth ministry that the youth worker has made.

In this five-level ministry environment, each level requires greater commitment from the student. *A student qualifies or disqualifies himself to participate in each level*. The student always has the prerogative to decide how far he is ready to commit himself. This factor increases the level of commitment and increases the maturity of the student.

Developing a five-stage environmental ministry primarily involves categorizing activities by what is *expected* from a student in each activity. Is the expectation merely that the student shows up? That he comes and listens? That he comes and is willing to grow? Is the expectation that he comes, grows, and learns to be a leader? Or is it that he comes and leads leaders? When a student makes a commitment to one of these levels of the environment, he understands what is going to take place in his life and in his training. And the youth worker knows at what level to direct his ministry efforts to that student.

In the environmental model of youth ministry, a youth worker can use one activity in several different ways, determined simply by how he challenges students to be involved. Consider for example, a "fifth quarter"—a student social following the high school football game. The youth worker might challenge *pool-of-humanity* type students to simply come and have fun. He might challenge *outreach* type students to come and to be open to hearing someone's testimony. He might challenge *growth-level* students to come and use the activity as an opportunity to grow in their evangelistic skills—by turning conversations with non-Christian students to the subject of Jesus Christ. The youth worker might involve *leadership-level* students in the same activity by asking them to help students at the growth level share their faith with others. Finally, *multiplication-level* students might be challenged to lead the entire activity. In this example, then, one activity is used five different ways to involve students at all levels of commitment.

In one sense, developing an environment is more a matter of analyzing activities and understanding how to use them than it is creating a new program. It's a matter of categorizing activities on the basis of how much commitment they require from students.

It is important that the youth leader communicates, by word and attitude, that the students on the leadership level are no more important to the ministry than the students on the outreach level. In reality, those on the leadership level have graduated to the "lower" position of "servant of all" (Mark 10:44).

The environment model is not a vehicle for judging students and determining their worth to the ministry. It is simply a device to help the youth worker clarify what he is expecting of students, how to challenge them to be involved in ministry activities, and how those activities can be used to reach students at various levels of growth and commitment. □

Cartoons © 1977 by J. Dennis Miller. Used by permission.

4 Youth Work—a Network of Relationships

by Ray Willey with Randy Sykes

Ray Willey *is founder and director of Cornerstone Ministries, a nondenominational youth organization based in Tucson, Arizona. An experienced youth worker, Ray has an extensive speaking ministry, serving both students and youth workers. He is a graduate of Biola College and has a master's degree from the University of Arizona.*

Each year Cornerstone Ministries sponsors regional youth workers' institutes across the United States. These institutes are designed to help local churches develop their ministries to youth. For more information, write to Cornerstone Ministries, Inc., 6601 E. 22nd St., Tucson, AZ 85710.

Randy Sykes *is the director of Youth in Action, a youth ministry consultation organization. Randy has over 15 years of youth ministry experience, including a stint as minister to students at the First Baptist Church of Lakewood, in Long Beach, California. He is a graduate of Biola College.*

This handbook contains a variety of practical helps for youth workers, and addresses various aspects of youth ministry. This particular chapter provides a perspective of youth ministry based on a single premise: that successful youth ministry in the local church largely depends on the development of a network of quality *relationships*. These relationships are examined, followed by the presentation of a *relationship model*.

The Pastoral Relationship

If you're a full-time youth worker, beware of involving yourself in a youth ministry that doesn't have a solid pastoral relationship. This relationship should be a strategic beginning point, out of which your ministry flows. A successful pastor-youth worker relationship goes beyond verbalizing "support" for each other.

1. It involves establishing a camaraderie with your pastor—a kindred spirit, not only in the Lord but also as fellow laborers in the church.

2. A successful pastor-youth worker relationship involves genuine pastoral support flowing out of fellowship. This support begins in part with honest, open communication. This means communicating not only about programs and tasks, but about personal goals and dreams. It means letting your pastor know *you* as you really are.

3. A successful pastor-youth worker relationship involves ministering to one another. You are in a position to minister to your pastor in a way no

one else can. You may be one of the few people who truly understands your pastor's frustrations and discouragements, his failures, and his weaknesses. You may understand him as only a fellow worker in the church context can.

Church Leaders

Develop trusting relationships with the leaders of your church (deacons, elders, governing board) by investing yourself in their lives. Work with and through them. Help them get to know you, your intentions, and your direction for the young people. As they come to know and trust you, you will be able to demonstrate to these leaders the value of youth work and illustrate the significant position it holds in the total church ministry.

Church Committees

As you work with various church committees (Christian education, youth, etc.) remember two things: First, committee members usually have a genuine concern for the church's ministry to young people. They do care. Second, many of them don't know a great deal about working with young people. They desperately need your assistance—your godly, knowledgeable leadership. Work with them.

NOTE: The practical outworking of youth ministry begins at the committee level. Programs and methods—the pragmatic decisions—are normally determined here. So, your relationship with these committees can have a significant effect on your ministry to youth.

Congregation

At this level, your relationships extend to the whole church body. As you get to know congregation members, they learn to appreciate you.

Not only should you give of yourself so that they come to know you, but you should also demonstrate integrity in your walk with Christ. Credibility is important. You can build credibility with your congregation through the many avenues that relationship provides.

Parents

As you minister to students, they will, in turn, influence their parents. Conversely, parental influence on teens inevitably affects your ministry to youth. Relationships with parents can directly influence your relationships with their children and vice versa. Obviously, parents are an important group to include in your ministering process.

Youth Staff

This level of relationships involves your contact with the volunteer youth workers, teachers, sponsors, and student leaders with whom you share the actual work of youth ministry. At this level, you have the opportunity to *multiply* your ministry through the lives of others. Pour your life into the lives of your youth staff and develop a close-knit unit.

The importance of these relationships is second only to your relationships with the students themselves.

Surround yourself with staff members who have a variety of strengths, interests, and abilities. Such diversity can make you more efficient in reaching the larger spectrum of students.

These workers will rally around you as you instill in them a vision and conviction for youth ministry. And you will discover your ministry growing in direct proportion to the growing development of your leadership base.

Youth

Here's the "bottom line." This is what your work is all about—to effectively minister to young people. Developing a relationship with each student in your group should be a priority.

A good way to measure your ministry's effectiveness is to evaluate your relationships with the students. You teach them. You guide them and provide activities for them. And yet, it's the quality of relationships that largely determines the success of any of these endeavors. Young people open up and begin to trust you as you develop a genuine followship for a common purpose. Programs, methods, numbers, and buildings are all important. They have their place. But only as they allow you to work with students. Your primary focus in the ministry must be *people*, not programs.

Minister to youth. And you will build not only a "successful program" or an effective ministry, but also a closeness, an affinity, a real oneness that symbolizes the relationship you share with your Lord.

A Relationship Model

Try viewing your relationships in terms of the inverted hourglass shown in the following diagram. In this model, the youth worker's network of relationships begins with the pastor and church staff. Flowing out of these relationships, exposure broadens to involve church leaders, various committees, and ultimately the congregation as a whole. At this point, the youth worker's relationships begin to intensify as they involve parents, the youth staff, and finally the students.

This relationship model does not assign the groups a numerical significance, as if to prioritize them by value. But it does demonstrate how each level of relationships builds on the previous level and how each calls for a different degree of commitment in terms of time and effort. ☐

"Successful youth ministry in the local church depends on the development of a network of quality relationships."

THE YOUTH WORKER

PASTOR (CHURCH STAFF)

CHURCH LEADERS

CHURCH COMMITTEES

CONGREGATION AT LARGE

PARENTS

YOUTH STAFF

YOUTH

5 The Intern Program

by Bill Stewart

Bill Stewart has been the minister of youth education at the First Baptist Church of Modesto, California since 1968. In addition to this responsibility for the junior high, high school, and college ministries; Bill is the coordinator of the church's intern program. Three full-time staff members, 12 interns, and 100 lay staff people look to Bill for supervision and training.

How can a potential "full-time" (or vocational) youth worker develop a practical, working knowledge of his field of ministry? One answer is the intern program, in which the youth worker develops ministry skills through the combination of academic training and supervised ministry experience in a local church.

In recent years, a number of intern programs have emerged representing various levels of commitment and involvement. Our intern program at the First Baptist Church of Modesto, California differs in several ways from programs which are designed for part-time and assistant workers: (1) Our particular program is designed for training "professional" workers for various areas of church ministry. (2) Training takes place prior to or during college/seminary training. (3) Goals and criteria are specific.

both by personal testimony and by the supportive witness of those who know him best. We also consider the length of time the applicant has been a Christian (1 Tim. 3:6).

2. The applicant must be convinced of, and able to demonstrate his call to the Gospel ministry.

3. The applicant should be aware of his spiritual gift(s), since his gift(s) determine where he will function most effectively in the body of Christ.

4. The applicant should be spiritually FAT: "F" (faithful), "A" (available), and "T" (teachable). In other words, his life prior to his applying for the program must have demonstrated that he is faithful in handling responsibility (Luke 16:10), available for the demands of ministry (John 4:34-36), and teachable (Col. 1:28).

5. The applicant must have proved himself in ministry prior to applying for entrance into the program. He will have

---

> *"The youth worker develops ministry skills through the combination of academic training and supervised ministry experience. . . ."*

Entrance Requirements

Because of the investment of time and money that goes into training an intern, we have set specific requirements for entrance into the intern program.

1. The applicant must have an assurance of his salvation through faith in Jesus Christ. He must be able to demonstrate his relationship with Christ

demonstrated in a practical way his call to the Gospel ministry. He must be a faithful person who is able to teach others (2 Tim. 2:2).

6. The applicant must be financially free. Heavy financial indebtedness will affect an intern's availability for productive involvement in the program.

7. The applicant must be a college senior or older. The program requires a certain level of maturity not frequently found in younger students.

8. The applicant must be supportive

of the local church. The program is intended to train workers for the ministry of building the *church* of Jesus Christ.

Program Requirements

1. The intern spends a minimum of either 10 or 20 hours weekly in ministries assigned by a staff supervisor. These hours do not include time spent in preparation for college courses.

2. The intern attends all regular church services plus all other churchwide services, such as evangelistic meetings.

3. The intern arranges a weekly meeting with his staff supervisor to report on the intern's ministries, plans, and needs. While his supervisor may introduce items for discussion at such meetings, it is the intern's responsibility to provide an agenda for discussion.

4. The intern takes a class in personal evangelism. If no such class is available in his church, he may receive training from a Christian college in the area or through a parachurch organization. Such a class should instruct the intern in how to lead others to a saving faith in Jesus Christ and to disciple new converts.

5. The intern should maintain a positive attitude toward the supervisory staff, the church family, and all other interns. He is to keep his heart spiritually sensitive to needs in the local body of Christ and do his part to meet those needs.

Assignment

Prospective interns are evaluated through written application, testing (the Taylor-Johnson Temperament Analysis test), and personal interview. When an intern is accepted into the program, he is assigned to one of the following departments: pastoral ministries (preaching and counseling), youth ministries, music and programming, Christian education (children's education, camping, conferences), adult ministries (adult classes, evangelism, discipleship), or business and administration. The intern spends most of his two-year internship working in one of these areas, under the direction of a staff supervisor who heads one of the departments listed above.

Evaluation

An intern's course of study lasts at least two years. Every six months, the staff supervisor evaluates the intern using a form to be returned to the intern coordinator. The intern uses a different form to evaluate his own experience and training in the program. With this information, the intern coordinator regularly interviews the intern to evaluate his progress.

Classification

Based on his means of financial support, academic involvement, and relationship to the local church, the intern is classified as follows:

The "A" class intern (scholarship and financial help). This intern receives full scholarship either to a local Christian college or to the closest seminary for up to 12 units per semester. The intern pays for his own textbooks, library fees, and other additional fees. In addition, he receives $110 per month for personal support. The "A" class intern spends a minimum of 20 hours per week working at a ministry assignment. He may not work at an outside job for more than 20 hours per week.

The "B" class intern (scholarship only).

This intern also receives a full scholarship to a local Christian college or seminary for up to 12 units per semester. The intern must pay for his own textbooks, library fees, and other additional fees. Unlike his "A" class counterpart, the "B" class intern receives no monetary support.

He must spend a minimum of 10 hours per week in a ministry assignment.

The "C" class intern (self-supporting). The self-supporting intern receives no scholarship aid or financial support. He spends a minimum of 10 hours of service time per week. The self-supporting intern may take a seminary or college class load not to exceed 12 units per semester. He also may work up to 40 hours a week at an outside job.

The "D" class intern (trainee from another church).

The intern who comes from another church to be trained by us spends a minimum of 20 hours per week in a ministry assignment. He is responsible for his total support including schooling and living expenses. He is also expected to pay $50 per week for staff training. (Churches requesting such training for an intern often absorb these expenses.) The "D" class intern may work up to 20 hours a week, if necessary, at an outside job.

Support

An intern's financial support must come from the local church where he is a member. We don't recommend he raise support from other churches because of potential problems with ethics and lack of accountability. We feel that the commitment should be within the body where the intern's service is given.

The Staff Supervisor

For any internship to be successful, the intern and his staff supervisor must be able to work together effectively. No one supervisor should have more interns than he can personally train. For each intern he does agree to train, the supervisor assumes responsibility for the following areas:

1. *Spending time with the intern.* The staff supervisor is to spend at least one hour weekly with each intern assigned to him. During these meetings, the supervisor makes ministry assignments, and checks on the intern's spiritual walk. The intern reports on progress and problems in his ministry of preceeding week(s). The intern and supervisor set personal goals, encourage each other, and evaluate the program.

2. *Outlining of the intern's areas of responsibility.* The staff supervisor outlines in writing the specific areas of responsibility for which the intern is accountable.

3. *Preparing a calendar of activities.* The staff supervisor helps the intern prepare a calendar of his activities including his ministry, schooling, and work load.

4. *Evaluating biblical priorities.* The staff supervisor helps the intern formulate and regularly evaluate the biblical priorities for his life and ministry.

5. *Training the intern.* The staff supervisor involves the intern in as much "side-by-side" training as possible. This often means ministering together.

6. *Reproducing.* The staff supervisor seeks to involve the intern in discipling one of the intern's peers. The objective is to prepare the intern to reproduce spiritually through a discipling ministry.

Tried and Proven

During their internships, many young people see their ministries tried and proven. Others find they're not cut out for vocational ministry. Those interns can then be encouraged to serve Christ in different fields. Though sometimes painful, such a discovery is better made at this stage of ministry than later. The intern program provides an ideal "proving ground" for potential vocational ministers. □

"Young people see their ministries tried and proven."

Recruiting Youth Sponsors | 6

by Phil D. Kennemer

"Once you're in, you'll never get out."

"It's too difficult a job."

"If anyone will do, why not get someone else?"

These are three common reasons, seldom verbalized but often felt, why church members say no to becoming youth sponsors. To overcome these attitudes, youth workers who have to recruit sponsors use a variety of techniques—from subtle manipulation to shameless begging.

The solution to sponsor recruitment often lies in adapting a long-range, *intentional approach* to recruitment.

people and give them the opportunity to fulfill their callings.

His task requires discipline and faith. First, he must spend a time getting to know the gifts and qualities to which students will respond. And finally, he must have faith to discern which church members have these gifts and qualities even in undeveloped forms.

The following guidelines can help you recruit sponsors on the basis of their gifts and qualities.

1. Create your own list of desired gifts and qualities. For example, the potential youth sponsor should:

> ## "Too many sponsors are left in youth ministry long beyond the point of effectiveness."

ment. Such an approach includes the following three elements: (1) There is no "random sample" recruiting. (2) Sponsors commit themselves to a one-year, self-renewable contract. (3) No recruit is asked to serve till he has received adequate basic training.

No Random Samples

God gives people a variety of gifts to carry out Christian ministry (1 Cor. 12). Not all are called to be evangelists or teachers. This truth should be considered when recruiting youth sponsors.

In the local church, God gives certain persons the gifts and qualities necessary to be successful in youth work. The recruiter must find these

- have had student-age youth living at home (knowledge),
- have had an attitude of understanding and tolerance toward youth (compassion),
- have strong faith in God,
- be F.A.T. (faithful, available, teachable).

Each youth sponsor position has unique needs. Your task is to list what you see as the needs of that position, then "translate" them into the gifts and qualities that meet these needs.

2. Write down the names of your potential sponsors, then list at least three specific qualities about each person (personality, experience, faith, etc.) that can be "translated" into gifts and qualities for youth ministry. If you can't come up with three such qualities, you probably don't know the person well enough, or he isn't right for the job.

3. Compare the list of potential spon-

Phil D. Kennemer *is pastor of Fulbright Memorial United Methodist Church in Houston, Texas. Before coming to Houston, Phil served as pastor of the First United Methodist Church of Elgin, Texas. He has also served as associate pastor in charge of youth and young adults in two different churches, and has been a guest lecturer at the National Youth Workers Convention. Phil holds a Graduate Degree of Theology from Austin Presbyterian Theological Seminary.*

sors and their qualities (no. 2 above) to the list of desired gifts and qualities (no. 1 above). If you've done your work prayerfully and carefully, you will begin to see the connection between the gifts and qualities needed and those present in potential sponsors.

4. *Approach each person who seems qualified.* Use a person-to-person conference or a personalized letter. Share specific reasons why you sense they are qualified to be in youth ministry. Ask them to pray about their involvement and to meet with you and others who may have a similar calling.

At this meeting, explain what becoming a youth sponsor involves. Afterward, potential sponsors can decide whether or not they are interested. Don't ask them for a response till they have had an opportunity to hear all of the facts. Go over the two remaining principles of the intentional purpose of recruitment (explained in the following material); then ask for a response.

your daily life and are willing to grow in the knowledge of this grace.
• You are actively involved in expanding your knowledge and personal application of the Scriptures.
• You will strive to plan and guide the learning process in such a way that students are able to discover and apply for themselves relevant biblical truths.
• You are not expected to have all the answers or to be a biblical scholar. Rather you are expected to grow in your understanding of the implications of your faith and help your students do the same.

Job Requirements:
• In preparation for teaching your class, spend a minimum of three hours developing a lesson plan.
• Meet with your class on a regular Sunday basis.
• Work hard to build Sunday School attendance.
• Occasionally organize special

No Involvement before Training

Too often, sponsors are expected to learn about youth ministry "on the job." In the intentional recruitment program, new sponsors are not asked to serve in any capacity till they have been adequately trained.

This training can be provided by the church staff, by some regional specialist in the youth field or, in small church situations, by church members who are former youth sponsors. Plan the training event at least three months in advance, and offer it at a time convenient for the greatest number of potential youth sponsors.

If the church is large, hold separate training events according to job functions (Sunday School teachers, growth group leaders, etc.) for junior high workers and high school workers. At the training events, deal with the following three questions:

1. *What can I expect from junior high youth or high school youth?* Explain what young people in these age levels are like. Include physical, mental, emotional, social, and spiritual characteristics of adolescent development.

2. *What resources are available?* Present the materials available to your sponsors for youth ministry. Include a survey of: curriculum materials (how to use, where to get); available reference materials (biblical and otherwise); supplies; and special equipment (films, projectors, record players).

3. *What skills must I develop?* Present those group-leading skills that are essential to working with youth. Allow potential recruits time in the training sessions to practice these skills and to receive constructive criticism. Seven such skills that ought to be considered are:

• *Goal setting.* Zero in on where you are going. Setting goals keeps programs and plans on target. Goals should be immediate as well as long-term.

"Sponsors commit themselves to a one-year, self-renewable contract."

One-year, Self-renewable Contract

Too many sponsors are left in youth ministry long beyond the point of effectiveness. Often they are given no idea of what is expected of them. An intentional recruitment program eliminates such problems with the following three policies:

1. *A youth sponsor's term of service is for one year only* (12 months from the time they actually begin service).

2. *Prior to beginning their service sponsors are given a full job description.* For example, a job description for a high school Sunday School teacher might include the following:

Qualifications:
• You are trusting God's love in

"fellowship outings" for your class.
• Get to know your students and, through your care and concern, communicate God's love for them.

3. *At the end of the 12-month period, no sponsor will be expected to stay for another year. If the sponsor wishes to continue, he must ask to be assigned for another 12 months. Otherwise, it is assumed that he should be replaced.*

This may be the hardest guideline of the intentional program to follow. The tendency is to relax once you have recruited youth sponsors. But doing so assures that the whole program will be back to square one in just a short time. So, force yourself to begin looking for next year's youth sponsors immediately after getting the year started. This guideline assures potential youth sponsors that they are not making a "lifetime" commitment.

• *Planning*. Formulate a procedure by which your goals are to be accomplished. In its most basic sense, planning answers the questions: what? who? when? and where? Planning also includes generating ways to involve youth in the planning process.

• *Finding resources*. Be on the lookout for ideas, events, persons, and activities which strengthen your youth ministry efforts. Not only should you order materials from time to time, but polish and refine materials you already have.

• *Priming the pump*. Create interest in youth activities by being mysterious, bold, and humorous.

• *Asking questions*. Ask questions that generate discussion. Remember to stay away from "yes and no" questions. Make the questions to the point, occasionally play devil's advocate, and give time for answers.

• *Facilitating group action*. Effectively move the group into, through, and out of an activity. Some key points to remember are: (1) Stand up and speak distinctly. (2) Be sure in your own mind about instructions; then present them clearly. (3) Relax and participate in the event or activity yourself. (4) When an activity has served its purpose, move to the next step. (5) Be confident.

• *Summarizing*. Help the group review what it has learned or observed from an activity.

Church Support

For an intentional program of youth sponsor recruitment to succeed, the recruiter must first obtain support of the program from the church's ruling body. This support should be secured in the form of a resolution or official statement, committing the local fellowship to an intentional program as described in this chapter.

Such a statement builds into the recruitment process both an accountability factor for the whole congregation and, most importantly, an understanding of what is expected of both the recruiter and of potential youth sponsors.

A statement of support reduces the credibility gap caused by previous recruitment programs in which youth workers were chosen according to willingness, not gifting; served as long as possible; and received little or no training.

A statement of support also acknowledges the ongoing, long-range nature of sponsor recruitment, relieving the recruiter of pressure to quickly fill positions.

The acceptance rate of potential sponsors recruited by the intentional recruitment method is high. Potential sponsors respond positively to a recruiter who has: (1) gotten the official backing of the local church, (2) offset potential sponsors' fears concerning expectations and training, (3) approached potential recruits on the basis of their own unique gifts and qualities. □

7 Equipping Leaders

by Joseph C. Aldrich

Dr. Joseph C. Aldrich *is president of Multnomah School of the Bible in Portland, Oregon. Before assuming this position, he taught at Dallas Theological Seminary and Talbot Seminary as well as at Multnomah. Dr. Aldrich has served as pastor of Mariners Church in Newport Beach, California. He is the author of* Secrets to Inner Beauty *and* Lifestyle Evangelism.

I've often wondered why weeds always look so healthy and green. Weeds do best when you ignore them. They thrive on neglect, perpetuating themselves without any human effort. But plant something that's worth growing, and a battle royal breaks out. Birds, bugs, beetles, and all kinds of beasts do their best to destroy the seed.

If leaders grew like weeds we'd soon be posting our church property with "no help wanted" signs. But leaders, like good seeds, don't grow unattended.

Our goal as youth workers is to equip young people for leadership. We want to raise a crop of young people grounded in their faith, equipped to share Christ with other people.

Belief and Value Systems

Such a goal demands that we influence both the belief systems and the value systems of young people. Ask a high school student whether he believes he should cheat on his exams, and he'll probably say no. His belief system says such behavior is inappropriate. Ask him if he ever cheats and it's likely he'll say yes. His value system overrides his belief system and determines his behavior. He values a passing grade and peer approval more than the dictates of his belief system.

Our hearts reside where our treasures are. We choose and act on the basis of what we cherish. Ideally, our belief and value systems should be totally synonymous. In reality they are not, and we often exist with large areas of inconsistency and conflict.

Our teaching, preaching, and exhorting usually appeal primarily to a teen's belief system. But his value system is primarily socially determined—he becomes like the people with whom he associates.

Two processes are thus involved in developing leadership. One is *conceptual*; the other *relational*. One is primarily a conscious process involving the intellectual processing of information. The other is an unconscious socialization process, not unlike cultural assimilation. A Japanese child doesn't have to be formally taught to be Japanese because, through assimilation, he becomes like those he associates with. If he grows up in a different culture, he will still be Japanese physiologically, but not culturally.

Napoleon said, "A man becomes the man of his uniform." The crucial question for anyone wanting to change behavior is, "How do we get him to change clothes?" Do we tell him he needs to change clothes and give him theologically sound reasons for such an action, or do we fold him into a small group of people wearing different uniforms and hope change takes place? I believe the second solution is the most effective. Let me illustrate: Here's a note I received from a student shortly after I broke my foot playing basketball:

"Dear Dr. Joe,

I learned a great deal about what kind of man you are when I played basketball with you the day you broke your foot. You really impressed me with your intensity and desire to excel. If you can show hustle and determination just in a pickup game with students, then you must live your whole life that way.

When you first hurt your foot, everyone thought you had just sprained it. You got up right away and tried to walk if off to get back into the game. It was obvious you were in great pain, but it seemed as if you weren't going to let an injury slow you down.

After witnessing that event, I'm proud to say that I look up to you and greatly respect you as a man and as a man of God. You are worthy of emulation, and I'd like to learn as much about your lifestyle as I can so I can follow your example. . . ."

My basketball buddy is a candidate for discipleship, for leadership development. Right or wrong, he has concluded that I am real, authentic, and worthy of emulation.

Emulation and Assimilation

Two processes seem to be involved in effective growth. The first is *emulation*; the second is *assimilation*. A junior high boy, who thinks you hung the moon, will walk with his hands in his pockets if you do. If you use certain figures of speech or laugh in a particular way, he will too. If you cheat and cut corners, he probably will too, even if his belief system says it's wrong.

His valuation of your friendship, interest, and personality and his emulation of you create a natural process of assimilation. He is a values vacuum cleaner. Our Lord said that when the student is fully taught, he will be like his teacher! (Luke 6:40)

Paul told Timothy to "continue in the things you have learned and become convinced of" (2 Tim. 3:14). Why? Why should Timothy continue? Paul had two reasons. First, continue because you know "from whom you have learned them" (2 Tim. 3:14). Second, continue because "from childhood you have known the sacred

writings" (2 Tim. 3:15).

What did Timothy know about Paul, his teacher? "You followed my teaching, conduct, purpose, faith, patience, love, perseverance, persecutions, sufferings, such as happened to me at Antioch, at Iconium, and at Lystra, what persecutions I endured" (2 Tim. 3:10-11).

Paul was saying to Timothy, "Keep going, my son, because your life has been grounded since infancy in authoritative revelation, and you have seen the implications of biblical truth lived out through the life of one who loves you. You have learned through studying the inspired epistles and the 'living epistles' who incarnate truth. Go and do likewise!"

Leadership Development

Since leadership development is not a mechanistic, assembly-line process, I will resist the temptation to list the "Seven Surefire Steps of Effective Discipleship." Instead, here are four general principles which I have found valuable in developing leaders:

1. Be a model! Be for real! If you want young people to bleed, you've got to hemorrhage! Be sure you are wearing the uniform you want them to change into. But please note that you are not called to be a model of *perfection*. Instead, let your *progress* be observable to all people, and progress assumes you haven't arrived yet!

Just as a serum has the essence of the disease in it, ministering effectively means your solution to a problem must include part of the problem. So, to encourage someone who's lonely, an effective solution should include a revelation of how *you* have coped with loneliness. If a problem is personal, part of the answer must be

personal. If you want students to be transparent, authentic, and open, you must be the same. This leads to a second principle.

2. Build mutually supportive relationships. The emphasis here is on the word *mutually*. You need relationship as much as the young person does.

I must confess I have problems with the "discipler—disciplee" concept if it's taken to the extreme. This concept often precludes real growth because the dynamics can be unhealthy.

Dick Underwood and I met every other Thursday for almost six years. His camper was the meeting place where we shared lunch, dreams, problems, possibilities, and just plain old-fashioned fun. I don't believe Dick was intimidated by my role as pastor. We met as equals, and shared openly and deeply concerning our successes and failures.

Dick Lippincott and I met on alternate Thursdays for two or more years. Sometimes we'd take a day and fly out to an abandoned airstrip, park the plane under a tree, spread out a blanket, and pour out our joys and sorrows to each other and the Lord. Lest

---

"You are not called to be a model of perfection."

---

you think we were "superspiritual," we usually took some guns along and ventilated some tin cans.

All of us have grown. Underwood and Lippincott and I shared the Word together. We shared prayer concerns. We shared and challenged each other as husbands and fathers. They knew of many of my personal inadequacies in those roles. We prayed regularly for each other's wives and children.

3. Help each young person find a dream and make it a reality. People feel successful when their dreams, in some measure, become reality. A major task everyone faces is to define his dream—his vision of adult accomplishment, and give it the proper place in his life structure.

Research shows that one of the key

factors in the success of such a quest is a mentor, a friend who supports and helps facilitate one's dream. The true mentor, the perceptive friend, fosters the other's development by believing in him, sharing in the developing dream, and giving it his blessing.

In developing leaders, someone must serve as transitional mentor to help mark the rites of passage from a "teacher—pupil" to an "adult—adult" relationship. Most of us will do anything for someone who believes in us. This supportive person creates a "boundary space" in which our hopefed imaginations can run wild and our creativity can flourish.

Dr. Howard Hendricks, known to his students as "Prof," played such a role in my life. He believed in me, encouraged me, helped me visualize the future use of my embryonic gifts and abilities. Many of the things God has allowed me to accomplish go back to seeds Dr. Hendricks planted and seedlings he nourished.

As mentors, we must make it our goal to listen well—to discover our young people's needs, feelings, problems, and especially their dreams.

To accomplish a dream, one often needs help in visualizing steps to achievement. Often a passed-over dream, banked like a fire, needs to be rekindled. Sometimes a person needs fresh, new challenges suggested by an outside source. Often the "new dream" focuses as the result of a friend's careful observation of temperament and abilities.

as possible, youth workers need to encourage young people to use their gifts. One of the fastest ways to encourage leadership development is to *let* leaders develop! Why does the "professional youth pastor" run the group's activities and services if he is committed to equipping the "laity" for their work of ministry? A youth

"Find a dream and link it to a young person's gift."

Shy and afraid of groups, one friend of mine is now speaking in churches and conferences because I sensed his abilities, planted some seeds, and then spent months and months working with him on the content, methodology, and style of his messages. I recently received a tape from him with two new messages he wants me to evaluate. How exciting!

Find a dream and link it to a young person's gift; then watch his gift grow and his motivation increase. The minds of men are not inflamed by small ideas!

4. Be a faithful steward of your young people's gifts. Keeping as low a profile

group will accomplish exactly what its leaders believe it can accomplish.

Encourage members of the youth staff to do what you plan to do, and then initiate relationships with young people which enable you to plant, cultivate, and harvest dreams.

A speaker at a secular seminar I attended startled me when he said, "People do not buy our products because they understand the product, people buy our products because they believe we understand them!" Want to build leaders? Know them, understand them, and stand back! Miracles will happen!

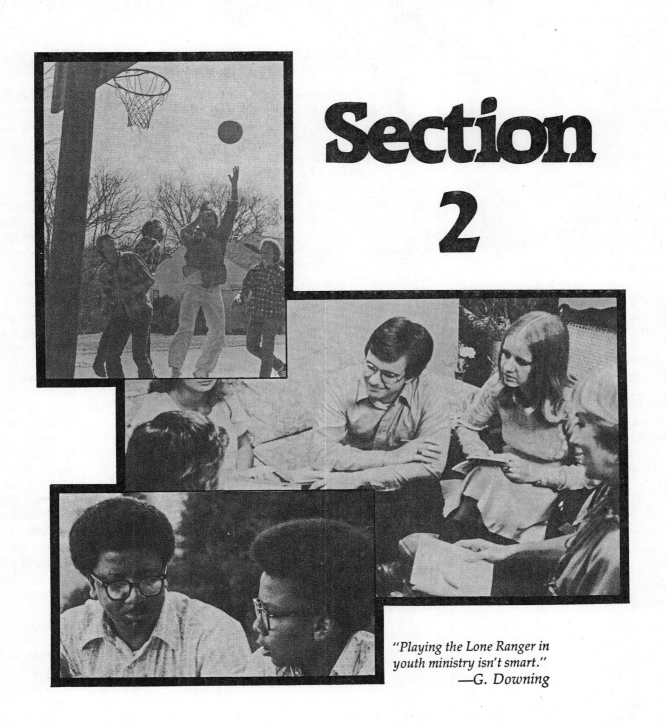

Section 2

"Playing the Lone Ranger in youth ministry isn't smart."
—G. Downing

8 The Care and Feeding of the Volunteer Youth Worker

by Gary Downing

Dr. Gary Downing *is executive director of Youth Leadership, a Minneapolis-based organization that trains youth workers. Gary also serves on the national training staff of Young Life and as a minister-at-large for Colonial Church of Edina, Minnesota. He is a graduate of Bethel College (B.A.), Bethel Seminary (M.Div.), and Luther-Northwestern Seminary (Doctor of Ministry). For information about Youth Leadership, contact: Dr. Gary Downing, Youth Leadership, 122 W. Franklin Ave., Minneapolis, MN 55404.*

I am a volunteer youth worker. I have often felt confused, overwhelmed, and inadequate around teenagers. I've sometimes felt lonely, frustrated, and even mad as a hornet around other youth leaders. At times I have wondered why I ever volunteered to work with youth.

I have also experienced times of caring, affirmation, support, and even celebration during the 13 years I've been involved with teenagers. Seeing young people experience the joy of new life in Christ, and then watching some of those same teenagers grow up and become youth leaders themselves, has been tremendously rewarding.

I got involved in youth ministry "by chance." While I was a junior in college, someone asked me to drive a school bus full of teens to a weekend youth retreat. I needed the extra money, so I agreed to drive. I brought a stack of books with me, planning to finish a term paper than was due. But I never came close to working on that paper! I spent the weekend walking around watching wide-eyed as those rowdy kids actually listened to a Christ-centered presentation of the Gospel and had a fun-filled weekend besides. (I had been raised in a setting where if anything was much fun, it was suspected to be unchristian.)

By the end of the weekend, I was hooked. Those kids were open and receptive to the Gospel, and I felt a warmth toward the staff as well. So I volunteered to help out on a more regular basis.

Within six months I was put in charge of leading the whole youth group. It all seemed so exciting and I was having too much fun to ask any technical questions like, "What am I supposed to do?" or "How much time should I spend?" or "Why are you putting *me* in charge of this ministry?" The answers to these questions came later, and then only through difficulty and disillusionment.

The excitement lasted about three more months. I was spending every spare minute being with the kids and directing the youth group. I didn't have time for personal devotions, my grades were dropping, and I hardly ever saw my family. I was beginning to feel all wrung out spiritually. And I didn't have time to really prepare for the youth meetings because I had gotten too involved with running the program.

One day I was driving to a youth group meeting, hastily trying to prepare a message. But nothing would come. All I could think about was how tired I was. And in spite of all the time I'd been spending with kids, I also felt very lonely. For the first time, I began to evaluate this ministry I'd so thoughtlessly jumped into. I realized how selfish my motivation had been. I saw that I wanted those kids to need *me*. I liked being around those good-looking high school girls. I enjoyed being treated with respect by those athletic guys. I began to wonder what in the world I was doing in youth ministry.

My case is probably extreme. Most volunteer youth workers don't have such mixed MOTIVES.. Most are not guilty of operating without a clear understanding of the MESSAGE they are called to deliver. And most probably have some awareness of the reasons behind the METHODS they use in their ministries. Yet, I've met enough volunteer leaders who have struggled with those "3 Ms" of ministry that I know I'm not totally alone. For the volunteer youth worker who can use some help in sorting out his *motives*, his *message*, and his *methods*, I offer the following hard-learned tips.

Don't Do It Alone

The first rule is: *Don't do it alone!* Some things are dangerous when done solo. It's never a good idea to go swimming alone, or to lift weights alone. Playing the Lone Ranger in youth ministry isn't smart either.

Christ sent His disciples out two by two. The Apostle Paul took somebody with him on his missionary journeys. Working in ministry with another person (or people) who shares a common vision is a practical way of "staying alive" in volunteer youth work.

Developing an adult "best friend in ministry" frees the youth worker from an unhealthy dependency on his youth group members' affirmation. So he can love them *unconditionally*, demanding nothing in return. Having a partner in ministry can sharpen vision, clean up motives, and increase effectiveness.

In my experience as a volunteer youth worker, there have been times of failure and discouragement. The support of a ministry partner and a little band of committed adults kept me going. We enjoyed being together, and we *knew* we needed each other.

In addition to the support it offers, the loving relationship of a few adults can be a powerful witness to students. It can serve as a living example of God's love in operation.

So don't do it alone. Find someone who will share your love for God and your desire to reach kids.

Priorities

A second rule is: *Don't make youth ministry too high a priority*. My own ranking, beginning with the area of highest priority, is as follows: God first, family second, church third, vocation fourth, youth ministry fifth. I have found that if my ministry comes any higher, other relationships—and my effectiveness with youth—*both suffer*. If youth ministry comes much lower in priority, I have trouble fulfilling my commitment to volunteer youth work.

At one time, such a ranking of priorities would have been unthinkable to me. "After all," I would have argued, "God wants me to give those kids my all." But an important part of my spiritual growth has come from reordering my priorities, and reorganizing my life to reflect those priorities.

I've discovered some significant results: The emotional and spiritual maturity gained by keeping priorities in order, results in a more holistic ministry to youth. Caring properly for one's family, and for brothers and sisters in the church, increases one's capacity for caring for youth. A proper focus on relationship with God develops a spiritual keenness that translates directly into youth ministry.

Through this prioritized network of relationships, the volunteer youth worker grows and is molded into the image of Christ. His ministry takes on more depth and power as he gives his life to kids as a fifth priority.

Have you ever done an inventory of your life's priorities? How do they match with what you believe are God's priorities for you? Don't let ego needs, or even kids' needs, squeeze you into giving your volunteer youth ministry a higher priority than God intends.

Vision for Ministry

The third rule for volunteer leadership with youth is: *Discover a personal vision for ministry*. Without a personal vision, the volunteer is easily tempted to lay back and leave the job to a

> "God has a place in ministry for all believers, not just for the hired church staff."

"hired gun"—the ministry professional. But God has a place in ministry for all believers, not just for the hired church staff.

The church too often resembles American spectator sports—22,000 people, badly in need of exercise, going to watch 22 people, badly in need of a rest, play ball. Christians can't afford to be spectators in a world that is so desperate for witness and service. The volunteer youth worker must determine what God wants him to accomplish, then be obedient to that vision.

For years I felt inferior as a youth worker because I couldn't perform as well as two of the professionals I

> "I couldn't perform as well as two of the professionals I knew."

knew. I didn't have the musical ability of one or the energetic humor of the other. I wondered if there was a place for me till I discovered the joy of just *being myself*. I realized that I had to take the risk of offering my life to students. I couldn't spend my time trying to be somebody else. I had to discover my own vision for ministry.

Stand in the Gap

A fourth rule for volunteer youth leaders is: *Learn how to "stand in the gap."*

After the Korean War, psychologists tried to discover why American GIs had been more susceptible to brainwashing in North Korean POW camps than had Turkish soldiers. One of North Korea's most effective techniques involved lining up an American platoon and giving an inhuman, ridiculous order. The North Koreans then threatened to kill the commissioned officer in charge if the command was not carried out immediately. When the platoon didn't respond, the guards hauled the officer in charge off behind the barracks. The rest of the men in the platoon heard several shots, then silence. This technique proved successful in manipulating the Americans into answering questions and divulging secrets.

But the Turkish troops responded differently. When the commanding officer was hauled off, the next person in the chain of command stepped into the gap and took control. As each leader refused to obey the clearly unlawful orders, he was hauled off—to be replaced by the next in command. This went on down the line until there was only one person in the platoon left to stand in the gap. What the soldiers didn't realize was that no one was really getting killed. The North Koreans were conducting a psychological ploy to undermine morale and to force the soldiers to divulge confidential information. The guards merely placed the "victims" in isolation in other POW camps.

The difference between the American and Turkish troops was that the Turks were willing to face death in order to "stand in the gap," instead of giving in to the enemy's demands.

The lesson for the youth worker, particularly the volunteer, is that often he will be called on to "stand in the gap." At times, he will feel as if God has given too big a vision, or too heavy a load, or too awesome a task.

But the beauty of taking on something that one is ill-equipped to handle is that it forces him to trust in God's power, not his own strength, to accomplish the mission God has called him to perform. Jesus "stood in the gap" and gave His life for the world. Will we volunteer to "stand in the gap" by being a bridge for divine reconciliation between young people and God? There is no higher calling!

The Support Team 9

by Chris Renzelman

One of the greatest threats to a youth ministry is the phenomenon of the "Phantom Youth Worker." When a youth worker is stricken by a Phantom mentality, he believes he can *do* and *be* all to his youth ministry—all by himself.

I've played the Phantom before, and periodically fall back into the role. At one time, my life became so packed with ministry activity that I was a nervous wreck. I was always on the go. One day I realized that my Irish setter had been running around the house a lot. Why? Because in just trying to keep up with me, that dog had adopted my frantic pace.

The Apostle Paul's instruction in 1 Timothy 2:2 and 1 Thessalonians 4:11 to lead a quiet and peaceful life (meaning tranquility arising both from without and within) seemed nonexistent in my life. Reading Romans 14:12, I began to wonder how I would respond to the Lord's question: "Chris, of those things I gave you to do, what did you get done?"

"Well, Lord, I did this and this and this. . . ."

"No, Chris, of the things *I gave you to do*, what did you get done?"

I felt sobered by the fact that my ultimate accountability lies with Him, not with the pressures that push me away from biblical priorities.

The Apostle Paul said to "therefore be careful how you walk, not as unwise men, but as wise, making the most of your time. . . . So then do not be foolish, but understand what the will of the Lord is" (Eph. 5:15-17). But I found that it's one thing to know what to do and another to be able to *do only that*, even with an understanding of the Spirit's role and en-

abling power. I've concentrated on time management from all angles, but it's still a struggle for me not to become overwhelmed by all that needs to be done.

Teamwork

Perhaps the most important action a youth worker can use to change this discouraging situation is to build a *support team*. Such a team consists of a group of volunteer adult sponsors and key student leaders who are actively involved in the *ministering* process.

The Apostle Paul wrote, "And the things you have heard me say in the presence of many witnesses entrust to reliable men who will also be qualified to teach others" (2 Tim. 2:2, NIV).

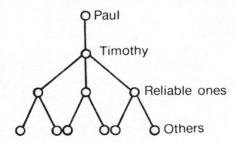

Delegation

Regardless of your ministry's size, there are people around who can effectively help you. If you have a multiplication mind-set, it becomes more natural to involve others in the ministering process. (For a definition of *multiplication*, see chapter 2, "A Philosophy of Youth Ministry.")

Chris Renzelman is the co-founder of Student Impact International, an organization that develops a variety of training materials for use with high school students. Currently, Chris oversees the development of H.U.B. ("Helping-U-Become") Resources, materials designed for training students how to evangelize and disciple on the high school campus. Chris also serves as minister to students and young adults at the Highland Community Church in Renton, Washington.

Involving others in the ministry is not always easy. You have to be willing to allow others the freedom to grow—and to fail! If you're *afraid* that your support team members are going to fail, you'll transmit that fear to the team. Fear of failure can cripple a support team ministry.

The stories of Gideon, Joshua, David, Nehemiah, and Moses illustrate how they worked through the fear of failure. Their successes ultimately came from a firm focus on what God had called them to accomplish, and from confidence in His promises.

Also, each of those men depended heavily on others to help him accom-

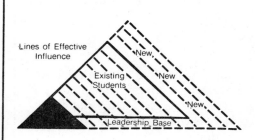

8. *Try to pay your workers in accordance with need and merit (1 Cor. 9:11-14; Luke 10:7; Matt. 10:10; 1 Tim. 5:17-18).* Yet don't discourage any volunteers from ministering as long as their needs are met and their service is to the Lord (Matt. 6:1). This is part of how the body works together.

God doesn't want you to minister alone. As you tap the source of God's given wealth in others, you find unlimited potential. But incorporating this philosophy of a support team into the church structure is not always easy. You may need to win your senior pastor and governing board's cooperation concerning your goals for building a support team.

"Be willing to allow others the freedom to grow—and to fail!"

---

plish God's purposes. Delegation is a must, not only to maintain the youth worker's sanity, but to accomplish God's purposes most effectively.

Developing a Support Team

The following guidelines can be helpful in building a support team:

1. *Remember that manpower resources are usually available.* Pray for "eyes to see."

2. *Help develop individual potential.* Don't get so caught up in programs that you miss the purpose—reaching and building *people.*

3. *Realize that a movement or organization experiences healthy growth in direct proportion to its leadership's effectiveness.*
It takes time to build solidly. Just compare the growth time and strength of a squash to an oak tree. Don't be

afraid to take time to develop leaders.

4. *Don't fear failure.* Worry is interest paid on an account that seldom comes due. Move out with confidence and realize who stands with you (Acts 4:13; 2 Kings 6:15-17).

5. *Demonstrate a balanced life (Mark 6:31; 1 Tim. 5:8).* Insure that you get time alone—"think time." The busier you become, the more essential think time becomes. During your think time, list all the activities you are presently involved in; then try to come up with 20 ways to do them better.

6. *Remember we all started somewhere; so begin where your team members are and build from there (Mark 4:33-34).*

7. *Pray for your support team (1 Tim. 2:1-3; Eph. 6:18-20).*

Convictions and Beliefs

Convictions, more than beliefs, are needed to bring about such changes. *Beliefs* are ideas and thoughts that you hold onto. *Convictions* are those ideas and thoughts that hold onto you. Your life revolves around convictions.

Surround yourself with individuals who share a support team leadership philosophy (Prov. 15:22; 20:18; 24:6). Bathe each step in prayer.

Remember that a particular *method* may work in one church, but not in another. Notice that's *method*—not *philosophy.* Philosophy can be applied in varying situations, but methods of implementation vary. Be creative based on where you are with your church's unique set of needs.☐

"The busier you become, the more essential think time becomes."

Developing a Team Ministry

10

by Tim Kimmel

The importance of developing a team for youth ministry has already been pointed out in chapter 9. We *can't* do the job alone. But if we have a team—a group of committed adults and student leaders, we can dramatically increase ministry effectiveness.

So many youth workers are out here all alone, not realizing the value of a team, afraid to put people around them, maybe even afraid to "share the limelight." Or they feel, "It's just easier to do it myself." But that's not the way we've been called to do it; and it's not the most effective way.

We've got to realize how essential it is to *spread* our ministry into the hands of others, and thereby reach more people for Christ than any one of us could alone. The Bible addresses this need. Some classic examples of team ministries are found in these passages:

● Moses and the judges (Ex. 18:13-26)
● Shadrach, Meshach, and Abednego (Dan. 3)
● Paul, Silas, and Timothy (Acts 15:36—16:5)
● Jesus and His disciples (Luke 6:12-16)

Following are some guidelines for developing an effective team ministry with adult and student leaders.

Selection

The most important aspect of developing a team ministry is selecting the right people. I have had students and young adults say to me, "Tim, I want to be in the ministry. I want to be involved." Unfortunately, they didn't have certain characteristics that I look for in team members. They may have had some enthusiasm, but lacked other crucial qualities.

In selecting team members, look for the following characteristics, through observation, prayer, and the Holy Spirit's leading:

● *Desire to serve.* Many people want to be in a flashy ministry, but they don't have servants' hearts. They want to be up front; but they don't want to pass out songbooks, or set up chairs, or drive kids home after a meeting. Those tasks are all part of the ministry. No one is too good to do any job. Someone might be better suited for a particular job; but ultimately, every team member should be willing to do what's necessary to meet the needs of youth.

● *Faithfulness.* If a person is not faithful in *little* things, how can he be trusted with much? (Luke 16:10)

An executive was on the verge of becoming the president of a large, prestigious bank. The job would have provided not only a high-paying salary, but tremendous responsibility.

A few hours before the board of directors was to present the position to him, the executive went to lunch with the board chairman. While going through a cafeteria line, the chairman saw the executive slip a couple of pats of butter underneath his napkin, to avoid having to pay for them. Just a

Tim Kimmel developed a burden to minister full-time to youth while leading a Young Life club in Dallas, Texas. He graduated from Bryan College and Dallas Theological Seminary, then served four years as youth minister at the Scottsdale Bible Church in Scottsdale, Arizona. Tim presently ministers as a conference speaker and writer of youth discipleship materials for Shepherd Productions.

"The most important aspect is selecting the right people."

few cents. But after the chairman saw the theft, he quickly called a meeting of the board. They immediately decided to drop the executive.

The reason? If they couldn't trust that bank officer with a few measly cents, they couldn't trust him with millions of dollars. The same principle is true for servants of Christ. We should look for people who have demonstrated *faithfulness* to God.

• *Availability*. A person comes to you and says he wants to be involved with you in ministry. "I appreciate your interest," you respond. "But you should be aware that in this particular

> ## *"Look for someone who's willing to bend and modify his lifestyle."*

ministry, you will need to attend a team meeting once a week. You'll need to meet once a month with all the coordinators. Also, you'll need to be here an hour early whenever we have a youth activity."

Suddenly the formerly willing volunteer begins to hedge: "Well, I've got this job; I've got to study, my friends want me to. . . ." The excuses may be entirely legitimate. But the point is, if the person is not going to be available and willing to bend his schedule some, he won't make a good team member. Look for somebody who's willing to bend and modify his lifestyle to benefit the ministry.

• *Teachability*. Someone else approaches you. This person is sharp and talented, but when it comes to letting someone teach him a new ministry skill or help him adjust to a new procedure, he's just not open. Such a person is not willing to grow. His unwillingness to be taught will hold back the success of your ministry team. A good way to combat this problem in others is to exemplify openness and teachability. (Show openness to being taught by your superiors and by those whom you oversee.)

One final warning about selecting a team member: Don't select someone just because he has the right spiritual gifts, raw talents, or personality for youth ministry. Make sure he also wants to serve, will be faithful, available, and teachable. A worker can have all the talent in the world, but without those character qualities he'll fail miserably.

Vision

Transfer your personal vision of youth ministry to your team. Rehearse it with them. Make sure they understand that their commitment is not to some program or building, but to students. Team members who catch a vision for working with youth will be motivated to carry on the ministry in your absence. And, if God leads one of your team members into another ministry somewhere else, your vision can be multiplied through him in a new location.

Team Relationships

Develop strong team relationships by spending time with your workers—inside and outside of ministry activities. Jesus socialized with His disciples. And yet He never spent His time unwisely. He developed His workers through whatever situation they happened to be in together—healing the sick or sharing a meal.

Going to a restaurant, ball game, or concert with your staff gives you opportunity to model godly behavior beyond the boundaries of "the ministry." When involved in a ministry activity, you're *expected* to live the Christian life. But it's good for your workers to see a leader who exhibits Christian qualities in the everday af-

fairs of life. Also, observing your staff in real-life situations helps you accurately evaluate their growth.

Your time together, inside and outside of the ministry, should be *fun*. Youth ministry always has its headaches and heartaches. But God has given you and your staff the Holy Spirit so you can be filled with joy, edify one another, and share one another's burdens.

Freedom to Fail

Give your workers the freedom to fail. They need to know they won't be rejected or fired just because they make mistakes. Team members shouldn't have the pressure of someone breathing down their necks, waiting for a blunder.

God is always willing to forgive, correct, and redirect. He is the God of the second chance when we make a mistake. And we should give the same grace to our staff.

Spending Time

Spend time with your key team members. If you have a large group of adult sponsors and student leaders, spending quality time with all of them is impossible. But try to spend time with several people who are especially close to you, who are directly accountable to you, and who have major responsibility in the ministry. Call them often, keep them informed of what's happening in your life, and vice versa. If they are graduating, or receiving an award, or being honored, etc., *be there*. Let them know you want to be involved in their lives.

On-the-Job Training

Take team members with you as you go places to minister. This gives them an opportunity to learn and to contribute, and ultimately relieves you of some ministerial burdens. Seeing you do the work of the ministry is an excellent way for team members to learn ministry skills. This form of on-the-job training is healthy for you and for them.

testimony.

- *Supplication*. Pray for one another's personal needs. This is not a time of prayer for the "ministry" as much as for the individuals involved in ministry. Bear one another's burdens through prayer.

- *Information*. Informally share with one another personal matters—things that are happening in your lives. Again, this sharing isn't necessarily related to the ministry, but involves matters that are important to you and your team members. Sharing this kind

those that have worked for me. But there's one other thing—one final caution—that I must pass along:

Remember that for the most part, team members are *ordinary people*. So, carefully avoid a "superstar" mentality. It's great to encourage your people and make them feel that you have confidence in them, but keep in mind that your workers are ordinary people in the hands of an extraordinary God! And what He can do with average people is phenomenal!

But if you project a superstar image, and your staff tries to emulate you, they can easily become discouraged. You may ask for something that's impossible, and so they try and fail. They may feel they can never do it the way you can; never say it the way you can; never have the confidence or charisma that you exhibit.

> *"Seeing you do the work of the ministry is an excellent way for team members to learn ministry skills."*

Short Accounts

Don't let anger, disappointment, or bitterness become deeply rooted in your team members' lives. Always clear the air as quickly as possible. The Word commands that you do not allow the sun to set on your wrath (Eph. 4:26). Be quick to reconcile any problem between you and a team member.

On occasion, you may need to work with team members to help settle disputes between them. Satan loves to divide and destroy. Defeat him by making sure you and your team members keep short accounts.

Team Meetings

Meet regularly as a team. Ideally, try to meet on a weekly basis. But most importantly, make your meetings regular. Aim to include the following ingredients in your meetings:

- *Reflection*. Share spiritual insights and principles that workers have gained. All can benefit from this time of shared fellowship and

of personal information provides another opportunity for team members to show a genuine interest in one another.

- *Evaluation*. Evaluate constantly. Always evaluate last week's activities and try to determine how close you and your staff are to accomplishing your objectives. Discuss areas which need to be improved. This can be a good time for you to carefully and lovingly strengthen weak areas in your workers.

- *Projection*. Look ahead to upcoming events, both immediate and long range. *Immediate projection* includes taking care of last minute details, and using an "inventory list" to help keep track of what needs to be done. *Long-range projection* includes finding out what needs to be done for future events. Use a master schedule calendar and individual personalized calendars for long-range planning.

Ordinary People

Other ingredients for developing and sustaining a vibrant team ministry could be mentioned. I have shared

Mr. Marriott, owner of a chain of hotels, told a story about Bing Crosby. Somebody asked Mr. Crosby why he thought so many people liked his voice. Crosby answered, "I think people like my voice because when they hear me sing, they think *they* can sing well too." Though few people could actually sing as well as Crosby, he made listeners feel as if he wasn't on some kind of pedestal, showing off his voice and skill.

The story is a good lesson to apply to team ministry. Your team members need to know that they are making a significant contribution. No matter *what* they do—handing out songbooks, or setting up chairs—their *faithful* commitment to their tasks is important!

Your team members also need to feel that they can succeed and that you are committed to helping them succeed in the ministry. You can give them the direction and confidence they need by spending time with them individually. Your support says to each one, "*We* are going to make it; you are not alone. *I'm* with you. The *team's* with you. The *Lord's* with you. And we're dedicated to succeeding in this ministry *together*."

Some Biblical Standards

● *"A pupil is not above his teacher, but everyone, after he has been fully trained, will be like his teacher"* (Luke 6:40).

As leaders we need to watch our walk with God. We need to be careful, realizing that all we do sets an example; that we are *always* witnesses, either for good or for bad. Our example must be worthy to follow.

● *"And the things which you have heard from me in the presence of many witnesses, these entrust to faithful men, who will be able to teach others also"* (2 Tim. 2:2).

The ultimate goal of team ministry is to develop abilities, skills, gifts, godly character, etc., in other people who will in turn give away what they have to others.

● *"So David departed from there and escaped to the cave of Adullam; and when his brothers and all of his father's household heard of it, they went down there to him. And everyone who was in distress, and everyone who was in debt, and everyone who was discontented, gathered to him; and he became captain over them. Now there were about 400 men with him"* (1 Sam. 22:1-2).

David surrounded himself with a "team"—people to carry on the vision and the responsibility that God had given him. This discontented, bankrupt, distressed group whom David picked, soon became "mighty men of valor"! David chose ordinary people, people with problems, broken hearts, and fears to carry on his work.

These mighty men of valor went out to battle many times. They returned victorious many times. But their greatest defeat, their worst humiliation, came as a result of David's sin (2 Sam. 16:5-13). The team lost when their leader sinned. Leader, your walk with God helps determine the effectiveness of your team and ministry. Walk closely with Him.   □

Student Leadership

11

by Jana Sundene with Dan Webster

Structuring a youth program to include students in the ministering process benefits the students, the youth worker, and ultimately contributes to the building of God's kingdom. Because using students in leadership positions encourages them to develop others; the youth ministry increases by *multiplication* instead of by addition.

Reaping the Benefits

1. Student leadership benefits a youth worker in several ways.

As students learn to share the youth worker's burdens and to work with him toward common goals, deep friendships naturally develop. The youth worker no longer just ministers *to*, but also *with* his students. The students' lives and ministries begin to challenge the youth worker. Also, students develop a deeper under-

a youth ministry which used student leadership, that I saw it was possible to serve God in a practical way.

I saw students my age and younger learning how to give, serve, and minister to those around them. And my involvement as a student leader taught me that only in *giving myself* can I mature in Christ.

But youth workers who want to involve students in ministering to their friends, sometimes stumble when trying to get this process in motion. Note that I said, "ministering to their friends," and not "evangelizing." Though teaching personal evangelism is important, it's not enough. A youth worker must not only teach students evangelism and the importance of becoming personal disciples of Jesus Christ, he must demonstrate the importance of becoming disciple*rs* for Christ.

How can you most effectively teach students to be disciplers? By *being* a discipler. Consider these three steps as you develop student leadership:

Jana Sundene is women's coordinator of the high school ministry of Garden Grove Community Church in Garden Grove, California. Jana co-directs Son City, the church's midweek outreach program to high schoolers. She is also discipling youth through the Son City team concept, producing key student leadership.

> ## "I saw students my own age and younger learning how to give, serve, and minister to those around them."

standing and appreciation of the youth worker as they experience firsthand the struggles and joys of ministry.

2. Student leadership also benefits the students involved. I've seen this fact proven in many students' lives, but I've seen it demonstrated most clearly in my own.

As a young Christian in my junior year of high school, I wanted desperately to serve God. It wasn't till my senior year, when I became a part of

(1) modeling discipleship, (2) entrusting the ministry to students, and (3) developing a team ministry.

Modeling Discipleship

"And the things which you have heard from me in the presence of many witnesses, these entrust to

Dan Webster is high school pastor of Willow Creek Community Church in Palatine, Illinois. A graduate of Biola College, Dan spent seven years directing the high school department at Garden Grove Community Church in Garden Grove, California. With Dawson McAllister, Dan coauthored Discussion Manual for Student Discipleship *and* Discussion Manual for Student Relationships. *He speaks nationwide to thousands of high school students each year.*

faithful men, who will be able to teach others also" (2 Tim. 2:2). Once God has revealed to you which students He wants in leadership, begin discipling them.

Model discipleship, biblically *teach* discipleship, and share your *vision* in ministry with your students. Christ shared with Peter not only Peter's responsibility as a disciple, but also Christ's vision for him (Mark 1:17; Matt. 16:18; John 21:15-19).

Remember, discipleship is a character-building relationship and not just a program (See chapter 14, "Discipleship," and chapter 15, "Discipling—a Holistic Ministry.") If you only teach a "method," your students will have a hard time understanding how to build fulfilling ministry relationships. *Model* discipleship for them in your relationships *with* them.

Entrusting Students

Webster's New Collegiate Dictionary defines *entrusting* as "surrendering something to another with confidence regarding his care, use, or disposal of it." In order to make student leadership a reality, you must be willing to trust faithful students to share in your ministry. It's also important that you trust a few key students enough to share some of your own fears, doubts, and victories with them—in other words, that you open up your life as you would to a friend. The deepest kind of giving, and one of the most fulfilling forms of learning, can only take place as you entrust yourself to others, and they to you.

Christ did *not* entrust Himself to all the people who followed His ministry (John 2:24). But on one occasion, He prayed all night before calling His disciples—the 12 men He would entrust Himself to (Luke 6:12). His example shows that entrusting is a serious matter that definitely needs God's guidance. As you build friendships with those in your group, wait prayerfully for the Holy Spirit to direct you to those He would have you entrust yourself to—those He wants to become leaders.

Developing a Team Ministry

Does it seem dangerous to actually turn over certain aspects of your ministry to students? It's not really, when you consider the Apostle Paul's words: "What then is Apollos? And what is Paul? Servants through whom you believed, even as the Lord gave *opportunity* to each one. I planted, Apollos watered, but *God was causing the growth*. So then neither the one who plants nor the one who waters is anything, but *God* who causes the growth" (1 Cor. 3:5-7, italics mine). What *is* a leader but a servant? And who is too young to be a servant?

As a student grows deeper in his relationship with Christ (aided most efficiently by the discipleship process), his life exhibits more and more of Christ's character. God can certainly honor this by giving the student respect in the eyes of his peers. On this basis, one student can lead others. Limiting a student's opportunity to grow and to serve others only hinders God's work.

A team ministry usually has two major characteristics. First, instead of just one "minister" (the youth worker) there is a small "team" of ministers. Second, each *minister* has a team of students.

In my case, my co-director and I have a team of six guys and six girls—ranging in age from juniors in high school to freshmen in college—and each set of team leaders (one guy and one girl) has a team of 30-60 high schoolers. Because of how our ministry is set up, we actually call each of the six groups "teams."

It isn't necessary to have such a large group to develop a team ministry, nor is it necessary to follow our format of ministry. You may want to begin by occasionally dividing into smaller groups for Bible study or outreach. The important thing is that group leaders have opportunities to "try their own hand" at leading the groups. Of course at first, you will need to give a lot of encouragement and direction. It might help to investigate how various ministries have used the principles I've described.

Remember, whatever you do, "Run in such a way that you may win" (1 Cor. 9:24). *Run* with your students; *invest* in them!

Christ looked out on the crowds and said, "The harvest is plentiful, but the workers are few. Therefore, beseech the Lord of the harvest to send out workers into His harvest" (Matt. 9:37-38). Through the strategy of student leadership, the Lord can send out many more laborers into His harvest. What a satisfying, effective way to reach young people! □

"The deepest kind of giving . . . can only take place as you entrust yourself to others."

Leading and Motivating Students

12

by Chuck Klein

One question youth workers often ask is, "How do I successfully lead and motivate young people?" Often, the person who asks this question has tried diligently to develop a successful youth program. He is committed. He works hard. But his activity is not producing fruitful results.

I believe the Lord has written some principles right into human nature which, when applied, can direct our activity to fruitful ends. These seven principles, which I've discovered in my own ministry to high schoolers, are basic—anyone can apply them. But they have helped me immensely in my objective of leading and motivating students to follow Jesus Christ.

Meet Students' Basic Needs

You don't have to be a psychologist or a psychiatrist to apply this principle. But you should be aware of some of the basic needs of your young people and try to meet them. Every young person has three basic kinds of needs. When you help meet these needs, the student usually begins to hear what you say.

1. *Personal needs—his relationship with himself.* Every young person needs to be loved and to love others. He needs to know who he is. The whole question of identity and self-image is a major issue in his life: "Who am I? Am I of any value or worth? Can I accomplish anything?"

Ask yourself these questions: Do my young people feel better about themselves as a result of spending time with me? Do they have a greater appreciation of their worth in God's eyes?

2. *Family needs—his relationship at home.* I believe the most important concept I've ever taught young people is that God works through parents to refine their children's lives and build godly character. It's especially exciting to see a student respond to his non-Christian parents as God's instruments. When a student begins to have the proper relationship and attitude toward his parents, he will usually mature in other areas as well.

3. *Spiritual needs—his relationship with God.* As I've studied God's Word, I've asked, "What basic ingredients (spiritual essentials) does a person need in order to grow spiritually?" To really grow spiritually, I believe young people need to know the following basic biblical truths:

- *In Christ, he is a new creature.* In other words, now that he's a Christian, who is he? What's his new identity? What's his spiritual heritage?

- *His needs and desires are not identical.* Often a young person wants things that appeal directly to his old nature, or that he really doesn't need. Other desires stem from legitimate needs that God wants to satisfy. It's important that the student sees this distinction.

- *Christ's love is unconditional.*

- *Every Christian is an ambassador for Jesus Christ.* The student needs to know that God wants him as a representative of Christ to his campus.

- *He has unlimited potential in Christ.* Each student needs to know that God has mighty things in store for him—things He wants to accomplish through the young person's life.

Remember, unless you're meeting some of the basic needs of students,

Chuck Klein is national director of High School Ministry, Campus Crusade for Christ, International. Chuck was involved in high school campus ministries on the local level for 10 years before assuming his present position. He also is director of the Department of Youth Ministry in the School of Theology, International Christian Graduate University. He is author of So You Want Solutions, *a series of books for youth.*

For information regarding Campus Crusade's High School Ministry, write to them at 9968 Hibert St., Suite 200, San Diego, CA 92131.

it's impossible to motivate them spiritually. You have to meet them where they're hurting. You don't have to be "Super Youth Worker," meeting every need of every student. Simply begin to meet some of those needs, and you'll see students motivated.

Be Free to Lead

Many youth leaders have forfeited their effectiveness because they haven't stood up and led their young people. God has put us in our positions as leaders because He knows that we have the ability to lead. God has ordained it; the kids expect it. They will look to us whether we recognize it or not. Students want to be led; they want someone to give direction.

As you lead, it's important to demonstrate a lifestyle of *dependence on Christ*. It's more important that students see your faith than your spiritual gifts. If they try to imitate your gifts, they will feel inadequate. But if

But in Christian work, too often we youth workers want to run everything. We want to do all the thinking, develop the program, and plan the strategy. Instead, we should be developing ministries that are *student led* but *staff directed*. We need to learn the balance of leading while helping students develop their own leadership potentials.

Your goals will never become *their* goals till your goals become part of their thinking. In order for this to happen, students need freedom to think, plan, and create.

Challenge Students

Most students are under challenged. But most youth workers are afraid to challenge kids for fear of alienating them: "We might lose them. They might not follow us anymore if we challenge them too much."

Use the following guidelines when challenging young people:

2. *Encourage students through positive reinforcement*. Before you can challenge a student, he must know you believe in him. One of the greatest encouragers in my life was a man who took the time to express his confidence in me. Because he encouraged me, he could challenge me. Not only could he challenge me, but he could confront me concerning different problems in my life. And I listened and responded to him because he took the time to encourage.

The Apostle Paul wrote that love believes all things (1 Cor. 13). Young people need someone to believe in them.

3. *Delegate responsibility*. Ministry multiplies as ministers delegate.

When we let young people share in "our" ministry, here's what they hear: "I approve of you. I believe in you. I trust you." When we don't delegate, young people hear the opposite: "I don't approve of you. I don't believe in you. You can't do anything right. I can do everything right."

4. *Build relationships*. Relationship validates challenge. Fellowship helps build the relationship needed for challenging young people. Youth leaders are often able to challenge their students in direct proportion to the amount of time they've spent building relationships.

5. *Challenge students with the ideals of the Christian life*. The Apostle Paul speaks of the transformed mind and the privilege of service (Rom. 12:1-2). A lot of students will respond to that kind of challenge, if we're willing to give it to them.

"It's more important that students see your faith than your spiritual gifts."

---

they try to imitate your life of faith, God will give them grace to do it (Heb. 13:7).

Make Room for Youth Leadership

A fine line exists between leading and dominating. In many high schools, students run their own clubs, doing their own thinking and planning. A teacher serves merely as an adviser.

1. *Help them look beyond themselves*. The average high schooler is bored with talking on the phone, cruising main street in his car, etc. He wants something beyond what he's experiencing right now. For you to be able to take a student beyond himself, you must view him with an eternal perspective. Having eternal perspective is simply seeing your student's potential—viewing him as God does. It is accepting him where he is, while seeing beyond to what he can become. It is being future oriented, but presently involved.

Develop a Positive Attitude

Young people respond to someone who's free enough to laugh at himself, someone who has a positive attitude about himself and others. An uptight youth worker is generally an unsuccessful leader and motivator.

"Before you can challenge a student, he must know you believe in him."

Make Room for Failure

Christ allowed His disciples to fail repeatedly. When they failed, Christ did not condemn them. Instead, He took time to correct them.

"He who never makes mistakes, never makes anything," someone has said. And "He who never fails, never does anything." If you expect students to grow, allow them to fail. Your continued trust, in spite of their failures, can be a powerful motivating influence.

Teach the Basics

Help each young person learn how to:
1. *Walk by faith.*
2. *Live a Spirit-controlled life.*
3. *Share his faith.*
4. *Study the Word.*

Learning to integrate these basic principles into his life does a couple of things for a student:

● *It gives him a sense of his own growth*. It gives him confidence in his capacity to mature spiritually.

● *It gives him the ability to take those basic truths and teach them to somebody else*. One of the most important things we can do is give young people easily transferable basics that they can integrate into their own lives, then pass onto others. It's a tremendous motivator.

Remember that we are to *model* these basics. If we assume an independent attitude toward basic spiritual truth, and just try to "wing it" all the time on our own human abilities, students will pick that up. They will take the basics seriously only if we show by our lives that they're important.

Several years ago, I was in charge of leading youth ministries on a number of high school campuses in Southern California. During the first couple of years, I learned some painful lessons. But as I struggled and learned, these seven principles emerged as the "bread-and-butter" of my ministry to youth: (1) Meet students' basic needs. (2) Be free to lead. (3) Make room for youth leadership. (4) Challenge students. (5) Develop a positive attitude. (6) Make room for failure. (7) Teach the basics.

I've found that as I consistently apply these principles, students respond to my leadership and become motivated to go on toward maturity in Christ. □

13 | The Parent Factor

by John Miller

John Miller is pastor of Northwest Bible Church in Tucson, Arizona. Previously, he was a youth pastor for 13 years in California and Arizona. John is a graduate of Long Beach State College and Talbot Theological Seminary. He has co-authored with Dawson McAllister, the Manual for Student Discipleship, Vol. 2.

It's a fact of life: Parents are one of the strongest human influences on a teenager. A person rarely comes through the parent-child relationship without having the world view of his parents solidly imprinted on his personality. So, a youth worker will find it difficult, if not impossible, to minister effectively to young people without the involvement and support of parents.

The Power of Example

Why is parental influence so great? Because *example* is such a great teacher. The way parents live often speaks so loudly that teens can't hear what parents, pastors, or youth leaders are saying.

Many parents push kids for achievement academically, athletically, musically, etc. Yet they give nominal lip service toward encouraging their children in personal devotions, Scripture memory, or witnessing at school. And the parents' own lives demonstrate that they place little value on those spiritual disciplines.

Between Parent and Teen

Where do you, the youth worker, fit into this dilemma? You're a *supportive bridge* between parents and teens. You have a unique opportunity to supplement parents' efforts to bring their children up in the Christian faith. Even when parents are not doing the job of Christian nurture that they should be doing, you must strive to be a *supplement*, not a substitute parent.

Getting Parents Involved

Following are some practical steps you can take to help parents take greater responsibility for the spiritual well-being of their children:

1. Organize a parents' support team. This group consists of interested parents who wish to support the youth ministry. Parents' participation includes critiquing and discussing the direction of the youth ministry. Caution: You may feel self-conscious with

---

"Spiritually, most young people will grow no faster or farther than their parents."

In an age of secularization and family breakdown, many parents look to the youth group to provide all the things they fall short of in regard to spiritual growth. Herein lies the problem: Spiritually, most young people will grow no faster or farther than their parents.

this procedure at first, but it is important to let parents air their feelings.

2. Begin a parents' newsletter. Once a month or once a quarter, mail out a newsletter describing coming events, curriculums, insights into the youth culture, national trends and thinking patterns of youth, and critiques on current youth-related films, music, and books. Also include short testimonies of some of the youth and a section for parents and youth to sound off on various subjects. Inject humor wherever possible.

3. *Offer parents' workshops.* Work-

Twice a year plan a potluck dinner at your home or the home of another youth worker/sponsor. This allows the parents to meet you, to meet other youth workers, and to meet each other in an informal and relaxed setting. The youth workers might work on a hu-

be cool or even hostile toward the church and youth workers. When facing such a situation, keep the following points in mind:

1. *God can use even the most inept parent to accomplish His redemptive purposes in the life of a young person.* Teens need to be reminded of this fact, and encouraged to view their parents as God's instruments.

2. *A young person with a poor home life often looks to the youth worker as a substitute parent.* Since it is impossible to fill the place of a parent (unless you plan to adopt), help the young person build Christian relationships beyond his relationship with you.

3. *Don't give up on parents.* And don't let young people give up on them either. When dealing with impossible parents, remember Luke 1:37: "For nothing will be impossible with God."

Ignoring the parent factor is unwise. And yet, seeing the counter-productive influence, the hypocrisy, and the inconsistency of some parents can be frustrating. Your calling is to meet the needs of your young people so they can establish solid relationships with Jesus Christ. You must seek ways to positively affect your students' total environment—friends, church, school, and *parents.*☐

"Strive to be a supplement, not a substitute parent."

shops can be used to help parents solve parenting problems and to teach youth workers and parents how to work together in ministering to youth. (See the "Basic Needs of Adolescents" outline at the end of this chapter.) Allow at least three hours for a workshop, either in one sitting or on three consecutive weeknights. Workshops might deal with basic needs of youth, their problems and pressures, and how the principles of God's Word relate to them. Or you might have a multi-topic workshop where you discuss such issues as dating, curfew, discipline, family devotions, personal freedom, priorities, drugs, and alcohol. Some good films on parenting are available and would work well here.

4. *Plan parent/teen socials and retreats.* Examples: (1) A picnic with several games involving competitiveness and togetherness. Find time for a parent to give a brief challenge and for a few young people to give short talks relating to the family. (2) An overnight trip for fathers and sons involving hiking, outdoor cooking, etc. Situations providing some stress or inconvenience draw parents and teens together. Use devotions led by parents, skits and games, and lots of free time together.

5. *Schedule mother/daughter, mother/ son, father/son, father/daughter banquets.* Use an appropriate speaker, film, or play. Include a puppet show, door prizes, gag gifts, sports films or short family films, appreciation testimonies, etc.

6. *Organize parents' fellowships.*

morous skit and follow up by sharing why they feel called to work with teenagers. Parents appreciate a special opportunity to be introduced to those who are working with their children.

7. *Visit parents in their homes.* Ask them, "Where can I be of the greatest benefit to your child's spiritual development? Are there any specific areas of concern you have about your son? What kind of future do you visualize for your daughter?" Also give parents ample opportunity to probe *your* life and ministry.

8. *Establish an open-door policy with parents.* Clearly communicate to parents that you are always open to their input and counsel.

9. *Publicly acknowledge parents' involvement.* Be generous with public recognition whenever a parent expends energy on behalf of the youth ministry. Use letters, as well as verbal expressions, to communicate appreciation.

The Impossible Parent

Sometimes, working with parents seems virtually impossible. For any number of reasons, some parents may

See outline on page 50.

"Communicate to parents that you are always open to their input and counsel."

Basic Needs of Adolescents

TEENS' NEEDS

A. *Need for acceptance* (Accept me for who I am.)
   Key: Age of masquerades, consequently teen:
   1. Lives at a fast pace; no time for family life.
   2. Fears revealing his real self.
   3. Conforms to be accepted ("be one of us").
   4. Accepts others conditionally (good looks, social standing, money, athletic ability, etc.).

B. *Need to be challenged* (something to live for.)
   Key: Age of apathy, consequently teen:
   1. Majors in minors.
   2. Is often lethargic, unmotivated.
   3. Lives for pleasure.

   4. Follows anyone with a cause.

C. *Need to have role models.*
   Key: Age of despair, consequently:
   1. Leaders are not leading.
   2. Teachers are not teaching.
   3. Parents are not parenting.

   4.. Peers have no direction.

PARENTS' RESPONSES

Key: Be honest, open, human.

1. Spend quality time (communicate).
2. Do not fear revealing your imperfections.
3. Let teen be himself.
4. De-emphasize worldly standards.

Key: Make own goals and dreams known:
1. Major in majors.
2. Give responsibility; require fulfillment.
3. Communicate consequences of hedonism, benefits of crucifying the flesh.
4. Speak of great men and women and the impact of their lives on the world.

Key: Be a source of hope and direction.
1. Be a leader.
2. Be a teacher.
3. Make parenting a higher priority than job or church activities.
4. Encourage meaningful relationships; discuss ways to strengthen Christian friendships (Prov. 13:20; 1 Cor. 15:33).

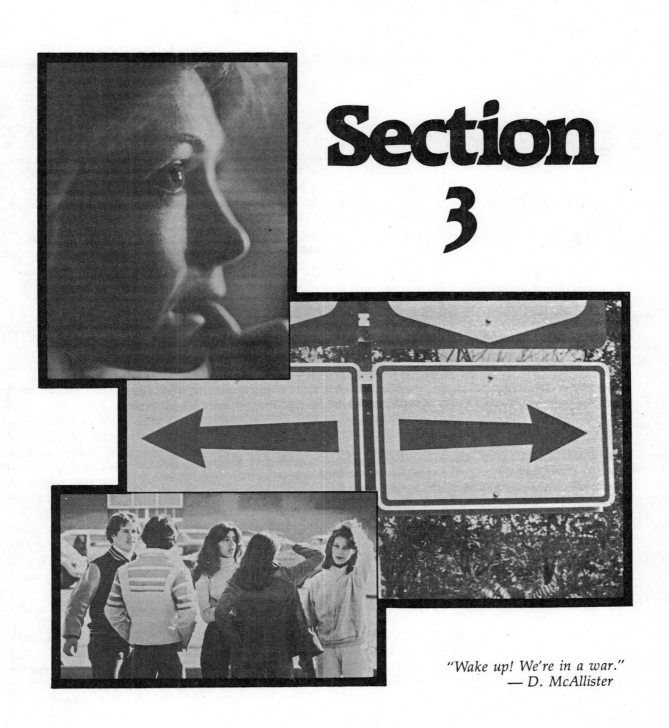

Section 3

"Wake up! We're in a war."
— D. McAllister

14 Discipleship

by Barry St. Clair

Barry St. Clair is founder and director of Reach Out Ministries. He has been director of youth evangelism for the Southern Baptist Home Mission Board, a member of the Athletes in Action basketball team, and named to Outstanding Young Men in America. The author of several books, including a series on student discipleship, Barry is a specialist in discipling high school students through church youth groups. He is a graduate of Southern Baptist Seminary in Louisville, Kentucky. For information on Reach Out Ministries, write to Reach Out Ministries, 3117 Majestic Circle, Avondale Estates, GA 30002.

The word *discipleship* is used a lot these days without being clearly defined. What is *discipleship*? It is: one maturing believer/reproducing other maturing believers/to the degree that they are also able to reproduce maturing believers.

The clear mandate of Jesus Christ to His followers is, "Go therefore and make disciples of all the nations" (Matt. 28:19). If we are going to have a lasting impact on the high school students we work with, we must obey our Lord's command.

Why Discipleship?

Why should youth workers be involved in a ministry of discipleship? Consider the following motivational factors:

1. *The motive of obedience (Matt. 28:19-20).* Christ commanded us to make disciples. That alone should be sufficient motivation. In *The Cost of Discipleship*, Dietrich Bonhoeffer makes this statement: "All the activity of the disciples is subject to the clear precept of their Lord. They are not left free to choose their own methods or adapt their own conception of their task. Their work is to be Christ-work, and therefore they are absolutely dependent on the will of Jesus."[1]

2. *The motive of producing fruit that remains (John 15:16).* Christ appointed us to go and bear fruit—fruit that lasts. If we want to produce students with a depth and quality of life in Christ, then discipleship is a must.

3. *The motive of multiplication of spiritual leaders (Matt. 9:37).* Again,

discipleship means reproducing maturing believers who are able to reproduce other maturing believers. The goal of discipleship is to produce fellow laborers for the harvest.

Clearly then, Scripture provides motivation for involvement in a discipleship ministry. The Bible also speaks clearly to the issue of *how* to develop people spiritually. This task must begin with the leader—the discipler.

The Leader's Relationship with Christ

Paul exhorted Timothy to "be strong in the grace that is in Christ Jesus" (2 Tim. 2:1, KJV). Before we can begin to produce disciples who will have an impact on the world, we must be right in our own relationships with Christ.

Too often, our relationships with Christ can be compared with the man who painted white stripes down the highway for the Department of Transportation. The first day, he painted five miles of stripes. The second day, he painted two miles; the third day, 576 feet; and the fourth day, only 180 feet. The boss called him in and asked him, "Are you sick?" "No," the painter replied. The boss then asked, "What's the problem?" The painter said, "I just keep getting farther and farther from the bucket."

For discipleship to be successful, as leaders, we must stay "close to the bucket" by being involved in a daily, personal walk with Jesus. How can this happen? The Apostle Paul gives us a clue: "The goal of our instruction is love from a pure heart and a good conscience and a sincere faith" (1 Tim. 1:5).

Paul and Timothy's goal for their ministries was love. They wanted their ministries to be characterized by the outflowing of God's *agapé* love from their lives to the people they ministered to. This should be our goal too. But this goal cannot be accomplished unless we have received God's agapé love in our own lives and are living in that love. Also, we need to be expressing our love back to God through obedience. Jesus tells us: "He who has My commandments and keeps them, he it is who loves Me; and he who loves Me shall be loved by My Father, and I will love him, and will disclose Myself to him" (John 14:21).

How do we reach the point where God's *agapé* love characterizes our ministry? First, to follow the order Paul gives in 1 Timothy 1:5, we need a "pure heart." We need to be washed of any sin that might be in our lives. We can do this by getting alone with God, confessing the sin, and then claiming the cleansing power of Christ: "If we confess our sins, He is faithful and righteous to forgive us our sins and to cleanse us from all unrighteousness" (1 John 1:9).

A "pure heart" also means that our hearts have a *single* preoccupation, and that preoccupation is Jesus Christ. Count Von Zinzendorf, the founder of the Moravian Church which had such a great influence on John Wesley, made this classic statement: "I have but one passion; it is He, He alone." The psalmist put it another way: "O God, Thou art my God; I shall seek Thee earnestly; my soul thirsts for Thee, my flesh yearns for Thee, in a dry and weary land where there is no water" (Ps. 63:1).

Second, Paul indicates, we need a "good conscience." Having a good conscience is knowing with confidence that we have no broken or strained relationships. We need to examine ourselves to make sure that our relationships are healthy ones. If they are not, Jesus has told us to first be reconciled to our brother, and then come and present our offerings (Matt. 5:24). We allow the Holy Spirit to show us those we have offended, then we go and make things right. Afterward, we can return and worship God with a "good conscience."

Third, we need a "sincere faith." Having a sincere faith means putting into practice the knowledge that we have. As one of my friends says, "You put into practice what you really believe. All the rest is just religious talk."

By being sincerely obedient to God, we can trust Him for His very best. When God commands, our response should be an enthusiastic, "Yes, Sir." When I ask my son Scott to do something, he often responds with, "Wait just a minute, Dad." I say, "No, Scott; just, 'Yes, sir.' " Often I respond to God the way Scott responds to me: "Wait a minute, Lord," when all He wants from me is a simple "Yes, Sir."

When we are clean-hearted, single-minded, with right relationships and obedient lives, then Jesus can use us as tools in a discipling ministry.

Relationships with Youth

It's clear that Paul had a close relationship with Timothy. He called him "my son" (2 Tim. 2:1) and he spoke of the things which Timothy had heard from him (2:2). Paul invested this fact. I met with them in a group setting, but I never associated with them outside of the group. We went through some materials and discussed them, but that was about all. After all the group meetings were over, one of my students, Lee, started going to confirmation class at the Jewish synagogue. I suspected then that I had made some mistakes. In evaluation, I saw that I had not invested my life in the students, but had merely held a class for them. I retraced my steps, and began to spend hours talking with Lee. I discovered that he really was looking for God.

We talked off and on for several months, getting down to some real problem areas in Lee's life. Soon he received Christ. After that, it took even more time to help him grow and become established in the faith.

Was it worth it? Yes! In high school, Lee won several people to Christ. In college, he led several discipleship groups, and numerous students accepted Christ as a result of his ministry. During his senior year of college, Lee was the leader of one of the Christian groups on his campus. Now he senses that God has called him into a pastoral ministry. You bet it was worth it!

Paul gives us a clear picture of the commitment required in a discipling relationship: "Having thus a fond affection for you, we were well-pleased to impart to you not only the Gospel of God but also our own lives,

> *"Discipleship means investing your life in your students' lives, not just meeting with them once a week for Bible study."*

his life in young Timothy. So, discipleship means investing your life in your students' lives, not just meeting with them once a week for Bible study.

An experience with my first high school discipleship group illustrates because you had become very dear to us" (1 Thes. 2:8).

Discipling is not a hit-or-miss ministry, but one in which we give away the most precious commodity we have—our time—in order to develop men and women of God.

Character Training

Our goal as disciple-makers is to produce disciples who have the character of Jesus. Paul said, "For our Gospel did not come to you in word only, but also in power and in the Holy Spirit and with full conviction; just as you know what kind of men we proved to be among you for your sake" (1 Thes. 1:5). Paul not only preached the Word, he lived it, and he taught as much through his actions as he did through his words.

A guiding principle should be: "And He has said to me, 'My grace is sufficient for you, for power is perfected in weakness.' Most gladly, therefore, I will rather boast about my weaknesses, that the power of Christ may dwell in me" (2 Cor. 12:9).

When we are vulnerable about our weaknesses, and when we are free to drop our "super-spiritual fronts," people feel more comfortable with us. People identify with us much more when we are open to share our problems. And people keep their eyes, not on some super-spiritual human leader, but on Jesus.

"Character training gets a disciple's obedience level up to his knowledge level."

Jesus illustrated this teaching method when He washed His disciples' feet (John 13). He not only told them that the greatest among them would be the servant. He demonstrated this truth. His example etched this truth on the tablet of their hearts. Character training gets a disciple's obedience level up to his knowledge level.

To Be Real

A discipling relationship develops a solid foundation when the disciple sees his leader in a variety of situations, especially in the leader's weaker moments.

A college girl I knew violated this principle with a classmate she led to Christ. While discipling her classmate, this older Christian never shared her struggles or failures. She wanted to be looked up to as a "mature Christian." But, the new Christian became very frustrated and discouraged because she *was* having struggles and failures, and didn't understand that they were part of every Christian's life.

Recruiting

Paul told Timothy to pass on the things Paul had taught him to "faithful men" (2 Tim. 2:2). We need to invest our lives in a few "faithful men." Thoroughly training a few workers is more effective than training many workers superficially.

What are the characteristics of faithful men and women which we need to look for? Faithful people are people who are 100 percent sold out to Jesus Christ. The psalmist gives us a picture of the kind of person we are to look for: "As the deer pants for the water brooks, so my soul pants for Thee, O God. My soul thirsts for God, for the living God; when shall I come and appear before God?" (Ps. 42:1-2) A good disciple has a thirst to know God. Not everyone has this. Seek those who do. As you look for these people, be open for God to point them out to you.

Multiplication

Paul mentions four generations of the discipleship process: Paul, Timothy, "faithful men," and "others also" (2 Tim. 2:2). By reproducing spiritual leaders, we *multiply* Christians in the world. Paul poured his life into Timothy. Timothy invested his life in "faithful men." And these "faithful men" invested their lives into other faithful men, and on and on. This process caused a far greater impact on the world than if Paul had just spent his time leading people to faith in Jesus Christ, but not taking them any farther than that.

Spiritual multiplication through discipleship is the tool to accomplish world evangelization in our day. If one Christian would lead one person to Christ every week for the next 16 years, 832 people would become Christians. Or if one Christian would lead one person to Christ every day for the next 16 years, 5,840 people would become Christians.

But, if one Christian would win one person and then disciple that person for the next six months so that person could win and train another, at the end of six months there would be only two people. Then if those two won two more and discipled them during the next six months, there would be four. . . .

At the end of the first year = 4 people
At the end of 1½ years = 16 people
At the end of 2 years = 32 people
At the end of 2½ years = 64 people
At the end of 3 years = 256 people
At the end of 4 years = 1,024 people
At the end of 5 years = 4,096 people
At the end of 6 years = 8,192 people
At the end of 16 years = 4,294,967,296 people

This is more than the entire population of the world!

Steps in Discipling

You might be asking at this point, "How do I go about beginning a discipleship ministry?" Here are seven basic steps that should help you as you seek to follow God in a ministry of investing your life in the lives of tudents:

1. Pray for conviction. Before you begin a ministry of discipleship, be absolutely sure it is God's ministry for you. Through prayer, let it become a conviction. Then, when you get down the road a few weeks and problems begin to crop up (and they will), knowing that you are involved in what God wants you involved in will give you the strength to keep on.

2. Pray for vision. Ask God to show you how He wants to use you to make an impact on your world. Dawson Trotman, founder of the Navigators, once said, "Why pray for peanuts when God wants to give us continents?" So often, our vision is limited to our own little world. But real vision is the ability to see that which is not yet seen.

Thomas Edison had a vision for harnessing electricity. He failed 1,000 times, but eventually produced the light bulb. Hudson Taylor had a vision for China. It cost him his wife, several children, and many hardships, but 2,000 faithful missionaries ministered in China during his lifetime as a result of his vision. Ask God to give you a vision!

3. Select the right group. Prayer is vitally important in finding the right people to disciple. Ask God to show you people you should be investing your life in. As you pray, keep your eyes open. Look for people who are hungry to grow into maturity in Jesus Christ. Look for responsible, faithful, teachable people.

Recruit people to a *cause*, not an organization. Never make people feel as if they will be another membership statistic. Tell them that the *cause* is Jesus Christ, and the *price* is their lives.

While you should be selective, don't be *exclusive* in announcing the opportunity. Announce to the whole youth group that you are beginning a discipleship group. Be clear about what it will cost them if they make the commitment. Present the commitment and let the people respond. The kind of discipling described in this chapter has been accused of fostering exclusivity. But such a charge can be avoided.

Make personal appointments with the people who you feel need to be in the group, and with the people who have indicated interest. Share with them your vision for the group. Ask them to pray about being in the group. Then get back in touch with them on a certain date to get their answer.

4. Ask for commitment. Ask the group members to make a fresh commitment to Jesus Christ and to each other as they begin the group. Important things to include in this commitment are: seeking to submit daily to the lordship of Christ, having a personal time alone with God each day, attending all group meetings, completing all assignments, being a witness for Christ, and supporting the local church through prayer and finances. Consider having a commitment sheet which members can sign as a visible symbol of this commitment.

After members make this commitment, hold them to it. It is a disservice to them and to others in the group to do anything less. The question often arises, "What if someone doesn't keep the commitment?"

• Be sensitive and loving.

• When you are alone with that person, say that you have noticed he hasn't kept the commitment, and that you are wondering if he is having some problems. If he is, help him with the problems. Encourage him to follow through with his commitment. Do this immediately when a problem arises.

• If the pattern persists, ask him what he feels he should do since he is not keeping the commitment. Often, a person realizes he has simply overcommitted himself, and at this point will choose to drop out of the group.

Periodically remind the group members of their commitment. This will make them more motivated to stick by their commitment.

5. Prepare for the group. Here are some practical areas to keep in mind when preparing to begin a discipleship group:

• The time of the meeting: The group can meet any time that is convenient for all members of the group. Make sure to clear the meeting time with the pastor or church secretary to avoid conflict with other meetings.

• The location of the meeting: Let the group help select the location. A home generally provides a more unstructured, neutral atmosphere than does a church building. An office or restaurant is another option.

• The length of the meeting: A discipleship group should normally meet for at least one hour at a time, but for not more than two hours. Try not to schedule the meeting back-to-back with other commitments.

• The group experience: Either before the group begins, or after the first meeting, plan a group experience. This can be an overnight retreat, a morning at the park, or an evening out together. It is a time for the group to begin to get to know each other informally. It helps the group to "jell" more easily.

• The proper materials: Order, in plenty of time, any study materials needed for the group. Nothing is more frustrating than needing the materials and not having them. Choose your materials according to the needs and interests of your group.

6. Set goals. Help the people whom you are discipling set goals. As you meet with each person before the group begins, and in the first few group meetings, find out where each

"Don't try to disciple someone who doesn't want to be discipled."

person is in his personal relationship with Jesus Christ. Find out how he is putting his faith into practice each day. Then begin to help him set goals. Goals might include having a consistent quiet time, learning to cultivate relationships with non-Christians, or learning to share his faith.

To help group members fulfill their goals, follow the example that Jesus set with His disciples. When Jesus taught His disciples to do something, He first *did it with them*, then He *went with them while they did it*, then He *sent them out to do it on their own*. Never just tell people how to do something and then send them out to do it.

A group of adults that I met with exemplified this principle. We spent two months talking about personal evangelism. I encouraged; I pleaded. We read books; we shared our frustrations. But I didn't take them with me to let them see how to share their faith in an actual situation. As a result, we spent two months being frustrated, and they didn't get the hang of actually sharing their faith.

7. Avoid the following dangers:
- Don't go too far too fast.
- Don't try to disciple someone who doesn't want to be discipled. Let him bail out when he wants to.
- Don't fail to follow up on broken commitments.
- Don't fail to meet with the group members individually.
- Don't create a negative atmosphere.
- Don't fail to meet with other discipleship group leaders to develop an overall fellowship and strategy.
- Don't fail to place discipleship within the local body of Christ.
- Don't fail to balance discipleship with evangelism.

Putting discipleship into practice will cost you hours of time and a lot of energy. Discipleship is not an *easy* method of youth ministry, but it is the most effective way to see students changed in a lasting, dynamic way for Jesus Christ. □

[1]Dietrich Bonhoeffer, *The Cost of Discipleship* (New York: McMillan, 1970), p. 228.

Discipling— a Holistic Ministry

15

by Chuck Miller

Having worked with youth for over 25 years, I've concluded that the discipling of high schoolers should be based on a commitment to the *total person*.

The Bible calls Christ *Saviour*. That word in the Greek means one who rescues; who brings to completion, fulness, fulfillment; who makes *whole*. Jesus Himself defined His mission in holistic terms: "The Spirit of the Lord is upon Me because He anointed Me to preach the Gospel to the poor. He has sent Me to proclaim release to the captives, and recovery of sight to the blind, to set free those who are downtrodden, to proclaim the favorable year of the Lord" (Luke 4:18-19). So, when you work with high schoolers, view them as Christ does—with concern for the total person.

Holistic Praying

Discipling should begin with finding out all you can about your students so you can know how to minister to their specific needs. A helpful way to initiate this process is to prayerfully consider each student, beginning with his *physical needs*: "Lord, how does she feel about her appearance? Help him with his weight problem, Lord."

Next, consider each students' *intellectual* needs: "Lord, where is he intellectually? Does he like to learn? What kinds of books does he read?"

In the *social* area, ask: "Does he have many friends? Does she only have friends of her own sex? Do boys pay attention to her? Who are his primary friends? Are they Christians or non-Christians?"

Think about and pray for an understanding of where students are *emotionally*: "Lord, every time that guy opens his mouth he's cutting someone down." Or, "She seems so irresponsible, so quick to make a commitment and never carry it through. Why, Lord? How can I help?"

Finally, think and pray about students' *spiritual* needs: "Lord, has he received You as Saviour? Help him to come to You. Lord, this one knows You, but where is she in the spiritual growth process? Has the Scripture become a part of her thinking so that, more and more, she thinks biblically instead of culturally?"

Often, by the time you've thought about and prayed for someone in these five areas, you realize: *I don't know this student very well. I have no idea whether he's an A or a C student, whether he never dates or if he's going steady.*

You realize you need to know certain students better. And your prayerful observation helps you know *specific areas* in which you need to fill the gaps in your knowledge. Your efforts in this area will pay off. The better you understand students, the more wisely you can shepherd them, and cooperate with the Holy Spirit to disciple them.

The Discipleship Group

One of the best environments in which holistic discipling can take place is the discipleship or "core" group. (See chapter 14, "Discipleship.") Here you begin to utilize the insights gained through prayerful

Chuck Miller has an extensive background in Christian education and youth ministry. He is pastor of the Highland Evangelical Free Church in Highland, California and director of Barnabas, Inc. He has served as director of Christian education at Fourth Presbyterian Church in Washington, D.C. and as minister to students at Lake Avenue Congregational Church in Pasadena, California. Chuck travels throughout the United States leading seminars on the discipling ministry. He is the author of several books, including Now That I'm a Christian.

consideration of students' physical, intellectual, social, emotional, and spiritual needs. You begin to help students establish individual and group goals. For example (in the *intellectual* area), if several group members consistently don't do their homework, discuss how many hours they're willing to commit to studying. Setting a goal of one hour of study per school night might be a big step of faith for some of these students.

An example of helping students set a goal based on a *spiritual* need might be in the area of Bible study. The problem might be not going to bed early enough to get up in the morning. In that case, the group might set up a small, measurable goal such as going to bed by 10 o'clock at least three nights per week. As group members support each other in setting and attaining goals, you grow into a team that cares for one another.

In addition to establishing *personal goals*, also establish *relational* goals. For example, group members know some Christians on the fringes of the youth group, in terms of their involvement. Since Bob and Tom have the same lunch hour as these "fringe kids," encourage Bob and Tom to eat lunch twice a week with these students who aren't involved. Meanwhile, the group prays for Bob and Tom's "ministry." And these two guys keep the group informed as to how God is working in the situation.

As a group, *pray* for personal needs, for other Christians, and for non-Christians. Ministry is *people*. So, involve the group in specific praying for people.

As you're discipling students, make sure your *motives* are pure—that you're not *using* students just to build your program. Students catch onto this situation. They know whether or not your love is conditional, your motives selfish.

Let's summarize briefly: You prayerfully consider students' physical, intellectual, social, emotional, and spiritual needs. You get to know students. You begin to see God surfacing

those students who are seriously committed to Jesus Christ. And you gather them together as a discipleship group. You ask God to mature your group and build you into a mutually supportive team. You trust Christ to bring others to Himself through your group members.

Those are the basics. In addition, consider the following two ministry concepts, *spectrum of ministry* and *phases of leadership*, as you develop a holistic discipling ministry.

Spectrum of Ministry

The *spectrum of ministry* concept relates to how you invest your time and effort in discipling students. Christ used His ministry time in three ways:

1. He occasionally ministered one-on-one. For example, John 3 records His one-on-one meeting with Nicodemus. But based on the Gospel accounts, Christ spent relatively little of His ministry in one-on-one situations.

2. He spent most of His ministry time working with a small group.

3. He also ministered frequently (with that small group) in the midst of masses of people.

Christ invested most of His ministry in discipling people in a small group context. So should we. Occasionally, because of the nature of a student's problem, you have to be alone with him. But normally it's better for students to share their problems and victories with the group. This enables students to experience the love and support of the whole "team." It also allows students to find help and strength from the Lord and from each other rather than from some superstar youth worker.

In addition to time spent working

on the group level, the *spectrum of ministry* approach also involves going with students into the *mass*—the high school campus. For example, you have lunch with kids at the high school cafeteria. Or you go with four or five students to a football game. Your goal is to reach out—and help your committed students reach out—beyond the discipleship group.

Phases of Leadership

As you disciple students holistically, it's also helpful to consider four *phases of leadership*. This concept facilitates the development of student leadership. The ministries of Paul and Barnabas illustrate these four phases.

Phase one: In phase one, "I do it completely by myself." There's no one to share the load of ministry. This phase is illustrated by Barnabas in Acts 4:36—11:25. As recorded here, Barnabas is alone—without a co-laborer. Then God raises up someone to minister with Barnabas.

Phase two: In phase two, "I do it, but you are with me." This phase of leadership is illustrated by Barnabas and Paul in Acts 11:26—13:12. In these passages, the phrase "Barnabas and Paul" (with Barnabas' name given first) is used frequently. One gets the impression that Saul (also known as Paul) is laboring alongside Barnabas, but that Barnabas is still in the driver's seat.

Phase three: In phase three, "You do it and I'm with you." Phase three involves the careful passing to another of the leadership reins. Beginning with Acts 13:42, the phrase "Paul and Barnabas" (with Paul's name given first) is used. In phase three, the leadership reins pass to another, but "I'm

> "Christ invested most of His ministry in discipling people in a small group context."

still there with him to encourage him, to support him if he needs help."

Phase four: In phase four, "You do it and I'm way in the background." With Paul and Barnabas, phase four is recorded in Acts 15:36-41, as God leads them to go in two separate directions.

Why is it important to think in terms of *phases of leadership*?

1. It encourages you to view the development of leadership as a primary goal of discipling.

2. It encourages you to thoroughly equip leaders *before* giving them too much responsibility.

The Long View

One final word about discipling as a holistic ministry: Have a *long view*—not a short view.

Because of the many years I've worked with young people, I've experienced the joy of chatting with a 32-year-old lady with whom I'd prayed to receive Christ when she was a teen. I've known the fulfillment of seeing people become ordained, become businessmen, teachers, coaches, mothers—and remembering when they professed Christ as high schoolers. I also remember when they joined a discipleship group and began to grow in the Lord.

What I'm saying is, don't just look at students as *high schoolers*. See them as *people* who you can influence for a lifetime.

And remember, successful discipling begins on your knees in prayer. There God will give you insight into the needs of your students. And He will help you minister to those needs as you disciple with a commitment to the *total person*. □

"Successful discipling begins on your knees. . . ."

16 Evangelism

by Mark Gold

Mark Gold is director of S.A.L.T. (Spreading Abundant Life to Teens) Ministries in Memphis, Tennessee. S.A.L.T. is a neighborhood evangelistic ministry reaching 400—500 teens weekly. Mark is also youth pastor of Broadway Baptist Church in Memphis.

I was happy and complacent in my youth ministry, rocking along with 125 junior high students, breaking attendance records week after week. Nobody in the city could touch my program or my numbers. What a year!

Then I blew it! I committed youth pastor suicide. I walked onto a junior high campus . . . and then another, and then another. I was confronted with reality: In my city, over 45,000 junior high students never attended a church—on any basis, regular or otherwise!

As this fact dawned, I experienced something similar to what I believe Jesus must have felt as He mourned the need He saw about Him: "But when He saw the multitudes, He was moved with compassion on them, because they fainted, and were scattered abroad, as sheep having no shepherd" (Matt. 9:36, KJV). I realized that the teens who most needed the Gospel never heard it. I began to ask God, "How in 'Your' world do we reach a city full of lost kids?" I began to grapple with the issue of evangelism.

"He that goeth forth and weepeth," I read, "bearing precious seed, shall doubtless come again with rejoicing, bringing his sheaves with him" (Ps. 126:6, KJV). God's plan of evangelism, I discovered, contains some basic ingredients:

Go Forth

The majority of lost teens are not clamoring for God. Comparatively few times in my Christian life have non-Christians stormed my "Ivory Palace" to demand that I share the Gospel with them. Sometimes kids have sought me out to ask how they could receive Christ. But in every case, someone else had gone to the non-Christian first, planting the seed and creating a hunger for the Lord.

Regardless of fears, or past programs, or budgets, or attitudes, or philosophies, or personalities, God's command is to *go!*

- "Go . . . and teach"
- "Go . . . and preach"
- "Go compel them to come in"
- "Even so send I you"
- "Ye shall be witnesses"

No matter how effective our personalities, our planning, and programming may be, the majority of teens won't come to us. We must go to them—at home, school, at the club, on the corner, wherever teens are—and uncompromisingly, lovingly, powerfully declare Christ Jesus as Lord.

How many young people do you have in your youth group? 3? 12? 180? What about the 145,000? Who's going to tell them?

If your answer is, "I must go and tell them," first consider how *not* to go. God's conditions for successful evangelism are *not*:

"The teens who most needed the Gospel never heard it."

1. *Personality*—"If you get saved, you'll become like me!"

That's an unscriptural concept that can rob the new believer of a proper foundation in Jesus Christ.

2. *Program*—"Join up with our Jesus-Sonshine-Hallelujah-Soon-to-Be-Crowned-King-Super-Banana-Split-Sunday-Youth-Group!"

What happens when all the banana splits are eaten and your convert fails 10th-grade math?

3. *Plywood*—"Get saved or I'll whack you over the head with this here plywood!"

As tempting a method as this may be, the Holy Spirit doesn't get too thrilled about it. How does God say to go?

ing, or tire-rolling contests. But He has promised that His Word will not return void (Isa. 55:11). We are called to bear the precious seed of God's Word (Mark 4:14).

In our Monday night ministry to "non-churched" young people, we include a 30-minute "open-up-the-Bible-and-look-at-God's-answers" time. Sometimes it involves preaching, sometimes teaching, sometimes discussing or getting involved in personal study, but *always*—it lasts at least 30 minutes! We don't trick anyone. People know beforehand that they are coming to a Bible study. In the four years that we have held our Monday night meetings all over the city, I cannot think of a dozen teens

the illicit relationship, but she moved back home and asked her mother's forgiveness. Talk about joy!

Just two days before I wrote this chapter, I dropped by to see my 73-year-old grandfather. He "casually" mentioned he didn't think he was saved. I "casually" shared the Gospel with him and, there in his living room, the Lord miraculously forgave him and came to live in his heart! You don't think there was joy?

God offers a joy in reaching lost people for Christ that can be found nowhere else. Paul understood this joy when he wrote, "For what is our hope, or joy, or crown of rejoicing? . . . For ye are our glory and joy" (1 Thes. 2:19-20, KJV).

> *"Allow your heart to be broken for the needs of unsaved teens, not for the size of your youth group."*

Weep

Allow your heart to be broken for the needs of unsaved teens, not for the size of your youth group. Young people *must* be saved! Without Jesus, they face this life and the next with no hope. The brokenness that God requires is not a worked-up, trumped-up, "oh, poor kids" brokenness, but a look through Jesus' eyes at what kids are, what they will become, and where they will spend eternity without Jesus.

Bear Precious Seed

God hasn't promised to bless our basketball-bouncing, bubble-gum chew-

that have been so offended by the Word that they didn't return.

Rejoice

The psalmist says, "He shall doubtless come again with rejoicing bringing his sheaves with him" (Ps. 126:6, KJV). I know of no more exciting or satisfying Christian experience (outside of my own personal salvation) than being present as God transforms a goat into a sheep! Or as God adopts a hell-bound sinner and makes him one of His very own children!

I recently saw God transform a 17-year-old girl, who had been living for two years with a 34-year-old man, into a young lady. She not only broke

What's Missing?

Evangelism has been in and out of style for the last 10 years. But it should never be a ministry "option." Evangelism is the *new life* of the church. It is the missing link and purpose that many youth ministries lack.

1. *Go forth,*
2. *Weep,*
3. *Bear precious seed,*
   and get ready to
4. *Rejoice!* □

17 | Training Youth for Evangelism

by John Musselman

John Musselman is currently the youth minister of Coral Ridge Presbyterian Church in Fort Lauderdale, Florida. Previously he served at the First Presbyterian Church of Gadsden, Alabama and Chapel Woods Presbyterian Church of Decatur, Georgia. John is a graduate of the University of Alabama and Reformed Theological Seminary.

Young people must be reached with the Gospel of Jesus Christ. And the most effective personnel for the job of youth evangelism are Christian young people. Unfortunately, churches too often view youth as the "future" of the church. Youth pastors and adult workers plan and execute programs designed to do something *for* youth till they pass the adolescent period.

> ## "Perhaps the church has been guilty of communicating to youth that they are on hold *till a better, more mature day.*"

Once teens grow up, so the thinking goes, *they* can begin to do the work of ministry.

Perhaps the church has been guilty of communicating to youth that they are *on hold* till a better, more mature day. One student put it this way, "I'm tired of people thinking of me as a dormant human being."

A Biblical Alternative

The Bible teaches that the pastor/teacher should equip the saints so that *they* can do the work of service and build the body of Christ (Eph. 4:11-12). It is not the pastor's responsibility to do all the work of ministry. Biblically, pastors are supposed to equip and train the people to do a potpourri of ministry functions. And in regard to this responsibility, nowhere does Scripture make a distinction between "pastor" and "youth pastor."

The implications of this truth for youth ministry are manifold. We will consider two.

First, it challenges the prevalent idea that the flamboyant, guitar thumping, wild and crazy guy makes the ideal youth pastor. By Ephesians 4 standards, the soft-spoken leader who understands the nature of the equipping ministry, who can train and delegate, may be far more effective than the charismatic personality.

Second, God's method of ministry suggests that youth who know Jesus Christ as Lord and Saviour should be busy doing the work of ministry. These young people are a part of the body of Christ. They can be trained to evangelize, serve, pray, lead Bible studies, and do many other ministry functions.

In regard to evangelism, youth can and must be enlisted in the army of Jesus Christ to participate in reaching the world with the Gospel. To prevent or hinder such enlistment will, without question, weaken Christ's church.

A Context for Evangelism

In our high school ministry, we discovered that an evangelism program can be successful only when it is built under the right conditions or, to say it another way, placed in proper context. The following suggestions may help you recognize and create the proper environment for a fruitful evangelism program:

1. *Demonstrate a genuine love for your students*. If you are building your own little kingdom to feed a deflated ego, you've missed the point. Youth pick up on selfish motivations. They soon know whether you sincerely care for them. Here are a few ways to demonstrate love to young people:

● Mail short notes telling students how much you enjoy seeing them each week.

● Send birthday cards to all students involved in the ministry.

● Visit students' homes.

● Appear at events they are participating in (e.g. sports events, cheerleader tryouts, drama presentations, etc.).

● Phone them to see how they are doing.

● Invite students to have dinner with you and your family.

● Fellowship with groups of students (8—12) in your home.

When they have been personally encouraged and loved, Christian students respond energetically to the challenge of evangelization.

2. *Avoid talking too openly with students about any future plans you may have of moving to another area of ministry*. Granted, some youth workers are called for short-term ministries and will no doubt move into other branches of service in God's kingdom. But this sharing of future intentions can destroy the motivation and momentum of a youth evangelism program. Once students know that you plan to leave, the question, "What will happen when he's gone?" can be a constant reminder of the ministry's uncertain future.

3. *Gain the trust of parents*. If parents don't trust you, they won't encourage their children to be involved in your ministry. A monthly newsletter to parents, occasional preaching before the local congregation, phone calls, and appointments all contribute toward the goal of building and maintaining trust. It's also beneficial

to have parents serve on your youth committee. This builds trust and provides valuable adult input.

4. *Provide adult models*. Are the adults in the church evangelizing? Are they winning their peers to Christ? Youth need mature models to follow. With few exceptions, I could not encourage a youth leader to begin an evangelism program in a church where the adults are not obeying the Great Commission. Threatened by the students' witnessing zeal, parents and church staff tend to discourage evangelism by the youth.

5. *Find a meeting facility youth can call their own*.

To increase the potential outreach to our community, we have chosen to locate away from the church building. Students who would not come close to a church are more easily persuaded to come to a 6,800 square foot warehouse we call "Gangway."

The location of our facility does not imply, however, that we are seeking to become some kind of "church within a church." We strongly encourage church membership, participation in youth choirs, and Sunday School enrollment. "Gangway" serves as a neutral ground where the claims of Christ can be presented in an informal atmosphere. The basement of someone's home might just as easily serve this function.

6. *Recruit other adult leaders to minister with you*. As more students come to know Christ, it will be impossible for one leader to minister to all the needs of the growing body. Training other leaders to work directly with the students will alleviate this problem.

Evangelism Training

Within the proper context, as described above, you may begin the next step of building a youth evangelism program—that of recruiting young people for evangelism training.

Our training and recruitment in-

volve several steps:

1. *Scheduling training sessions*. We plan two training programs a year. The first begins in September and runs 14 weeks. Our second training class begins in January and runs till May. Though our training periods are the same number of weeks each year, the dates vary according to the trainees' school schedules.

At the beginning of each school year, we write a letter to the numerous schools in our area, requesting a calendar for the upcoming school year. We look for vacations, teacher workshop days, holidays, and other times when a student may have an opportunity to leave the area. We then plan our training cycle around these dates. This planning procedure has dramatically cut down on student absenteeism from training sessions.

2. *Sending information letters*. We begin our actual recruitment by sending a letter to all the youth in our ministry. This letter describes the training program, giving information on the length of training, how to enroll, etc. The letter creates an awareness of the program.

3. *Encouraging students to recruit their peers for evangelism training*. Students who have previously been trained in evangelism are asked to recruit untrained young people to form training teams. Each trained student recruits two other persons to become a part of his/her three-member team. Trainees are selected on the basis of their Christian character, faithfulness, ability to stick with a commitment, and their sincere desire to see the lost won to Christ. During the training program the trainer (previously trained student) oversees the trainees' progress.

4. *Making contacts*. The youth worker should plan on obtaining a broad range of youth contacts.

We obtain prospects from church attendance cards filled out during Sunday morning and evening services, calls from parents or friends, a youth concert series, city-wide outreaches, our regular weekly outreach, and camp-outs.

5. *Teaching by example*. Part of the evangelism training for youth includes classroom instruction. But it's not enough to hold classes on witnessing. Youth must be *shown* how to witness. They should learn by observing an experienced person evangelizing someone else. The youth leader should model personal evangelism by taking trainees with him as he shares the Gospel with someone.

In an initial training session, for example, the youth leader might take two students with him. Then in the next training period there should be two new evangelism groups led by previously trained students, and so on. This process of equipping leads to rapid multiplication.

6. *Enjoying the result*. Once students begin to see their friends coming to know Christ, their enthusiasm mushrooms. They want to tell other students about the Person who has changed their lives. As they train their friends to share this same Good News with others, the army grows larger and stronger. The youth ministry staff gathers the new Christians into small classes designed for growth, and invites them to participate in the various ministry opportunities for fellowship with newfound friends in the Lord.

"Youth must be shown how to witness."

The effects of leaders adopting this "equipping" approach to youth ministry could be momentous. Just imagine an army of Christian high school students—trained and motivated to reach their campuses for Christ. Imagine the secular college campuses of America being infiltrated each year by new freshmen who are equipped to evangelize.

We can no longer leave to the parachurch organization the task of training students. Youth leaders must not give up their God-given responsibility to train students in personal evangelism within the framework of the local church. Let's carry out the job description God has given us. High school students are ready to be trained! ☐

Full-cycle Evangelism

18

by Don Cousins

The primary goal of a biblically based youth ministry is to produce disciples of Jesus Christ. The Lord's Great Commission is, "Go therefore and make disciples of all the nations, baptizing them in the name of the Father and the Son and the Holy Spirit, teaching them to observe all that I commanded you; and lo, I am with you always, even to the end of the age" (Matt. 28:19-20).

A study of the church in the Book of Acts reveals two fundamental phases of disciple-making: (1) *evangelism*—bringing the non-Christian to a saving knowledge of Jesus Christ, and (2) *edification*—teaching the new believer all that Jesus commanded. In our ministry, we have found that two meetings a week are most helpful in accomplishing these two objectives:

The outreach meeting (for evangelism) is a tool for our Christian students which aids them in their attempts to win their friends to Christ.

The core group meeting (for edification) consists of Christian students who desire to be disciples of Jesus Christ. This meeting involves teaching, fellowship, prayer, and Communion (Acts 2:42).

In our ministry to students, these two phases of disciple-making—evangelism and edification—are incorporated into a process which we call *full-cycle evangelism*. This full-cycle process begins with Christian students who have been discipled to a point where they are ready to begin discipling others for Christ. The youth worker's role in the full-cycle process is primarily one of equipping and assisting these "discipled students" in their task of winning and discipling their peers for Jesus Christ. Full-cycle evangelism includes the following steps: (1) friendship, (2) verbal witness, (3) outreach program, (4) conversion, (5) body-life program, (6) discipleship, (7) spiritual parenthood.

Friendship

People win people to Christ. Programs are nothing more than tools in the hands of God's people. So, the first step of full-cycle evangelism involves Christian students building friendships with non-Christian students.

The Christian student identifies a non-Christian friend he wants to see become a Christian. If he doesn't have a non-Christian friend, he ventures out and builds a friendship with a non-Christian at school.

Paul says Christians are to be out *in* the world, but not *of* the world (1 Cor. 5:9-10). Christians are temporary residents of this planet with a godly mission of attracting others to Christ. We are His ambassadors. It's true that the believer's values, attitudes, behavior, and lifestyle are not

Don Cousins is one of the originators of Son City, an innovative style of youth ministry which has become widely used throughout the United States. A graduate of Trinity College, Don directed the expansion program of Son City in churches around the country. Presently he is director of the Son City program of Willow Creek Community Church in Palatine, Illinois and is developing a similar model ministry to college-age students. For information and materials regarding the Son City style of ministry, write to: Don Cousins, Son City, Willow Creek Community Church, 863 S. Vermont, Palatine, IL 60067.

"The youth worker's role . . . is one of equipping and assisting 'discipled students' in their task of winning and discipling their peers for Jesus Christ."

to be worldly. But so often the only people who have friendships with non-Christians are other non-Christians. To reach non-Christian students for Christ, a Christian student must be prepared to establish friendships at school.

Verbal Witness

As friendship and trust grow between a Christian student and his non-Christian friend, the Holy Spirit motivates the Christian to verbally share his testimony. The Christian student might say, "You know, there's been a change in my life . . . and that change has been brought about by Jesus Christ." The non-Christian student often needs that personal tug.

This second step of full-cycle evangelism involves knowing the right time to share Christ simply and honestly. Religious jargon only confuses. "Let your speech always be with grace, seasoned, as it were, with salt, so that you may know how you should respond to each person" (Col. 4:6). Witnessing for Christ means being genuine and vibrant about saying, "*My* life has been changed; my sins have been forgiven." The witnessing student needs to keep Christ central, highlighting what *He* has done.

The best way for students to succeed at giving a verbal witness is by actually doing it. By repetition, verbal witnessing becomes natural. The youth worker can help students get started by leading practice witnessing sessions in the core group meeting.

Outreach Program

The next step involves a Christian student bringing his non-Christian friend to the weekly outreach meeting or activity. This step attempts to break down a non-Christian's misconceptions about Christ and then reintro-duce him to Christ in a positive way.

The "Son City" evening has proved very successful for us. We use music, drama, multimedia, and a Gospel message to present Christ in a positive, creative way. Each Son City evening includes Christian fun and acceptance, and provides a positive uplifting experience. Midweek is usually a good time for this outreach meeting so that as many as possible can attend.

This outreach evening provides a nonthreatening environment where a Christian student can get a helping hand in telling his non-Christian friend about Christ. Such fellowship supplements the personal witness with an environment filled with God's love and acceptance.

Conversion

FRIENDSHIP + VERBAL WITNESS + OUTREACH PROGRAM + THE POWER OF THE HOLY SPIRIT = CONVERSION.

Conversion happens when the non-Christian student receives Christ as his personal Saviour and Lord. Conversion often takes place through:

1. A personal relationship between the Christian and non-Christian. A Christian student personally leads his friend to Christ.

2. A decision made at a weekly outreach meeting. Periodically, the outreach meeting should give students an opportunity to invite Christ into their lives. Here are some practical suggestions for providing such an opportunity:

● Have core group members, individually and collectively, pray for each outreach evening, especially for the meeting when a conversion decision will be called for.

● For a period of weeks, deliver messages that point toward the need for decision and build a "groundwork" for presenting an opportunity to receive Christ.

● Give any student who wants to make a decision the opportunity to talk with someone about it privately.

● Teach each core group member how to lead someone into a relationship with Christ.

● Present the opportunity for decision in a relaxed, low-key manner. A student from a non-Christian background already has many negative ideas about evangelism; he is skeptical. Don't reinforce that skepticism. NOTE: These first four steps—friendship, verbal witness, outreach program, and conversion—make up the *evangelism* phase of the full-cycle process. For each student who receives Christ, growth continues with the next three steps, the *edification* phase.

Body-life Program

The Christian student now invites his newly converted friend to a core group meeting or Bible study. The core group meeting gives opportunity for students to learn how to function as the body of Christ, and serves as the base and foundation for outreach functions. This program puts Acts 2:42 in practice: "And they were continually devoting themselves to the apostles' teaching and to fellowship, to the breaking of bread and to prayer."

We call our body-life program "Son Village." It's a time to pray, worship, fellowship, and learn from God's Word each week.

Discipleship

At this point, the new Christian also needs to be personally discipled. Jesus' time with His disciples exemplifies what it means to invest one's life in someone. The new Christian's friend, who has led him through this whole process, needs to be a Christ-like model and spend time with the new Christian:

● discussing their spiritual lives;

- reading the Bible and praying;
- having fun together;
- discussing problem areas in their lives and seeking Christ-centered solutions.

NOTE: The youth worker should encourage and guide the students in finding Christ-centered solutions.

Spiritual Parenthood

The concept of spiritual parenthood comes from 1 Corinthians 4:14-21. Spiritual parenting means producing discipled spiritual offspring . . . not just conceiving them, but rearing them in the ways of the Lord. At this point, the Christian student has become that "spiritual parent" to his new Christian friend. The process comes *full cycle* as the new Christian gains the maturity to reach out in friendship to another non-Christian student. NOTE: Full-cycle evangelism is not a short-term process. It takes a substantial investment of time and effort to go full cycle, but if properly done, this process can yield a bountiful harvest.

In conclusion, full-cycle evangelism is a process, not a program. As the Christian student invests his life in a non-Christian friend and then sees the converted friend invest his life in another, together they utilize God's most effective method—multiplication—to accomplish the Great Commission.

> *"The process comes full cycle as the new Christian gains the maturity to reach out in friendship to another non-Christian student."*

Full-cycle evangelism begins with the Christian student's friendship with a non-Christian, a sharing of his verbal testimony, and the support of outreach program efforts. The combination of these steps, together with prayer and the power of the Holy Spirit, brings the non-Christian friend to the point of conversion.

As a new Christian, he then experiences growth in Christ through the core group and personal discipleship. Finally, he comes full cycle and begins to win his non-Christian friends to Christ. And the cycle begins anew. (For a description of how full-cycle evangelism can be incorporated into a ministry to students on the high school campus, see Chapter 22, "Campus Ministry.") ☐

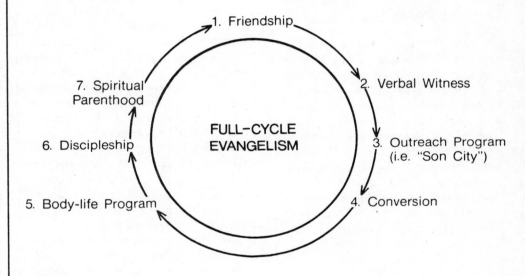

1. Friendship
2. Verbal Witness
3. Outreach Program (i.e. "Son City")
4. Conversion
5. Body-life Program
6. Discipleship
7. Spiritual Parenthood

FULL-CYCLE EVANGELISM

19 Youth Trends
An Analysis of Youth in the Church

by Pat Hurley

Pat Hurley *is former president of Spectrum Ministries, a youth leadership development organization. As a traveling speaker, he has spoken to over 300,000 young people in 300 cities during the past six years. In addition, Pat's television appearances have expanded his outreach to include some 30 million TV viewers. (He is seen regularly on ABC's "Kids Are People Too.") Pat is the author of three Power Paks for youth workers:* The Magic Bubble, Penetrating the Magic Bubble, *and* The Penetrators.

The greatest hope for our world tomorrow is the youth in the church today. There is no question about it. The church must understand and develop her youth, and motivate them toward a lifestyle of Christian discipleship in a sinful and dying world.

Unfortunately, the church loses far too many of its young people before they ever learn to walk with Christ. As soon as they move on to college or to a full-time job, the formal dropout occurs. But often this is merely the formal towing-away process. In reality, the girls started dropping out the summer following their sophomore years of high school; the guys started turning off in junior high.

The youth years are when people need to become grounded in a committed, personal relationship with Jesus Christ. Youth workers must be aware of the pressures that contribute to this "great youth turn-off." We must know how to lead youth toward an acceptance of a Christ-centered value system.

With these imperatives in mind, let's look at four major philosophies that affect youth in the church: *humanism,* the belief that man rather than God is the center of the universe; *relativism,* the belief that there are no objective moral standards; *subjectivism,* the idea that right and wrong can

"I'm Number 1" (Humanism)

"I control my own destiny."
"Man can do anything."
"I . . . I . . . I . . . ."
"Me . . . Me . . . Me. . . ."

Youth in our churches live in a world saturated by humanistic thinking. What are the main influences that propagate this philosophy?

1. Television. The power of the tube shouldn't be underestimated. A few statistics:

- The average American watches TV 3 ½ hours a day.
- By the time a child reaches kindergarten, he will have seen 1,500 murders on TV.
- By the time a child reaches fifth grade, he will have spent more time in front of a television set than he will in school classrooms from kindergarten through college!
- Between the hours of 10-12 at night over 3 million children between the ages of 2-11 are watching TV. After midnight this age-group is still over 1 million.
- By the time a student graduates from high school, he will have viewed 15,000 hours of TV and approximately the same number of murders.
- The average child will watch over 15,000 commercials in one year.

"Youth in our churches live in a world saturated by humanistic thinking."

---

be determined merely by how a person feels about an action; and *negativism,* the cynical outlook on life.

On the screen and off, kids see superstars who are successful without God. If these role models can be talented, rich, good-looking, and powerful through self-effort, why does anyone need God? When TV heroes do fail, they fail because they didn't plan their actions properly, or because of some other miscalculation. There is no mention of sin, repentance, or the Bible.

One of Satan's major delights is TV's stereotyping of Christians. Christians shown on the screen are usually losers, squares, fanatics, or hypocrites. In the world of junior and senior high school youth, where *image* is so vital, the Hollywood version of a Christian doesn't look very appealing.

2. *Madison Avenue*. Advertisers propogate a humanistic mentality through a preoccupation with materialism, status, and sex:

• Materialism; We need to buy, buy, buy, says advertising, so we can have at least everything!

• Status: Ads tell youth what they need to buy to be liked, to be successful, to have sex appeal. "Everybody" who's anybody buys certain brands of jeans, makeup, sound systems, cars, and sports equipment.

• Sex: Advertising constantly bombards youth with sexually suggestive messages. And, predictably, an increasing number of young people are giving up their virginity, taking the pill, turning to homosexuality, and contributing to the success of the pornography market.

3. *Peer pressure*: The media and Madison Avenue provide the ammunition, but the *peer group* supplies the gun.

The average Christian young person adopts the values of his peer group because he has a deeper relationship with the group than he does with Jesus Christ. He strives for peer acceptance because his values are human-centered. The key here is for the Christian parent or youth worker not to put the child's friends down. If the teen is forced to decide between adults and his friends, he'll usually choose his friends. The goal should be to present Jesus Christ more and more

clearly. As the young person recognizes Jesus as his Master, he will listen to His voice and the peer group will take its proper place.

Countering Humanism

It's sad that we live in a humanistic world—one that has turned its back on God. Yet, there is hope because Jesus Christ can penetrate the hearts of people. We can do our part to counter the affects of humanism on our young people. But this requires building relationships of mutual trust. The place to start building such relationships is with dialogue. And what better place to start the dialogue than in a local church?

How to build a trusting relationship with youth:

1. *Be yourself*. Be honest with young people. Let them know what you're thinking and feeling—even what's bugging you.

2. *Really listen*. "What's that? Yeah, I hear what you said." But did you really, or were you thinking how you were going to answer?

3. *Accept them for who they are*. To-

day's young people are characterized by a lack of identity, a fear of the future, and a deep-seated distrust of almost everything and everyone around them. They will not respond positively to you unless you accept them for who they are now (yet never lose sight of what Jesus can do with their lives).

4. *Be vulnerable*. Let them know that you are human. Let them know that you too have to depend on Jesus Christ for the strength and courage to

stand up to the negative effects of TV, Madison Avenue, and peer pressure.

"What's Wrong for Him May Be Right for Me!" (Relativism)

One day in a philosophy class, my teacher posed a serious question concerning a "profound aspect of philosophical truth." The teacher turned to my best friend for an answer. My friend thought a moment, shrugged his shoulders, and replied, "I don't know."

The teacher stared momentarily and then leaped with joy. "That's right—we don't know!" He'd gotten the answer he wanted: *Truth is relative—so there are no right answers*.

It's called copping out, rationalizing, expediency, or just plain sin. Many young people don't want to know the truth. If the truth is clear, they will be responsible for it. And responsibility requires a moral commitment. If they don't want to be moral, they can just pretend that truth doesn't exist or that they don't under-

stand it. Then they have an excuse.

"If it feels good, do it!" Satan's greatest tool is deception. And he floods the airwaves with it. Through the clouding of right and wrong, the young person begins to believe there is no absolute truth—so he ends up believing his own version of the "truth." That's what Adam and Eve did. That's what students all across the country are doing.

Any society has basic foundations which support the function of a civi-

> *"Through the clouding of right and wrong, the young person begins to believe there is no absolute truth."*

lization. The most basic are the *church*, the *state*, the *family*, and *education*. When these institutions lose their credibility, the entire society and its values are thrown into chaos.

When these institutions are unstable, the young person doubts the credibility of God and the Bible as well. When he doubts the things he sees, he *more easily* doubts what he doesn't see. He can't trust God because he doesn't trust anything else. Let's examine this credibility problem by looking at the church, the government, the family, and education in our society.

1. The church. Once the church becomes *optional*, the *truth* of Jesus Christ becomes optional too. Once a churchgoing teenager becomes aware that kids at school don't really think church is an important factor in their lives, he begins to "tolerate" Sunday mornings and Sunday nights. But the electricity, the enthusiasm, and the relevance of the Christian life drain away.

Between 1960 and 1970 church attendance in America dropped from 49 percent to 40 percent! That period was also known as the "what-is-right-for-you-is-right" generation among students. When the church loses its credibility, young people turn to "doing their own thing" because they feel they only have themselves to trust.

God knew young adults long before George Gallup did. In a Gallup poll, researchers asked college students what qualities were most important to them. They listed love, happiness, and inner peace. "The fruit of the Spirit is love, joy, peace, patience . . . gentleness, self-control" (Gal. 5:22-23).

What young people desire—freedom from guilt, security, assurance of life after death, independence, a sense of worth, and the ability to love and be loved—are found in Jesus Christ. Most young people just don't realize it. They are searching everywhere for what the church should be giving. The church must reevaluate her commitment to relevantly communicating the person of Jesus Christ to a youth cul-

ture that is struggling to survive.

2. The government. The majority of the students of the '80s are neither politically conservative nor liberal—they are *apathetic*. They don't believe that their participation in government can make society better. John F. Kennedy's exhortation, "Ask not what your country can do for you; ask what you can do for your country" has become a quaint notion from a bygone era. Government and its politicians lack credibility.

3. The family. A few statistics: During the American Revolution the divorce rate was 1 in 500. During the Civil War the divorce rate was 1 in 100. Today it is 1 in 2. The average father spends seven minutes a week with his son.

The family is in trouble. And not only is this true outside the church. The divorce rate in Christian families continues to climb.

4. Education. Education, like other of our institutions, is under fire: teachers' strikes, busing riots, crime (in a recent year 77,000 teachers were assaulted in our public school system and that figure is growing yearly), and the lowered Scholastic Aptitude Test (SAT) scores are a few of the major problems facing today's educators.

A national administrator of the SAT program said, "The low scores of students today are the result of many factors; the primary one being the stress placed on them by an unstable society in which they live."

Countering Relativism

This societal instability makes a young person want to quit caring about right and wrong. He isn't always conscious of this but you can see his cynicism about these various institutions. And if he cannot depend on basic institutions, there's nothing to cling to but self-protection.

If a young person is not a Spirit-filled Christian, that is *exactly* what

he will do. The disintegration of a once unified people leads to chaos. That's why Babylon, Greece, and Rome fell. America should keep her eyes open. And Christians should be holding Jesus Christ up for her to see.

Not only do we need to evaluate secular education in terms of its credibility, but also Christian education. We know that the absolute standards given in God's Word hold the answer to relativism. But are we being personal, creative, and motivating when we relate the Word of God to young people? Key phrases are: *absolute truth, creative communication, personal communication,* and *prayerful evaluation.*

"I Feel Good about It— It Must Be Good" (Subjectivism)

Closely related to the problem of relativism is subjectivism: "If there are no moral absolutes, then I will base my behavior on what *feels* right for me."

Why are so many youth susceptible to this philosophy? Here are a few reasons:

1. Man is an emotional being. Made in the image of God, man is an emotional being. Unless controlled by the Spirit, man's emotions are fed by lust—man's effort to please himself. That's why young people look for something that gives them thrills—the headphones, the drugs, the sexual experiences.

They know these aren't the things that should be getting their emotions excited. But their Christian lifestyles are often sterile, boring, and unsatisfactory. So they turn to sensual thrills to find emotional fulfillment.

2. Non-expressive people. Many people don't know how to express their true inner feelings. So little conversation takes place in families be-

...ause young people are cut off from intimate verbal communication with their parents—and vice versa. Young people are finding other ways they can have that expression—through sensual experiences.

3. The coldness of modern technology. Computerization is increasing in every area of our lives. Young people feel the coldness—they feel they are numbers instead of people. They are forced to look for something that will make their lives more personal—sensual thrills and excitement.

4. The development of a mobile society. In the past, people attended church, went shopping, went to school, and had friends and activities all in the same general location. But with the proliferation of freeways and automobile ownership, many kids find their lives spread over a 30-or 40-mile area. They go to church in one area, school in another, and so on. As a result, they have no roots.

Time magazine reported that the average middle class family moves once every four years. Alvin Toffler, author of *Future Shock*, calls this moving about, "transient disaffiliation." which is characterized by a lack of commitment to friends as well as a "care-less" attitude toward neighbors and community.

Church has ceased to be an important factor partially because of this phenomenon of rootlessness. In previous generations teenagers spent Friday or Saturday nights at church activities with their families. Not today.

5. The increasing acceptance of athetic evolution. The subtle teaching of evolution has made young people feel that they are nothing more than products of chance. Many believe there is no such thing as being made in God's image, because there might not even be a God—everything can be explained scientifically. This gives a young person total "freedom" to live by instinct rather than by conscience. Finally, increasing numbers of young people don't care what happens after they die because "life" is supposedly a product of chemicals haphazardly forming together.

Take a quick look at subjectivism in *movies, music,* and *teenage lifestyles*:

• *Movies.* Movie producers understand today's youth culture better than many youth workers. These producers have thoughtfully said, "Hey, we know you don't know what you're doing, so *escape* with us."

"What if a large city in the United States had a major earthquake? What if a skyscraper suddenly caught on fire—and you were involved in it?" A wave of "disaster" films was the forerunner of the scary-sensationalist movies: "What if a giant killer shark decided to eat you for lunch?" Movies about dogs, rats, and birds that suddenly turned into monsters and threatened the human condition—anything that appealed to people's fears—made millions of dollars.

Along with violence and disaster films came movies about the occult: *The Exorcist, Parts 1 and 2; The Omen; Carrie; The Demon-Seed*. These films were box office hits because the producers said, "Because life is so weird, let's come from another angle—and give you a 'solution.' "

Alex Haley wrote *Roots*, and it became one of the most highly watched movies of all time. People were fascinated with the story. It was geared toward an entire race of people trying to find its identity. *Star Wars* came along and said, "Escape with us into the future."

Movie and TV producers are playing Ping-Pong with kids' emotions. They're bouncing our young people from one extreme to the other to make money. They're saying, "Maybe this will work after this flood of movies— let's try hitting them with this approach." It's like bowling—you set them up and then you knock them down. This subtle approach of manipulating the weaknesses, fears, and insecurities of students today makes millions of dollars for marketing experts.

• *Music.* Rock and roll made its debut in the '50s when Elvis Presley came on the scene representing the rumblings of growing teenage rebellion. Kids got behind this new movement and said, "Hey, we'd like to be out there doing our own thing too. This is cool!" Tradition suddenly became the object of teen wrecking crews.

The '50s, while reflecting the comfort and security of the Eisenhower period, also uncovered a giant market for music promoters—affluent teenagers. Money could be made from rock heroes, with their T-shirts, pennants, lunch boxes, bumper stickers—you name it.

In the early '60s music hit somewhat of an identity crisis. Then suddenly the English invaded America. The Beatles, the Rolling Stones, the Animals, the Dave Clark Five, and The Who crossed the Atlantic and everything broke loose.

The Beatles' music was a phenomenon. They started with simple love lyrics like, "I want to hold your hand," "She loves you," "I saw her standing there"—songs most kids could relate to. As the '60s evolved and youth culture became more complex, the Beatles' music evolved along with it. They progressed from those simple love songs to songs about revolution, drugs, and death.

The Rolling Stones built their rock format around sex and satanism and other groups followed suit. During the mid-'60s rock stars not only sang about death, but also experienced it as the "ultimate trip." Janis Joplin, Jim Morrison, Jimi Hendrix, and Brian Jones all met untimely deaths because of their "free" lifestyles.

The entire spectrum of music in the '80s reflects a no-holds-barred philosophy. Songs and rock groups today represent every single condition of human desperation. Songs glorify extramarital affairs, neuroses, and paranoia.

The music groups take student minds and open them to the point where kids ask, "What is real?" Sex is openly exploited, drugs are freely encouraged, Satan is a hero, and fantasy is the ultimate trip.

• *Lifestyles*. The progression from one escape to another moves on. Many churchgoing young people attend the parties where drugs are being taken. When they hear of someone who has lost his/her virginity, they often say, "If they love each other, it's right."

The progression continues. That's why kids are into TM (Transcendental Meditation), biorhythm, tarot cards, and Ouija boards, astral projection—anything to do with spiritism, the unknown, and the afterlife—has gained popularity and acceptance.

What will teens be like when you're 65 (or 29 or 32 or 45)? If the major institutions continue to break down, the lives of our youth will become even more devastated: The crime rate among junior high and high school students is already appalling. Youth from ages 10 to 17 comprise only 16 percent of the population but account for nearly 50 percent of all persons arrested for serious crimes. Of all crimes solved by the FBI, 31 percent involve persons under 18. Kids are looking for a thrill. Crime and murder will remain major expressions of that search.

Demon possession will occur on a much larger scale. Suicide will continue to be a top killer of our young people. Since 1950 there has been a 150 percent increase in teenage suicides.

Homosexuality will explode on high school campuses. It will express a craving for emotional security from students who come from unstable home backgrounds.

"We may not even recognize the American family in 20 years."

If present trends continue, we will probably see the continued disintegration of the traditional family. We may not even recognize the American family in 20 years.

"Listening is so important because teenagers help form their identities by expressing themselves."

Countering Subjectivism

What can be done? Members of your youth groups need to see that relationships with Jesus Christ *can be experienced*. They need to see beyond the regular meetings and activities to the *person* of Christ. Here are some things you should be aware of as you work with students in your church who are constantly looking for excitement in life:

1. *Freedom is doing what we ought to do—not just doing what we want.* Kids who get bored fastest are those who live the most permissive lifestyles. The more they ignore responsibility, the less they are satisfied with their lives.

2. *The greatest experience is to be loved.* Most young people have trouble comprehending God's acceptance. They need to be convinced of their importance to the Lord. If they constantly feel a lack of communication with God, they are going to seek other ways to gain this feeling of love—maybe in another person, drugs, money, or a job.

3. *Listening is perhaps the most effective weapon to combat the problems of subjectivism.* Certain kids in your youth group constantly give signals in attempts to gain your attention. If you don't catch these signals on the first few tries, the signals often become more extreme.

Listening is so important because teenagers help form their identities by expressing themselves. So they need a caring listener. When a true listener is absent, young people seek expression through other outlets: a pill, a bottle, a fast car. Expression will be found; that isn't the issue. The question is, "Will it come through a responsible source?" Teens' problems are often solved when someone really listens.

"That's the Stupidest Thing I Ever Heard" (Negativism)

The number one cause of negativism is guilt. The more guilty someone feels, the more apt he is to blame someone else, in an attempt to escape responsibility for his guilt. Negativism also results from unbelief. Instead of taking a stand on something, a youth reacts to whatever position someone else takes. Instead of standing for anything, he just criticizes what everyone else stands for.

Major symptoms of negativism: *boredom, lack of follow-through*, and *apathy*.

1. *Boredom*. Many young people feel that their lives are empty and meaningless. Bored because they're not trusting Jesus Christ to live through them, they often look for thrills and activities to fill up their lives. They feel guilty and bored because they are substituting their way for God's way and it doesn't fulfill them.

2. *Lack of follow-through*. Many of today's youth lack the desire to do things thoroughly. They give up easily. This lack of follow-through is a glaring symptom of negativism.

3. *Apathy*. The most obvious symptom of negativism is the "I-couldn't-care-less-about-anything" attitude

that is so prevalent today. "I'm bored" is the password to the crowded club of apathetic youth. If a young person finds nothing positive in today's world, then why get excited about anything?

The results of negativism are:

1. No more heroes. The negativism of the media has resulted in a loss of real heroes in our society. This attitude has even begun to destroy the image of past heroes. George Washington and Abraham Lincoln used to be respected because of their honesty. But the media causes society to question their validity as heroes by asking leading questions such as "Didn't George Washington have a mistress? Is it true that Abraham Lincoln was a bigot? He only freed the slaves to insure a place in history for himself, didn't he?"

Modern-day heroes, from an Elvis Presley to a John Kennedy to a Jackie Kennedy Onassis have been dissected by the media. As a result, we cannot expect anyone to be a "hero" for long.

2. Fall of traditions. The holidays are prime examples. Christmas, Easter, and the Fourth of July used to have greater meanings. Christmas is now called "winter vacation." Easter is "spring break." Most holidays in our calendar year have been reduced to nothing more than three-day weekends. People aren't excited about what commemorative days stand for, whether it's Memorial Day or Veteran's Day.

3. What's in it for me? Life in much of America is no longer based on principle but on *principal*. If you've got money you don't need feelings. If you've got money, you don't need friendship. Negativism is such a dominant philosophy because we've replaced honesty, integrity, and loyalty with the question, "What can I get out of this financially?"

Countering Negativism

Because young people often have poor self-images and because their image of God is so limited, they do not believe they can accomplish much—so they don't try. Yet they need a way of expressing themselves. With no purpose in life and an overabundance of energy, they end up leading helter-skelter lifestyles.

The root of failure is almost always *lack of acceptance*. Few people—teachers, youth workers, or parents—ever seriously say, "I believe in you. You are a significant person to me."

Parents need to look into areas of their child's life that could cause feelings of failure: How do they handle their child's report card? How do they handle their attitudes toward their son's or daughter's dating life? What about their child's weight? Can they communicate the right things to do about his weight and not make him feel like a failure?

Don't be negative with youth affected by negativism. Don't condemn cynical students. If the youth in your group tend to be cynical and apathetic, what they don't need is more preaching. They don't need punishment either. They already feel *guilty*. That's why they think they are failures; and they're afraid of becoming worse failures. Guilt is why they live the way they do.

They need to comprehend that God *really* cares for them as individuals. They need to see God's character. They need to see God's nature. They need to see God's compassion. They need to experience His forgiveness and acceptance. They need to see Jesus Christ, not just hanging on a cross, but living in their daily lives. □

Adapted by permission from The Magic Bubble *by Pat Hurley, published by Victor Books,* © *1978 by SP Publications, Inc.*

20 The American Student—Misery in the "Me" Generation

by Dawson McAllister

Dawson McAllister *is founder and president of Shepherd Productions, Inc., an interdenominational organization dedicated to helping students grow in their personal relationships with Jesus Christ. During the past 10 years, Dawson has spoken to more than a million high school students and has written six books that deal with teenage relationships. He is a graduate of Bethel College and Talbot Theological Seminary. For information regarding Shepherd Productions, address them at: P. O. Box 512, Englewood, CO 80151.*

By the end of the 1970s, the word "me" had become one of the most fashionable in the popular vocabulary. Looking out for "Number One" had become an acceptable basis for behavior. Adults and young people unashamedly flaunted their obsession with self. As a result of this trend, the '70s came to be called the "me decade."

Whatever label is given to describe the '80s, the philosophy of "me-ism" seems firmly entrenched in modern society. This philosophy is likely to influence the youth culture for some time to come.

At its root, "me-ism" is anti-god. The "me-ist" says, "I am the center of the universe. I don't need God telling me what to do. I can meet my own needs, take care of myself, and enjoy all the pleasures available to me. Absolutes are nonexistent. I will become my own value system. I will answer only to me."

"Me-ism" and the Home

The symptoms of this "me-centered" philosophy are tragically manifesting themselves in the home. Many parents today are increasingly self-oriented. They lack commitment to their children and thus are not inclined to make sacrifices for them. Discipline disappears from the home as parents become increasingly permissive.

The growing number of working mothers is to some extent a manifestation of the "me-ist" mentality. While some mothers need to work to survive, others work outside the home simply to satisfy their materialistic appetites or to portray the image of liberated women.

Another example of "me-ism" in the home is the growing tragedy of divorce and the single-parent family. In 1978, the U.S. Census Bureau recorded 8 million homes in which the mother was the only parent, and 1.6 million homes where the father was the only parent. According to the bureau's report, over half of all the children born today will live in a single-parent family.

Children who have lost parents through divorce suffer the consequences of poor parental modeling in the areas of problem-solving and communication. They suffer the trauma of choosing between two people, both of whom they want to love.

"Me-ism" and the Media

The communications media also encourages the high school student to have selfish attitudes. Through 12 years of school, an average student will spend 15,000 hours watching television compared to 12,000 hours spent in a classroom.[1] What values are being impressed on the teenager as he watches those 15,000 hours of TV?

Newsweek reported: "Contemporary video entertainment, especially the sitcom, is running directly counter to traditional American values and institutions. Television's favorite black hats . . . are businessmen, military officials, and the small-town power structure; on the other hand, criminals, the poor, and the hyperkinetic style of urban life are almost invariably portrayed with sympathetic strokes. This 'coherent, anti-Establishment ideology' . . . is largely the result of a left-of-center bias that has come to dominate the medium's creative community."[2]

An actual or implied sexual occurrence hits the American student 2.7 times during every hour of TV viewing and 88 percent of all sex presented on television is sex outside of marriage. In 1978 the number of instances of implied sexual intercourse, sex-related comments, and suggestive sexual scenes appearing on network television totaled over 20,000.[3]

"Me-ism" and Alcohol

The consumption of alcohol depicted on television is also on the rise. In fact, someone drinks alcohol 3.5 times per hour on television—4 times per hour during prime time. For every one time coffee is consumed, alcohol is consumed 10 times. For every time milk is consumed, alcohol is consumed 44 times. Water is consumed once for every 48 times that someone drinks alcohol.[4]

Obviously, students cannot be constantly bombarded with a "me-ist" philosophy without sooner or later allowing it to affect their lives. One consequence of "me-ism" is a "partying spirit" lifestyle among many American teenagers. The "partying spirit" way of life says, "Let's not deal with the pain and reality of life. Let's assume the minimal responsibility to survive—until party time."

This way of thinking was one reason for the popularity of *disco* in the late '70s. With disco, if the music blared and the lights dazzled, one could forget the drudgeries of reality.

Consequently, the "me" generation was saying, "I do not want to think. It will only lead me to despair. So I'll party, party, party."

The "party spirit" shows itself in the alcohol craze of the "me" generation. Joseph Califano, former Secretary of Health, Education, and Welfare, reported that more than 3 million youths experience problems at home, school, or on the highways as a result of alcohol consumption.[5]

"Me-ism," Violence, and Sex

Another sad consequence of "me-ist" thinking is increasing violence and cruelty. The home, once a haven of rest, is no longer a peaceful oasis. Every year, 6.5 million children are physically harmed by a parent or family member. Annually, 8 million children, or 18 out of every 100, assault their parents.[6]

The violence in junior high and high schools is even more alarming. For example, the National Institute of Education estimates that each year 5,200 junior high and senior high teachers are attacked, 6,000 are robbed by force, 282,000 junior and senior high students are assaulted, and 112,000 robbed.[7]

While "me-ism" has fueled the crime rate, it has also desecrated sexual expression. "Me-ism" makes young people forget love and commitment in a frantic pursuit of sexual pleasure outside of marriage. The De-

partment of Health, Education, and Welfare reports that 1 million girls between the ages of 15 and 19 become pregnant each year—370,000 of these pregnancies end in abortion. Some 234,000 result in illegitimate births, and 100,000 pregnant teens try to legitimize their situation by a marriage that is likely to end in divorce. One out of every five new mothers today is a teenager—30,000 are age 15 or younger.[8]

If those figures aren't alarming enough, in 1978, 5,000 teenagers and young adults committed suicide.[9] Psychologists say that for every teenager who succeeded, 50 tried.[10] Over a quarter of a million young people tried to take their lives in that year.

The eruption of these tragic problems has occurred because young people cannot handle the license that "me-ism" grants. Their home lives have been wrecked. They have given up on church; they have given up on government; and now they're left to rely solely on themselves.

And what does God say about this tragedy? He says, "Wake up! We're in a war." The battle is for the hearts and minds of American teenagers. The war will not be won simply by telling students to behave as Christians. Many of them don't know what that means anymore. The battle will be won only as Christ's followers allow His love to melt the hearts of selfishness that have become so prominent in our society.

The American student must somehow come to recognize that God is holy and that this same holy God will one day judge the world. He must come to realize, therefore, that if he lives only for himself, ignoring God, he will have to pay the price. God hates rebellion and the cheap independence of "me-ism."

I believe that the 1980s must be a time when the Christian church

---

"Eighty-eight percent of all sex presented on television is sex outside of marriage."

"The battle is for the hearts and minds of American teenagers."

---

echoes, in word and life, the statement of the Apostle Paul: "For I determined to know nothing among you except Jesus Christ, and Him crucified" (1 Cor. 2:2).

Many youth workers have become so caught up in the activity of ministry that we've forgotten the source of our spiritual power. Our methods have replaced prayer. Advertisements have replaced personal evangelism. Rap groups have replaced Bible studies.

The Christian student must be trained to share the Gospel of Christ crucified, and he must be prepared to defend his Christian lifestyle with Scripture. In short, the Christian student—and all of us—must be living and practicing manifestations of the Christian life. The only way this sleeping "me" generation will stir from its stupor and turn to the Saviour is if it sees Christians living the God-centered, supernatural lifestyle of Jesus Christ.   □

[1] *Youth Letter*, (Published by Evangelical Ministries, Inc., Philadelphia), May, 1978.
[2] "TV Comedy: What It's Teaching the Kids," *Newsweek*, May 7, 1979, p. 67.
[3] *National Federation for Decency Report*, Fall, 1978.
[4] *Ibid.*
[5] "New Alcohol Program to Focus on Women, Teenagers," *Los Angeles Times*, May 2, 1979.
[6] *Youth Letter*, July, 1979.
[7] *Youth Letter*, July, 1979.
[8] *Family Circle*, June 26, 1979.
[9] *Good Housekeeping*, May, 1979.
[10] *U.S. News and World Report*, July 10, 1978.

by Dan Maltby

The youth culture in America is a simmering tea kettle, ready to rattle its lid and whistle loudly sometime in the 1980s. That's the evaluation of our Campus Crusade for Christ High School Ministry staff, a conclusion reached after careful analysis of current national trends. During this decade, we expect to see a period of quiet contemplation followed by a storm of violent reaction to the failure of society to meet youth's "felt" needs for personal peace, pleasure, and affluence.

A Selfish Age?

The '80s have begun as a period of quiet nostalgia—a return to pre-1960s values. Career planning has replaced demonstrations; pursuit of individual success has replaced mob violence. Youth today are into themselves, not social change. They are out to beat the system rather than destroy it.

In the halls of high schools and colleges across the country, the unifying revolutionary causes are gone. The student council leaders are more concerned with how their positions appear to their friends and on their job applications than whether any real

think our opinion is that most Americans are a lot of dummies. They've seen everybody obeying orders but nobody wanting to change any."

Secular Humanism

This uneasy lethargy cannot last. The revolt of the '60s was a warning for the future. The '50s marked an era of peace and prosperity with parents instructing their children in values of right and wrong, in things that were proper and improper. But by the '60s, the basis for right and wrong had been lost in the landslide toward secular humanism, the dominant philosophy of America today.

Without the foundation of a personal God and His authoritative Word, the reason for what parents said and did was gone. Suddenly, in the midst of expanding war, assassinations, and economic crisis, someone asked the generation of the '50s, "Why . . . ?" There was no reply. Radical change and violence answered the silence.

The pendulum has swung again. Today's young people are seeking more "traditional" values. They want to find some security—an anchor or rock—to build a life on. But the pen-

Dan Maltby is a graduate of the University of Missouri with a bachelor's degree in chemistry and a master's degree in business administration. Following two years of employment in the chemical industry, Dan joined the high school ministry staff of Campus Crusade for Christ, International in 1973. Dan is currently their assistant director.

"Some of the values may look pre-1960, but the philosophical foundations have changed."

change results. The founder of one of England's punk rock groups summed up his group's feelings at the conclusion of an American concert tour: "I

dulum cannot swing back on the same plane. Some of the values may look pre-1960, but the philosophical foundations have changed.

The Family Structure

The family structure has deteriorated substantially. With nearly 6 out of 10 children in broken homes, children lack parental role models. Their increased feelings of rejection produce higher and higher levels of hurt, anger, and despair. The school—the newly assigned surrogate parent—cannot meet these needs. But if the answers to life's frustrations are not to be found in the educational system or the values of parents, where can we expect youth to look? The faddishness of our culture makes it difficult to say. But some factors are clear. The pendulum will not again swing back to the radical but idealistic mind-set of the '60s. Youth's sense of idealism has deteriorated (compare the '50s with the present in this regard).

The upheaval of the '80s will be characterized by disdain and disgust rather than by ideals. Meaningless violence will represent an end in itself for many.

Grim Predictions

In the '80s expect youth to mount an effort for significance and meaning within the system through a fight for legal rights within their schools and families. Yet hopelessness will mount. Many more students will seek solace in the supernatural, the bizarre, the out-of-this-world experiences—the existentialist leap. The early warnings are here—punk rock, UFOs, and out-of-the-body experiences.

Entertainment, a giant influence in the youth culture today, will reach new heights of thrill-seeking adventure. Death-defying, dare-devil, and perverted amusements will become the vehicles of young searchers who hope to find meaning in subjective experience.

Government will again receive the brunt of the reaction to come. The anger, hurt, and hopelessness now simmering will express itself in irrational acts of violence.

What Can We Do?

Things look grim for the youth of today. A potentially explosive situation is before us. But the Gospel is still a rock of hope. The calm before the storm—the quiet searching now going on—is fertile ground in which spiritual reaping may take place.

As youth workers we must remind ourselves that the trends forecast in this article are not set in concrete. By God's grace and our faithfulness, we can change this course of history.

Whatever criticism may be directed at the evangelical thrusts of the past several years, something remarkable has taken place in the attitude of Americans toward a faith in God. In the '60s, theologians predicted the imminent death of God and the church. Neither has happened. Based on current indicators, a youth culture with truth validated purely by experience, and violence as a lifestyle, seems a likely prospect. *It need not happen.*

"Go therefore and make disciples of all the nations, baptizing them in the name of the Father and the Son and the Holy Spirit, teaching them to observe all that I commanded you; and lo, I am with you always, even to the end of the age" (Matt. 28:19-20). □

> *"The pendulum will not again swing back to the radical but idealistic mind-set of the '60s."*

Campus Ministry | 22

by Keith Braley

A campus ministry's *objective* is to present the opportunity of receiving Christ to every student within a reasonably defined geographic area. Its *method* is to recruit, challenge, and mobilize students to a ministry of evangelism and discipleship, beginning with students from the local church out of which the ministry operates.

Where Do I Start?

Any person who begins a ministry with the purpose of making Jesus Christ an issue on every local high school campus will soon become overwhelmed with the magnitude of the task, unless he has help.

In my present ministry, I have had the support of approximately 40 college and career-aged people, some married and some single, who share the vision of reaching students for Christ. But help didn't come overnight. The first 10 months of ministry were given almost entirely to recruiting and training staff members, many of whom came from within the local church. As staff were recruited, they were divided into "campus teams"—groups of volunteers committed to working with students from one specific high school. These volunteers formed the foundation for an effective campus outreach.

Ministry Goals

Staff recruitment and training are basic components of campus ministry. But even more basic is *vision*. You can't mobilize a staff unless you know where you're going. Can you imagine the response the Apostle Paul would have gotten if he had said, "Follow me as I try to figure out what I'm doing"? Paul was not indecisive. He was in the business of following Christ and of challenging others to do the same.

Do you know your objectives in ministry? Do you know how you are going to accomplish those objectives? Let me suggest some steps you can take to clarify and transfer your goals to your staff.

1. Evaluate your personal and ministry activities in light of your stated purpose for being involved in ministry to youth. Try to determine what percentage of your activities contributes directly to your ministry goals. Then determine what percentage of your activities are spent on meetings or random activities which do not meet your stated goals. Work toward eliminating those activities which do not advance your goals and objectives.

2. If your goals include a ministry to the campus, plan your programming to aid your staff in reaching high school students for Christ. Remember that staff teams—not meetings—are the basic units of campus ministry. The purpose of meetings should be to complement the ministry of your staff.

3. Equip your staff with the necessary tools to have ongoing personal ministries. This means that staff people should have some basic skills. They

Keith Braley *is youth minister at Village Baptist Church in Portland, Oregon. He and his volunteer staff helped develop a Son City philosophy of high school ministry which now serves as a model for youth workers throughout the West Coast. Before coming to Village Baptist, Keith was involved with a ministry to college students. Later he was minister of youth at Arcade Baptist Church in Sacramento, California. He is a graduate of Western Conservative Baptist Seminary.*

should know how to: share their faith in a concise way, follow up new Christians, make campus contacts, lead a Bible study.

4. *Challenge your staff and students with a clear presentation of an aggressive campus ministry.* Acts 1:8 records Christ's instruction concerning the receiving of power in order to be His witnesses, "both in Jerusalem, and in all Judea and Samaria, and even to the remotest part of the earth." One of the tremendous strengths of the campus ministry is that this goal of reaching a *specific geographic area* for Christ can be transmitted from staff to students. As staff are properly trained and equipped, they can raise up students to evangelize and disciple their own campuses.

Natural Groups

For a staff person or a high school student to maintain a vision for reaching his world for Christ, he must first discover that he has a "Jerusalem" (i.e. Acts 1:8) for which he is personally

> *"We challenge each of our students to build a friendship with another student who is not a Christian."*

when presenting the challenge of the Great Commission; this is a student's "Jerusalem."

A Ministry Model

Many students become motivated by the idea of presenting Christ to their locker partners or to their friends in drama class or choir. But they need a plan to help them see the dream become reality. A pattern that we suggest to our staff and students is called *full-cycle evangelism.* (See chapter 18.) This model has seven phases which are explained below.

1. *Friendship.* We challenge each of our students to build a friendship with another student who is not a Christian.

2. *Spiritual friendship.* The second step involves the student turning that

> *"Think of the campus in terms of groups of students who are related through common interests or abilities."*

responsible. Vision converges with reality when ministry is measured in bite-sized chunks.

I challenge students and staff to think of the campus in terms of groups of students who are related through common interests or abilities. For example, the members of the football team are a natural group, as are the student council members. The students who produce the yearbook are another natural group; the cheerleaders and drill team a fourth. Every student in your youth group belongs to at least one natural group on his or her campus. This is the place to start

relationship into a spiritual friendship by discussing Christ. This does not mean that the Christian student pulls out a tract and makes a formal presentation. But as friends discuss concerns and interests, natural opportunities arise in which a Christian perspective on life can be expressed. Often the Christian's beliefs surface when he talks with his friends about personal struggles. The Apostle Paul tells us to "make the most of the opportunity" (Col. 4:5). That is the intention of phase two of the cycle.

3. *Communicating the Gospel.* The third step in the process is to initiate

a way either to share the claims of Christ with the friend, or to place the friend in a situation where someone else does. This step should involve an opportunity to *respond* to the presentation. Sharing what Christ has done in one's life without confronting another student with his or her responsibility to respond to that information is inadequate. For example, a woman on our staff team related the following story:

One of her most committed campus ministry students was Kathy. Over the years, Kathy told her friends about her relationship with Christ and about her church, but she never told her friends how they could have a personal relationship with Jesus.

Finally, the staff member invited Kathy and several of her friends to a meeting where adult leaders gave a clear presentation of the Gospel and an opportunity to respond. The response was overwhelmingly positive. In fact, Kathy's best friend later told the staff member, "I always wanted to know why Kathy was so sure of where she was going, but she never told me. Thank you for telling me how I can have my own relationship with Christ."

Non-Christians are dependent on Christians to tell them how to have new life. Be bold in challenging students to share Christ in a loving, but forthright way. However, many times a student will not confront a friend because he or she doesn't know how. To help students and staff with their personal ministries on campus, we have created a weekly evangelistic meeting where Christ is shared in a nonthreatening context.

During this meeting, we use a variety of approaches to present our message. These approaches include the use of drama, a stage band, and multimedia shows to create an atmosphere where the student will feel free to enjoy himself without feeling pressured, and yet at the same time be confronted with the issues of Christianity and the need for personal response. Thus the third step in the cycle, sharing the claims of Christ, can take place on a personal or a group level.

4. Conversion. This step is dependent on the work of the Holy Spirit, supported by prayer. Christians can and must share their faith, but only the Holy Spirit can convict a person to the point of response.

Many of our students ask, "But what do I do if my friend doesn't respond to the presentation?"

The Apostle Paul tells us that love never gives up (1 Cor. 13). So, when a non-Christian gives the Christian student a negative response to his Gospel presentation, we point him back to step one of the cycle. We encourage him to persevere in the relationship with his friend. Often students will respond negatively when first confronted with an opportunity to receive Christ, and then respond readily at a later time.

Encourage your Christian students with the fact that they are only responsible to share Christ; their friends are responsible for their decisions whether or not to receive Christ.

This is important because goal-oriented students often view negative response as failures. And they are tempted to give up on building relationships with the non-Christians involved.

5. Maturation. The fifth step in the cycle begins at the point of conversion. When this occurs, the Christian student has a new goal in mind for his or her friend—that of leading the new Christian toward maturity in Christ. The Apostle Paul said, "We proclaim Him, admonishing and teaching everyone with all wisdom, so that we may present everyone perfect in Christ" (Col. 1:28, NIV).

But how do we practically accomplish this task, given that many high school students have no church backgrounds and may be turned off to the church? We have found that an intermediate step can help ease the student into church fellowship. That step, in our ministry, is a body-life meeting held each Sunday evening.

The meeting consists of fellowship centered around worship songs, prayers for one another, and teaching of the Word. In this atmosphere the new Christian is nurtured in the faith. He learns some of the skills necessary to live the Christian life, such as prayer and Bible study. And he comes to understand the necessity of fellowship with God and with God's people.

6. Discipleship. Once a student has shown a consistent response to the Word and to fellowship, we encourage him to become involved in step six of the cycle—discipleship. Most often, discipleship occurs through individual time spent with a campus staff person. Occasionally in our ministry, mature high school students disciple younger ones.

The immediate goal of discipleship is to meet a student's individual needs in order to facilitate growth. The longer-range goal of discipleship is multiplication. Discipled students should be able to share their faith and lead others to maturity in Christ.

7. Coming full cycle. The seventh step in the cycle is actually step one repeated in the life of another student. It occurs when the newly discipled person develops a friendship with the purpose of eventually sharing Christ. At this point, a student has come "full cycle."

Initiating a Campus Work

Can high schoolers really accomplish the goals set forth by the full-cycle evangelism model? Any youth worker knows that demands from parents and teachers, sports and social activities pull high schoolers away from the ministry activities which the youth worker considers important. Teens influenced by emotional and social developmental factors, often lack the stability needed to sustain an effective campus ministry. For these reasons I have found it necessary to commit the building of campus ministry to college and career-age staff. Working with enthusiastic high school students, older staff provide the maturity needed to accomplish the goal of bringing students to maturity in Christ through full-cycle evangelism.

In closing, here are three practical steps which a staff person can use to begin a ministry on the high school campus:

1. Collecting names. When you assign a volunteer staff person to a campus, any contacts you can give him or her will help in the process of developing relationships with students. Names can be collected from a variety of sources. Old Sunday School role books, registration cards taken at evangelistic meetings, camp rosters, visitor lists from once-a-year special events, all are likely sources from which contacts can be collected.

2. Contacting students. Challenge your staff person to contact each student whose name has been collected and find out at what level of Christian commitment, if any, the student is living. Encourage the staff member to set a target date for meeting each of the students on his or her list.

3. Forming a strategy. After a staff person has met with all the students whose names he has been given, he will get a reasonable idea of which students are discipleship material, which ones are lukewarm in their Christian commitment, and which ones are not Christians at all. On the basis of this knowledge, the staff person can then begin to pray that God will raise up students to minister on campus, that He will challenge them to discipleship, and that Christian students will begin to develop relationships with other students on campus.

Summary

A campus ministry's objective is to present the claims of Jesus Christ to every high school student within a given geographic location. This objective is accomplished by providing volunteer young adult staff and Christian students with the necessary skills for effectively presenting Christ to non-Christian students. Campus ministry also involves the nurturing of new believers and the growth to maturity of older Christian students. These students become multipliers of the Christian life and walk.

The full-cycle evangelism model is an effective means of imparting a vision and strategy for campus ministry to both high school students and young adult staff members. ☐

Access to the Public Campus
Knowing Your Legal Rights

by John Whitehead

"**Y**ou can't meet with students at this school because of the separation of church and state."

"Your classroom talks will be monitored. If you step out of line, we'll cancel you."

"No student can walk out of this auditorium with a greater desire to know Christ than he had when he walked in."

If the administrators or teachers on your high school campus confronted you with those comments, would you be without an answer? You don't have to be. Your legal rights as a non-student who works with students are substantial. Under proper conditions, you have the right to be on campus. You have the right to speak in classrooms when invited. You have the right to help establish Christian clubs and to initiate religious activities for students. But you need to know why and how.

Often, however, relating to the faculty and administration of your high school campus is difficult enough without introducing the touchy issue of "legal rights." You don't want to alienate the very people you seek to serve by staunchly advocating your "rights."

But you do yourself—and the students and faculty you serve—a favor by knowing what the law says about religious expression in public education. Keep in mind that one reason the Christian viewpoint is not included more often in the public schools—despite your legal rights—is that interpretation of the law is left to local school authorities. So, laws are applied, correctly or incorrectly, by administrators who may be uninformed of the full implications and freedoms of each law. If you know the law, you may be able to gently point out faulty thinking on the part of school administrators. Your understanding of the law and its implications can be a helpful resource to them.

Also, your ministry can be enhanced as you apply your legal knowledge in loving, understanding, and appreciative gestures toward the faculty and administration.

Let's look at your legal rights (they really are easy to understand) and then consider some ideas that may be helpful to remember as you incorporate them into your ministry.

Three Unconstitutional Practices

First, when considering your legal rights, the most important fact to remember is that there are only three practices that are unconstitutional, as a result of the U.S. Supreme Court's *Schempp* decision of 1963. These are:

1. State-directed and required prayer.

2. State-directed and required Bible reading.

3. State-directed and required on-premises religious training.

NOTE: The key elements in each of these situations is that they are "state-directed" and "required."

Though this decision clearly makes it unconstitutional for the public schools to initiate and sponsor religious activities, it obviously does not restrict religious activities from taking place on the school premises when sponsored by someone else. Nor does

John Whitehead is a practicing attorney in Washington, D.C., specializing in constitutional law. He previously has served as the special constitutional consultant to the Center for Law and Religious Freedom of the Christian Legal Society in Oak Park, Illinois. He is now on the Advisory Board of the Center for Law and Religious Freedom. Mr. Whitehead is a frequent conference speaker and author of two books and numerous magazine articles.

it ban non-students or off-campus speakers from speaking on religious topics when they have been invited in to lecture. While the *Schempp* decision abolishes required prayer, required Bible reading, and required Bible study, it says nothing to prohibit voluntary religious expression and participation—an important difference.

Neutral, Not Hostile

A second point to remember also stems from the *Schempp* decision. The *Schempp* case does more than clarify the three unconstitutional situations. It labels the relationship between the church and state as "neutral," not hostile. The legal term used is "accommodation neutrality," which means that government institutions (such as the public schools) may accommodate (or aid) religion in certain instances. The public schools are warned not to act with hostility by turning a deaf ear or blocking religious activities merely because they are religious. Why?

"That would be preferring those who believe in no religion over those who do believe . . ." remarked former Supreme Court Justice William O. Douglass concerning the *Zorach VS Clauson* case of 1952. "But we find no constitutional requirement which makes it necessary for government to be hostile to religion and to throw its weight against efforts to widen the effective scope of religious influence."

Right to Hear

A third point to remember is that students are considered *persons* under

our constitution. Therefore, they have two important rights:

1. They have the right to hear all sides of an issue (including religion).

2. They have the freedom to express themselves on these issues in an orderly manner.

Both of these rights were specified and guaranteed by the Supreme Court in 1969 in the *Tinker VS Des Moines Community School District* ruling.

NOTE: This means that school authorities don't possess absolute authority over their students. They may not dictate the content of ideas that students hear. In school or out, students have the right to hear about and express themselves on all sides of an issue.

How does this decision affect you? Because of this ruling, students have the right to hear you. Probably the best way of presenting the Christian perspective to students is as an invited guest lecturer in the classroom. This is an appropriate atmosphere for sharing ideas, and it's entirely legal.

Right to Teach

A fourth legal point guarantees rights to teachers. In the *James VS Board of Education* verdict of 1972, teachers were given broad discretion in selecting study materials and using appropriate teaching methods to teach subject matter. Teachers' rights allow them even to defy higher school authorities in selecting and using what they feel to be appropriate teaching materials. This right also gives teachers the freedom to invite guest speakers into the classroom to present their viewpoints as a way of teaching the course material.

Teachers too are free to express their views on controversial issues, though they may not indoctrinate students to their views. Since the classroom presents a marketplace of ideas, teachers are free to present any and all views objectively. Indeed, an excellent way to present subject matter objectively is to invite outside speakers into the classroom to speak on a topic from a particular point of view. Because of teachers' rights to use their own teaching methods and to express their own viewpoints, they are free to invite you into their classrooms as a guest lecturer on a religious topic.

These four legal points can increase your confidence in your high school campus ministry. But, though it's beneficial to vocalize your legal rights, a few words of caution are needed.

Concentrate on Relationships

First, when the going gets rough, advocating and insisting on your legal rights should be your last resort. Pulling legal levers almost never builds close, friendly rapport with faculty or administrators. After all, your objective as a minister to youth is not to win legal battles, but to win, build, and send high school students for the cause of the Gospel.

For this objective to happen, relationships with administration and faculty are of prime importance. You need to do all you can to nurture encouraging, appreciative, supportive relationships with teachers and administrators. Even at the expense of your rights. Even if you're told you can't share the Gospel on campus. Even if unfair restrictions limit your ministry there.

Friends, Not Opponents

Second, it's important that you don't view the faculty and administration as your opponents who stand in your way of ministering to students. Nor do you want the faculty and administration to consider you as their opponent. They are people who need your support, help, and friendship. They are potential disciples and part of the school to which God has called you to minister. And they need to see

battle. Leave the legal lever as a last resort. Let God use you as a servant to those at your school.

Are you experiencing problems as you seek access to campus? Here are a few suggestions that may be helpful:

1. Pray and ask the Lord to work in your situation and to show you if your rights are worth risking a confrontation. Involve others in prayer also. It's possible that as you take time to pray, God will begin to change the hearts of school authorities.

4. Consult other churches and Christian movements (Campus Life, Young Life, Campus Crusade for Christ) that have active ministries with students to get valuable hints and insights.

5. Find an influential principal, teacher, business executive, or parent who will stand behind what you're doing.

6. If the situation does not improve, form a committee of parents. Explain what is happening, describe your legal rights, and ask them to give you counsel. If they agree with you, have a representative go to the principal to express the concerns of the group. This representative should approach him in a loving, gracious manner without being pushy. Attempt to reach a satisfactory conclusion without the principal deferring to the school district, where a decision affects all schools, not just one.

7. Seek legal counsel if you still are not getting a satisfactory response from the school authorities. □

"Government institutions (such as public schools) may accommodate (or aid) religion in certain instances."

---

the glory of Christ reflected in your life as much as the students do.

As you can see, you can be confident about your legal rights as you minister to high school students—the law is on your side. But your legal rights should be of secondary concern when they threaten the delicate relationships you've taken care to establish. Make it your practice to take a relational approach. It will accomplish more in a shorter time period and will be more effective than a court

2. Know the school district's policies regarding religious activities. Decide if you can live with those policies and still reach your goals on campus. Remember that school authorities occasionally make decisions without a clear understanding of what the policies actually say. They may benefit from your knowledge.

3. Keep up to date on information regarding your legal rights. Familiarize yourself with the resources that are available to you.

Reprinted by permission from Insight *(Vol. 3, No. 3)* © *1981 by Campus Crusade for Christ, Inc.*

See chart on page 86.

Four Key Cases

Whether you are a youth worker, teacher, or student, there are certain legal rights that enable you to present the claims of Christ on the high school campus. Following are three U.S. Supreme Court cases that guarantee to you four important legal rights. Take time to memorize them so that you can be confident as you minister to students. There may be instances when the mere mention of these cases (in a loving and gracious manner) may help clarify the school administration's misconceptions and help keep doors open without legal hassles.

The Law

1. *School District of Abington Township VS Schempp*, 1963—In this case the Supreme Court clarified that the state could not direct or require three practices of religion: state prayer, Bible reading, and on-premises religious training

2. *School District of Abington Township VS Schempp*, 1963—This decision also defined the relationship between church and state as "neutral," not hostile.

3. *Tinker VS Des Moines Independent Community School District*, 1969—The Supreme Court ruled in this case that the student has certain constitutional rights, such as the right to express himself in a way that does not disrupt or violate the rights of others.

4. *James VS Board of Education*, 1972—This case gives the teacher the constitutional right to make known those views he feels strongly about, as long as he doesn't try to indoctrinate the class.

Your Right

1. This law means that your presence on campus may not be construed as illegal simply because: (1) you are not there under the sponsorship of the government (school), and (2) your ministry is not initiated by the government.

2. This case said that the government may accommodate religious activities and should not prohibit such activities merely because they are religious.

3. This case gives a student the right to share his religious beliefs with other students, even in the classroom with the permission of the teacher. The case also recognizes the student's "right to hear" all sides of an issue.

4. A teacher has the right to share his religious views in the classroom. This right includes his having an outside speaker come to present the Christian perspective on a topic.

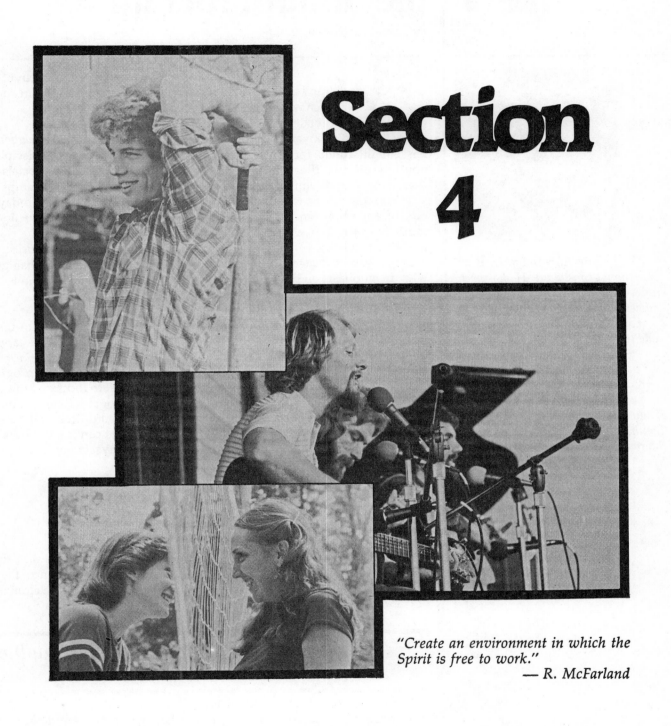

Section 4

"*Create an environment in which the Spirit is free to work.*"
— R. McFarland

24 | Financing the Youth Program

by Leland A. Hamby, Jr.

Leland A. Hamby, Jr. is an educational consultant. He has been involved in local church work as the minister of education at churches in both California and Colorado. In addition, Lee has taught at Western Bible College and Conservative Baptist Theological Seminary. A graduate of Arizona College of the Bible and Talbot Theological Seminary, Lee has been active in the Southwest Baptist Conference as the chairman of the camp committee and Christian education board.

"We can't afford it." "How much will it cost?" "The church has other expenses, you know." If you're a youth leader who has sought funds for your church's youth ministry, these phrases undoubtedly sound familiar.

This chapter deals with three methods of securing funds for a youth ministry in the local church. The first method, receiving funding from the church's *general budget*, is discussed with an emphasis on how to plan and present a youth ministry budget to a church budget committee. The second method, *special funding*, is viewed in terms of how this method fits into the overall operation of youth ministry financing. The third method described is *youth funding*, which gives the youth department 50—100 percent of all its young people's offerings.

General Budget Funding

In most churches, the general church budget is the primary source of funding for youth ministry. The best way to present your youth ministry's financial needs to the appropriate board or committee is to establish a clear set

the various program activities. Some areas to be considered in such a plan might include:

Instructional	Relational
Sunday School	Discipleship
Bible studies	Socials
Club programs	Camps
Leadership training	Sunday evening

Service	Musical
Outreach projects	Small groups
Missions	Choir
Visitation	

In your presentation to the budget committee, specify the appropriate dollar amounts needed for each component of the youth program. But don't forget to focus on how each facet of the program will benefit youth. Budget committees allocate dollars where they can see the best "return" on their investment.

Parents and Pastors

The parents of youth and the senior pastor greatly influence the general budget funding in the church. So, the kinds of relationships a youth worker

---

"Youth have a great deal of expendable money."

---

of objectives for the youth program. Meet with the leaders in the youth division to prepare a program plan for the entire year. This plan should emphasize what you want to see happen in the lives of your youth through

has with parents and pastor often affect his success in getting youth program funding.

Parents are vitally interested in how the youth ministry benefits their children. Having periodic parents' meetings is a good way to receive feedback about the youth group and to let parents know about program plans and financial needs. Such meetings frequently prompt parents to help support the youth ministry.

Many youth programs experience financial difficulty because the youth leader has avoided contact with the senior pastor. Usually, the pastor wants to see the youth program succeed. But since he is responsible for all areas of the church, he is often the one who has to suggest that some things be postponed or modified in order to keep the total church ministry in balance.

So, both the pastor and the youth leader need to have understanding attitudes and good rapport. A solid, close relationship with the pastor is essential. Ultimately, this relationship can have considerable positive impact on youth ministry funding.

Special Funding Projects

Church youth ministries supplement general budget funding with any number of special funding projects:

1. *Special fund raisers:* Car washes, slave days, spaghetti feeds, etc.

2. *Merchandise sales:* T-shirts, candy, literature, candles, etc.

3. *Sponsorships:* Adults sponsor students by the hour to work at church, or to help a needy family, etc.

4. *Donations:* The youth worker solicits funds from groups such as business organizations or companies.

5. *Specials:* The youth program hosts a special youth activity designed to raise funds, such as a youth workers' educational seminar, or a student conference.

All of these methods can legitimately be used to finance youth ministry. But the youth worker should monitor them closely, watching for any unbalanced dependency. Such dependency can create a financial monster that will overshadow his ministry, become too cumbersome to administrate, and worst of all, impede the other primary sources of funding. Special funding projects work best for *special* projects and *special* needs.

Youth Funding

The third method of funding for youth ministry is one which I have used successfully in three different churches. It's called youth funding because it involves young people financially supporting their own ministry.

The guiding principle behind youth funding is that 50—100 percent of all offerings collected in the youth division go into a special youth fund. The remaining percentage, if any, goes into the regular church budget. These offerings represent money collected in regular *youth* meetings such as a Sunday School class, a Bible study, or a discipleship time.

Why Have Youth Funding?

1. *Youth have a great deal of expendable money.* Watch who spends the most the next time you and your youth go to a social outing; it won't be you!

2. *Youth need to be challenged to give to the Lord and to His work.*

3. *Students need to learn what it costs to provide for various programs in the youth department.*

4. *The youths' increased giving will benefit the church.* In each of the three churches where I used this approach, the giving in the youth division eventually exceeded the church budget for youth ministry.

Methods of Youth Funding

Though methods will differ from church to church, the following guidelines are suggested for implementing and running a program of youth funding:

1. *Establish a written policy to regulate youth funding operations.* This policy, including the following points, should be approved by the ruling body of the church.

• The youth fund shall be administered by the youth leaders and officers of the Youth Department. An outside board (such as the board of Christian education) shall review all expenditures.

• Funds shall be used for youth-related projects, programs, or materials.

• All youth fund offerings shall be deposited into the church's general account. The church treasurer shall issue checks for youth fund expenditures and shall keep ledger accounts of youth fund deposits and disbursements. The treasurer shall issue to the youth department heads a monthly statement of youth fund deposits and disbursements.

• Youth funding shall be used as a training aid, helping students learn the cost of running youth ministry programs.

• Students serving as youth group officers shall be involved in the process of setting up a youth fund budget and in the approval and review of expenditures.

2. *Develop a list of materials and ac-*

> *"Budget committees allocate dollars where they can see the best 'return' on their investment."*

89

tivities to be supported by youth fund monies. Such a list might include the following items:

Operational Expenses
- Youth telephone
- Youth stationery
- Mailings, postage, promotions
- Printing
- Transportation, maintenance

Program Expenses
- Honorariums for speakers, music groups, specials
- Follow-up materials
- Training materials for outreach, officers, sponsors
- Baby-sitters for sponsors

- Officers' retreats
- Curriculum, books, magazines
- Athletic equipment
- Media equipment, films, slides, projectors, lighting
- Camping

Outreach Expenses
- Local mission projects
- Foreign mission projects
- Service projects

3. *Develop an education program regarding biblical principles of giving.* Establish a regular time of sharing the scriptural view of stewardship with the youth. Present the budget to the group and explain that it will be met through their regular giving of tithes and offerings. Many young people have jobs or allowances from which they should be taught to give to God's work.

4. *Develop a continuing program of promotion to youth.* The youth fund will continually have to be put before the group in various ways. You can publish a weekly report, put it on a poster, write it on a chalkboard, give a verbal report of the giving, etc. When the group undertakes a special project, take pictures and have involved youth give reports on the results of the project. When funds are not meeting the budget, let the youth know and then challenge them to give.

Publicizing Youth Activities 25

by Mark Zier

No universal laws or far-out theories can guarantee success in publicizing youth ministry activities. Hard work and strategic planning can help. So might these seven axioms of youth ministry promotion:

Analyze Your Goals

Carefully decide what you want to achieve with your promotion. Write your goals on paper or record them on cassette tape. Then evaluate your ideas, amplifying and revising, till you have a list of goals that are clear in focus and direction.

Find a Supporting Cast

Get the support of adults and recruit students to help in your promotional efforts. Listen to their suggestions. Students can provide invaluable input as to how other young people are likely to respond to various forms of publicity. But most importantly, they can provide enthusiastic *verbal pub-*

feel worthwhile. Enthusiasm is contagious—nothing can replace excited people!

Also, *never* assume everyone is doing his job. Follow up on those to whom you have assigned a project or responsibility. Train and lead your supporting cast well.

Match Media to Needs

Choose a particular promotional medium based on your promotional goals and your audience's needs and tastes. A poster campaign may be just what's needed to promote a musical group in Tempe, Arizona. But in Coral Springs, Florida, distributing handouts on the high school campus might do a better job of promoting a similar event. Occasional changes in promotional methods can also be quite refreshing.

Keep It Short, Sweet, and Simple

The first sentence you use in a letter, handout, or poster should jump out,

Mark Zier serves on the staff of Youth for Christ and Campus Life in Ft. Lauderdale, Florida. He is also president of the Visual Sports Network, Coral Springs, Florida. Previously, Mark served as youth pastor at Grace Baptist Church in Newhall, California and at Grace Community Church in Tempe, Arizona.

> *"The best publicity is a group of turned-on young people who support your ministry."*

licity on their campus, at work, and in the community. The best publicity is a group of turned-on young people who support your ministry. Fire those kids up! Be sure all students who want to help have special jobs. Make them

grab the reader, and stimulate his imagination. If the opening does not intrigue the reader, he will read no farther.

Minimize your word content. In some cases, certain musical groups and personalities need no introduction—their names alone will carry the copy. For others who need a brief statement of introduction, give an honest, positive, and imaginative statement. Don't water down your message with a lot of busy words, logos, or excessive use of photos. Keep your message strong, clear, and simple.

Promote Regularly

Publicize weekly, monthly, or quarterly; but develop some kind of consistency in the way you promote youth activities. The more frequent the publicity, the more likely the kids are to respond.

Examples:

1. *Weekly handout,* such as a youth bulletin or flyer

2. *Monthly "look in advance,"* publicizing future activities

3. *Calendar,* datelining events for the next six months or year

"Develop consistency in the way you promote youth activities."

Make It Positive, Creative, and Neat

Let these adjectives be an accurate description of your publicity pieces. This needs no explanation; simply abide by it.

Keep an Idea File

Never discard an idea that might be used in promotion. Store it somewhere so you can come back to it later. You'll be surprised how often you'll return to those creative bursts of genius. □

Reaching Youth through Music

26

by John Bowers

Music is one of the most powerful and effective mediums for communicating the Gospel. Nearly every teen enjoys music. It's a universal language. Also, music is a readily accessible tool for most youth workers. An incredibly broad variety of Christian music is available today, a full range suited to almost every taste. This wide range of popular contemporary styles makes music a relevant, ready tool for those who want to reach the hearts and minds of youth.

A Brief Theology

God seems to be especially pleased with music as a means to *worship Him.* "I will praise God's name in song and glorify Him with thanksgiving. This will please the Lord more than an ox, more than a bull with its horns and hoofs" (Ps. 69:30-31, NIV). "Sing for joy to God our strength; shout aloud to the God of Jacob! Begin the music, strike the tambourine, play the melodious harp and lyre. Sound the ram's horn at the New Moon, and when the moon is full, on the day of our Feast; this is a decree for Israel, an ordinance of the God of Jacob" (Ps. 81:1-4, NIV).

God is also pleased with music used to *proclaim His truth to others.* "David . . . set apart some . . . for the ministry of prophesying, accompanied by harps, lyres, and cymbals . . . (1 Chron. 25:1, NIV). "Sing to the Lord a new song; sing to the Lord, all the earth. Sing to the Lord, praise His name; proclaim His salvation day after day. Declare His glory among the nations, His marvelous deeds among all peoples" (Ps. 96:1-3, NIV).

In itself, music is a neutral tool—it can be used for good or evil. Used correctly, music can reach students and bring glory to God. So the Lord is concerned both with our heart attitude and with the content of music we use. "Let the Word of Christ dwell in you richly as you teach and admonish one another with all wisdom, and as you sing psalms, hymns, and spiritual songs with gratitude in your hearts to God" (Col. 3:16, NIV).

How then can a youth worker use this tool of music most effectively in youth ministry?

Music has long been an integral part of most youth ministries. Its use has ranged from the traditional church youth choir to the informal analysis of secular rock music, in which students learn to filter popular song lyrics through a biblical grid. This chapter, however, will focus primarily on how to use a musical concert or performance in youth ministry.

Determine Your Audience

Who do you want to reach? Identify them as specifically as possible. For

John Bowers is the founder and director of Anno Domini Ministries, Inc. (Portland, Oregon) as well as staff coordinator of musical outreach ministries for Western Conservative Baptist Seminary. In previous years he has been involved with Campus Crusade for Christ, International, the Forerunners musical group in Europe, and the Anno Domini musical group.

"In itself, music is a neutral tool—it can be used for good or evil."

example, suppose you define your primary audience as "non-Christian students at Adams High School." You would have other "audiences" as well—students in your own youth group, your sponsors, and possibly your deacons/elders; but you dare not lose sight of your primary audience. Your musical performance should minister directly to them.

Determine Your Message

What do you want to say to your audience? In other words: What do you want them to be thinking about when they leave?—the Gospel?—your church?—your youth group?—their own lives? You may wish to do some pre-evangelism—to raise thoughtful questions, entertain, or encourage so you can establish and nurture long-term relationships. On the other hand, you may want to bring people to a crisis point where they'll realize their need to make decisions.

Be sure to consider those questions *before* you go too far with concert plans, as the answers will determine the atmosphere and musical messenger you will use. Will your purpose best be met by a big-name artist in a 5,000-seat auditorium or by a folk duo in an intimate living room? Either can be effective, depending on what you want the performance to accomplish.

It's usually wise to sponsor smaller concert groups or individual singers for your own youth group, or an outreach to their friends. An individual performer can minister on a more personal basis to a smaller group. This type of concert removes the obstacles and difficulties of trying to sponsor a huge, expensive show. Such a show is normally handled best by a professional promoter who has the financial funding and the expertise needed in this highly competitive field.

The beauty of the smaller performance is that you can leave the "big-time" concerts to somebody else, and

simply plug your kids into them. But do schedule your yearly calendar to include a couple of the bigger city-wide concerts—concerts that no one group is capable of pulling off, but that can benefit all. Your students will feel confident in inviting their non-Christian friends to such a professional concert, plus it will allow your students to meet other Christian students in the community.

How to Promote a Concert

1. Musicians. Contact the musicians who will best communicate in the context you have determined; be sure that they fit into your strategy and ministry needs. It is usually essential to reserve a date with them first, and go from there. Also be sure to allow yourself ample time to properly promote the performance, depending on the type and scope of your concert.

2. Location. The most common error committed by beginners in concert planning is selecting a poor location. When you advertise, people will quickly discern your expectations of attendance and will assign status to your event based on the location. For example, if you're advertising a nine-member group to perform in Chemistry Lecture Hall Room 305-B, chances are excellent that hundreds will stay home! Concerts normally should be held in auditoriums or in other places where similar functions commonly take place. Even if you have in mind something small and intimate, locate in a room that is conducive to your purpose.

As a general rule, use your *own* facilities whenever possible. You'll find that your own church auditorium, gymnasium, youth room, or grass lawn can be quite appropriate and also inexpensive. For the average youth ministry, *renting* a special facility is almost never necessary. Occasionally, you may want to consider some other

suitable locations that are both inexpensive and "neutral," such as a nearby school yard, a park, a big backyard, or even a business facility.

3. Publicity. Students decide whether or not to attend a performance based on a combination of *personal contacts* and *media input* (advertising). For example, a student may see a concert advertised all over town, but not be interested because he's never heard the group or anything about them—that is, till a good friend says, "I've heard them and they are *awesome!*" In the same way, a student's best friend may drive him crazy talking about some great new group, and yet the student has never heard of them—that is, till he sees a full-page newspaper ad on them. So, whether you're using a famous popular artist, or an unknown local group, the principle is the same: Attractive, concise advertising *and* effective word-of-mouth are always the key ingredients. (See chapter 25, "Publicizing Youth Activities," for further information).

Here's something to remember: *People reach people.* Whether it's word-of-mouth enthusiasm or displaying posters and flyers, you need to involve *your youth group* in the process. To properly publicize your concert, excite your sponsors and students with a vision for the event! Show them how this concert can affect them—and their friends. Demonstrate its value to the group. They in turn will multiply your efforts and reach out to many others.

One last thought on publicity: Be sure to utilize the *free* publicity you can get through newspapers and radio stations in the form of P.S.A.s and P.B.A.s (Public Service Announcements and Public Broadcast Announcements).

4. Budget. This area comes last by design. You've started by determining your audience, messages, and how to best reach that audience. Now you must figure out how much it will cost. If the cost seems prohibitive, don't start cutting corners (like printing cheap posters). That's only a short-cut to failure. But if necessary, go back to the beginning and start over. Scale down the type of concert so it's within your budget but still has a valid place in your ministry. Find that delicate balance between your ability to pay and to apply faith to your finances. The Lord will honor such an approach.

Follow-up

Plan your follow-up *before* the day of the concert. Comment or response cards are excellent, non-threatening ways to make contacts. You can use plain 3" X 5" cards or a prepared card, but ask the audience to write what they thought about the event. This will help you evaluate and plan for the future. Ask for names and addresses. (If they're not willing to be contacted, you should make them feel free not to give that information.) Such cards can be used to record decisions as well. You may want to request more specific information such as, "I would be interested in a Bible study," etc.

Whether or not you use cards, you should definitely use *sponsors*. Your sponsors should be ready to move in and counsel or share with individuals who may respond to an invitation. Sponsors should be trained in this area of counseling and provided with a practice situation prior to the concert. Music is a strong, moving tool that can result in *decisions*. Be ready to follow up and work with people. Don't waste the opportunity! NOTE: You may find that with a minimum of training, your key students will do well as counselors.

Bridging the gap from an event like

permanent, but you also probably had a low profile at the concert. One way to help overcome this problem is to have those involved in the program—the musicians in the group—stay in your area for an extra day or two and help with follow-up. Send out teams composed of one musician and one of your own group members to meet the contacts so those contacts will identify with your group personally.

In many cases this approach won't be possible because of the musicians' tight time frame. The next best thing would be to expose the group to your students before and after the concert. Remember, it's important to relate

> ## "It's important to relate your concert to your entire ministry (and its objectives)."

a concert to your ongoing ministry is often difficult. You typically will have used musicians who were highly visible in concert, but who are also highly temporary—here for the concert, gone the next day. As a sponsor you are your concert to your entire ministry (and its objectives), so be precise in your follow-up; use it to touch base with your *own* kids, and seek to plug in the new contacts as well. ☐

27 Music or Missions?

by Keith Green

Keith Green *is a recording artist, director of Last Days Ministries, and editor of "The Last Days Newsletter." Keith's recordings include* For Him Who Has Ears to Hear, No Compromise, So You Wanna Go Back to Egypt, *and* The Keith Green Collection. *For information regarding Last Days Ministries, contact: Last Days Ministries, P.O. Box 40, Lindale, TX 75771.*

So many people ask me how they can start a music ministry. At concerts, I get countless questions about this, and I get lots of letters and even some long-distance phone calls from people who feel they have been "called" into the music ministry. One day, I began to ask myself why nobody ever asks me how to disciple a new believer, or how to become a missionary or street preacher. Most people seem to prefer the "bright lights" of what they think a music ministry would be, rather than the obscurity of the mission field or the dirty streets of the ghetto, or even the spiritual sweetness of just being a nobody whom the Lord can use mightily!

Are You Willing?

My answer to this question is almost always the same: "Are you willing to never play music again? Are you willing to be a nothing? Are you willing to go anywhere and do anything for Christ? Are you willing to stay right where you are and let the Lord do great things through you, though nobody seems to care or notice?" Usually the answer is a quick yes! But I really doubt if these would-be performers know what their answer entails. . . .

> *"Most people prefer the 'bright lights' of what they think a music ministry would be, rather than the obscurity of the mission field. . . ."*

Star Struck

Why are many Christians so star struck? Why do we idolize Christian singers and speakers?

It's true that the Holy Spirit has anointed men and women to minister to His people and to the unsaved. But Satan is getting a great victory as we worship these tape and record ministers, and clamor to get their autographs in churches and concert halls from coast to coast.

In reality, such hero worship hurts those ministers. They try desperately to tell us that they don't deserve to be praised, but we squeal with delight and praise them all the more. We smother them, making it almost impossible for them to see that only Jesus deserves the honor and glory. We crush their humility and grieve the Spirit that is trying to keep their eyes on Jesus.

> *"Are you willing to never play music again?"*

Of course, we idolize what we ourselves want to become. A lot of us want to be just like our favorite Gospel singer and performers. In idolizing them, we insult the Spirit of grace and try to make a place for ourselves rather than a place for Jesus.

A Thankless Job

Why do so few Christians "idolize" the missionaries who live in poverty, endangering their lives and their families? Why do so few Christians shower praise on the ghetto preachers and prison ministers who never take up an offering; for if they did, they would either laugh (or cry) at what they received?

Why? Because from early on, society teaches that being comfortable and being liked are two terribly important things. Who lives more comfortably and is more well liked than the latest bright and shining Gospel star? Who has lived less comfortably and has had less supporters than the missionaries and soul-winners who have died untimely, premature deaths trying to win souls to Christ?

Do we really believe we're living in the end times? Then why do many of us spend more money on Gospel records and concerts than we give to organizations that feed the poor or to the missionaries our churches support?

I repent of ever having recorded one single song, and ever having played even one concert if my music and (more importantly) my life have not provoked listeners to sell out completely to Jesus!

Let's quit trying to make gods out of music ministers, and quit desiring to become like them. The Lord commands, "Deny yourself, take up your cross daily, and follow Me" (Luke 9:23, author's paraphrase). My piano is not my cross; it is my tool. I'd never play it again if God would show me a more effective tool for proclaiming His Gospel.

To finish, let's be reminded that the Lord will say, "Well done, good and faithful servant" (Matt. 25:21, NIV) only to those music ministers who glorify Jesus and Jesus only. Let's all repent of idolizing Christian performers and seeking a comfortable "rewarding" life while we are supposed to be passing through like strangers and pilgrims in this world (Heb. 11:13). For our reward is in heaven, and our due service to the Lord is "not only to believe in Him, but also to suffer for His sake" (Phil. 1:29). □

28 Involving Youth in Missions

by Mel Bittner

Mel Bittner *and his wife Jan are missionaries to France with the Conservative Baptist Foreign Mission Society. Their main work is with evangelism and church planting. Before going to France, Mel served eight years as director of Christian education and youth at churches in California and Arizona.*

You're the sponsor, the leader, the youth worker, and you want to instill in your young people a burden for missions. How do you go about it?

Develop a Burden

Before you try to interest young people in missions, check out your own attitudes. Do you think of having a missionary speak to the youth group as a necessary evil, something to be endured during an occasional church missionary conference? Are you actively involved in supporting missions? The point, obviously, is that you can't instill a burden you don't have.

Pray for Missionaries

Whether for yourself or your young people, a good way to start developing a burden for missions is by praying knowledgeably for missions and missionaries. This kind of praying goes beyond the hackneyed, "Lord, bless the missionaries on the foreign fields and the homelands. Amen." Gordon England has suggested the following guidelines for knowledgeable missionary praying:

About *you*:
● Believe that God can meet the missionary's needs.
● Be informed about his ministry.

● Take time to pray regularly.
About *the missionary*:

● Know that character development should be his most important single goal. Pray that God will conform the missionary to the image of His Son.
● Pray that he receives spiritual discernment and wisdom.
● Pray that he will be gracious, especially under pressure.

About *his family*:
● Pray that they will have adaptability and flexibility.
● Pray that they will have a happy home—one that gives a good testimony.
● Pray for the needs of the children. Remember that sometimes the only place they feel at home is in an airplane between countries.
● Pray for balance in maintaining an equilibrium in the roles of work responsibilities and family responsibilities.
● Pray for the family's health and safety.

About *his work*:
● Pray that Satan would not be able to hinder the missionary's work.
● Ask God to give the expertise needed to do the job.
● Pray for his national colleagues.
● Pray for good interpersonal relationships among the missionaries.

These are general guidelines. They should be supplemented with more precise information from your missionary. This information can be obtained through prayer letters, personal letters, tapes, or talking with mission representatives. Another excellent but expensive way to be informed about a missionary's work is to visit the field yourself.

Serve at Home

Once you and your youth are praying intelligently for missions, you may feel a need for more immediate involvement. Before you head out for "the uttermost part of the earth," you might consider being missionaries to *your* Jerusalem. (See Acts 1:8.) Knock on those doors right around your church. (You won't have to bus your converts so far.) Then lift up your eyes to *your* Judea (Mexico? An Indian reservation? A minority group near you?) You probably have many foreign-speaking people in your town who would welcome some friendship.

Teach your young people how to lead someone to Jesus Christ. Take one or two students with you as you evangelize. Nothing teaches as well as example. Be that example. If a young person is active and productive in his local church, he will more likely be productive in a cross-cultural situation.

A Christian student from Africa told an American church about the spread of the Gospel in his country. Afterward someone said to him, "You know, I believe I'd like to be a missionary in Africa."

"What are you doing now?" inquired the speaker.

"Not much of anything," was the reply.

"Then please," replied the speaker, "don't go to Africa to do it."

> *"Knowing the calling of God is important, but an emphasis on 'the call' can confuse the issue."*

Know God's Calling

This leads me to my next subject—the fabled "missionary call." Knowing the calling of God is important, but an emphasis on "the call" can confuse the issue.

In *Let's Quit Kidding Ourselves about Missions*, Jim Weber correctly points out that the marching orders of the church in Matthew 28:19 should read, "Going . . . teach all nations," and not "Go therefore. . . ." Young people need to know that their primary "call" is to the Lord Jesus Christ and that the will of God for their lives is that they be conformed to the image of His Son. *Where* they exercise their gifts or practice their vocations is not as important as being available to God wherever they are. Wherever they *go*, they should be involved in the missionary task of disciple-making.

Paul had been a missionary for many years when he received the "Macedonian call." The late Dr. Brushwyler said, "Missionaries have just one thing in common regarding their 'calls.' The Holy Spirit has confirmed it to each one in His own unique way. And each one knows it."

Involve Youth in Serving

Assume that you have some young people who would like to serve the Lord in a cross-cultural situation. How could you equip them?

1. *Help them develop Christlike qualities in their lives.* (Of course you want this for all of your young people.) Some of these qualities are a servant's heart, submission to authority, a clear conscience, a forgiving spirit.

2. *Feed them biographies of missionaries.* These can edify believers tremendously, often next only to the Word of God.

3. *Help them find opportunities for short-term work abroad.*

4. *Help them learn to appreciate the differences between cultures.*

5. *Encourage them to pray for specific countries.*

6. *Teach them how to be disciplined in their thought life, devotional life, finances, and speech.*

Home churches often fail in their support of missions in the following areas:

- keeping informed
- recruiting new missionaries
- giving money
- praying
- evangelizing at home

You can help alleviate these problems by putting the kind of creative energy into the support of missions that you put into other programs for young people.

There are many missionary opportunities around the world. As a youth worker, aim to open your young people's eyes to these possibilities. Your rewards will be great. □

> *"If a young person is active and productive in his local church, he will more likely be productive in a cross-cultural situation."*

29 Designing a Christian Camp Program

by Richard McFarland

Richard McFarland is youth minister at Bethany Bible Church in Phoenix, Arizona. Previously, Richard served for three years as a youth minister at Palm Springs Community Church in Palm Springs, California. Richard has worked a great deal with student-led camping. He is a graduate of Whitworth Bible College.

A successful Christian camp program is *goal-oriented*. It is a program designed, through thoughtful planning, to develop campers in one or more of the following areas: evangelism, spiritual growth, leadership, discipleship.

Nine areas to consider in designing a camp program are: (1) creating an environment, (2) analyzing needs, (3) establishing an objective, (4) training counselors, (5) developing activities, (6) using student counselors, (7) defining counselor responsibilities, (8) following up decisions, (9) evaluating performance.

Creating an Environment

Ultimately, programs don't change lives; God does. A camp program should create an environment in which the Holy Spirit is free to work in the campers' lives. Every component of the program, whether meals, free time, or teaching time, should be designed with this principle in mind. Create an environment in which the Spirit is free to work; He will!

Analyzing Needs

Analyze the needs of campers, giving consideration to two basic types of needs: earthly needs and spiritual needs.

Earthly needs. Earthly needs are usually *physical* (i.e. food and shelter); *social* (i.e. friends, acceptance, boy/girl relationships); *emotional* (i.e. love, fear of failure). An analysis of earthly needs will affect such practical matters as housing facilities, food, cabin placement, and recreational activities. Effective handling of the earthly needs of campers creates a greater openness to God's dealing with their spiritual needs.

Spiritual needs. The Bible sheds light on the types of spiritual needs adolescent campers face. (See Eph. 4—6; 1 Tim. 3:2-7; 1 Peter 5:1-7; Acts 6:3-5; and Titus 1:7-9.) Considering the following questions in light of these Scriptures can help determine the spiritual needs which your camp program should focus on: (1) To what life goals should the camper be committed? (i.e. to be Christlike) (2) What decisions should campers be able to make in the following areas of their lives: physical (Do I need exercise?) personal (What career should I pursue?) social (Who should I date?) and spiritual (Do I want to grow?) (3) What ministry skills should campers learn? (i.e. how to study the Bible) (4) What relational skills should campers develop? (i.e. submission to authority)

Establishing an Objective

Establish a measurable camp objective. Don't design a program to change the total person in one week or weekend when time barely allows for successfully affecting a single area of change. Instead, create an entire program to achieve a *single* objective. For example, if you want to focus on evangelism, structure the whole camp around the objective of evangelizing campers. Or, if you feel the most important need is for the spiritual growth of believers, focus your program to help campers develop a particular quality or ministry skill.

Why have a *single* objective? It defines clearly where change is to take place. It defines clearly the responsibility of counselors. It gives staff members a basis for evaluating the camp.

Training Counselors

Once you have analyzed needs and established objectives, then camp counselors must be trained to help run the camp program. Often it helps to involve counselors in the process of establishing the objective. Not only should counselors know the objective, they should be instructed in how to work with campers to accomplish the objective. For example, if the objective is to help campers grow in love for others, then the counselor should be instructed in how to demonstrate that quality to the campers he works with.

Developing Activities

Camp activities are the environment in which the Holy Spirit operates to change lives. Every activity should work toward meeting the campers' needs and developing a spiritual quality in their lives. For example, football becomes not just a game, but an environment in which to work on

"A camp program should include a plan for following up campers who make decisions for Christ during camp."

such qualities as patience, unity, and teamwork.

Using Student Counselors

Every adult counselor should be assigned at least one student counselor who can serve as his assistant. Why student counselors? It gives them opportunity to learn leadership skills. It lets them experience what being the authority figure is like. Having students assist adult counselors develops counselors for future camps. It also provides the other students with peer models.

Defining Counselor Responsibilities

Counselor responsibilities should be well defined, and counselors should be committed to fulfilling these responsibilities. (See the sample outline of "Counselor Responsibilities" on page 102.)

Following Up Decisions

A camp program should include a plan for following up campers who make decisions for Christ during camp. Follow-up activities might include a

Bible study, discipleship group meetings, building friendships, or a single activity designed to bring counselors and campers together again following camp. A follow-up plan should also make provision for campers who, because of distance or religious background, may not be able to attend your church. Following up these campers might involve developing a packet of materials designed to help them grow spiritually, or getting them in contact with other churches or Christian groups.

Evaluating Effectiveness

Was the camp successful? You won't really know without conducting some form of evaluation. The camp director(s) should evaluate counselors to determine how effectively they carried out their responsibilities. Counselors should evaluate campers to determine to what extent the program objective was realized with each camper.

The following questions can be useful in evaluating the effectiveness of the camp program: Did the camp program accomplish its objective? What "physical" problems occurred (food, housing, recreational facilities, etc.)? Did the Holy Spirit use the camp to produce change in the campers' lives? What should be done differently at the next camp? □

See outline on page 102.

"Every activity should work toward meeting the campers' needs and developing a spiritual quality in their lives."

Counselor Responsibilities
(Sample Outline)

I. Before camp:
- A. Pray about the camp and your role in counseling high school young people.
- B. Seek to line up a team of parents and friends who will pray for you and for those with whom you will be involved at camp.
- C. Prepare devotionals that deal with each days's theme for each morning of camp.
- D. Choose an assistant student counselor.
- E. Delegate responsibility to your assistant counselor. Make certain the assistant counselor follows through.
- F. Meet or call those who have been assigned to your cabin so that they will sense your interest in them.
- G. Attend all planning meetings.

II. During camp:
- A. Realize that the half hour each morning before breakfast devoted to prayer and evaluation is of special importance.
- B. Conduct, along with your assistant counselor, a morning cabin devotional that relates to each day's theme.
- C. Plan to spend counseling time (a minimum of 20 minutes for each camper in your cabin) some time during the week.
  - 1. Confront and assist the camper in reaching the objective for each day.
  - 2. Give the camper a personal example of how you are striving to reach the objective for each day.
  - 3. In some way, indicate to the camper that you love him and care about him.
- D. On the last morning of camp, have a debriefing session as a part of your devotional. Attempt to find out what camp has meant to each camper.

III. After camp:
- A. Follow up any from your cabin who have made decisions for Christ.
- B. Call all those in your cabin and let them know again of your interest in them.
- C. Thank your assistant counselor and any other young people who may have been of help to you.
- D. Be available to help the camp directors with equipment and cleanup.
- E. Keep a notebook of how the camp objective was or was not reached. This will be evaluated for use at the next camp.
- F. Thank God for what happened at camp.

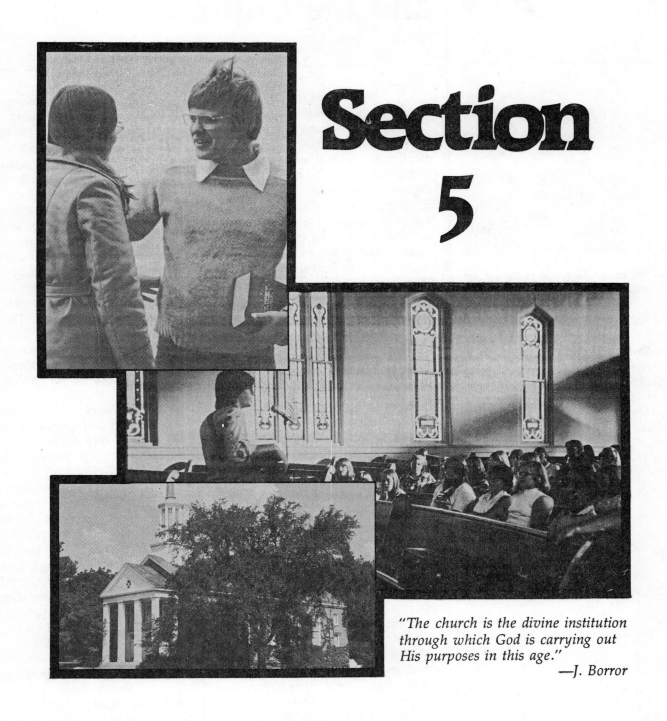

Section 5

"The church is the divine institution through which God is carrying out His purposes in this age."
—J. Borror

30 | The Youth Worker and the Church

by James Borror

Dr. James A. Borror is pastor of the First Baptist Church of Lakewood in Long Beach, California. Before coming to Long Beach, he began a church in Scottsdale, Arizona. Dr. Borror is a graduate of Bob Jones University and Dallas Theological Seminary where he received both his Master of Theology and Doctor of Theology degrees. He is a popular speaker at pastors' seminars, camps, and Bible conferences.

The church is the divine institution through which God is carrying out His purposes in this age. In spite of this obvious New Testament fact, rarely does a manual on youth ministry contain a thorough discussion of the church. Perhaps one of the reasons for this neglect is the confusion many people feel concerning the nature and purpose of the church. The question, "What is the church?" is, as Emil Brunner puts it, "the unsolved problem of Protestantism."

What the Church Is Not

There are a number of false ideas as to what the church is:

1. *The church is a building.* Though not many believe this in theory, some still act as if the essential nature of a church is brick and mortar. Church buildings are useful for housing the fellowship of God's people, but the church is not defined by walls and stained glass windows.

2. *The church is a social club.* Unfortunately, some service clubs, lodges, and even bars provide more genuine intimate fellowship, personal interaction, and social satisfaction than some churches.

3. *The church is a fellowship.* Closely allied to the social club idea is the notion, based on a misinterpretation of Matthew 18:20, that the church is merely a loose fellowship created whenever two or three believers get together. Proponents of this view believe that they are fulfilling the obligation of Hebrews 10:25 and other New Testament passages relating to the church by merely getting together with a few Christian friends.

4. *The church is a social service agency.* Though the church provides a valuable social service to the world, it is more than an agency for social change.

5. *The church is a theatrical production.* Spectators watch a weekly performance. The chief actor is the preacher. The church members are the spectators—and the critics.

6. *The church is a religious clinic.* Persons can go there for strength and emotional reinforcement. Though this definition touches on a part of what the church is, it overemphasizes what the church can *do* for people as opposed to what people can *give* to the church.

7. *The church is a commemoration.* This definition presents the church as something like a historical society, perpetuating the memory of a great life.

8. *The church is a reproduction.* This idea is popular with those who always want to go back to the first-century, New Testament church. But the New Testament shows that the early church had many failings. Though the New Testament gives basic principles concerning the nature and function of the church, the Scripture also presents the church as a dynamic, growing cell, not a reproduction.

9. *The church is a classroom.* Without question, one of the church's major functions is studying God's Word. But this definition ignores the fact that God's love should also be communicated through the exciting, dynamic fellowship of God's family.

10. *The church is invisible.* This definition, though partly true, ignores the importance of the visible local body.

All of these viewpoints are inadequate definitions of the church. The church may have many of these aspects. For example, it does have a social dimension; it does care for the needs of other people; it does in a sense have an audience; and it is concerned about wholeness and health, even as it commemorates Christ. But each of those definitions is inadequate in itself.

The Nature of the Church

The word *church* appears 112 times in the New Testament, and biblical writers use it in two primary ways:

1. In reference to *time*, the church consists of all believers united with Christ and His body by the Spirit, from Pentecost to the Rapture.

2. In reference to *location*, the "local" church consists of all believers who live in one locality and who are organized for corporate worship, evangelism, and edification.

Invisible and Local

The important question is, "How are these two entities—the invisible church and the local church—related to each other?" In the New Testament, biblical writers use at least six figures of speech to refer to the church: body, temple, bride, flock, branches, and priesthood. Four of these figures of speech refer to the local church as well as the total body of Christ:

1. God's temple (1 Cor. 3:16-17)
2. A body (1 Cor. 12:27; Acts 9:4; compare 8:3)
3. A bride (2 Cor. 11:2)
4. A flock (1 Peter 5:2-4)

The local congregation is the local, temporal, physical expression of what the total body of Christ is in its ideal, spiritual, and invisible pattern throughout this age. The local church is the visible part of a larger "rock"—the church composed of all true believers. As the visible part of a rock formation is of the same nature as the larger formation, so the local congregation shares the *nature* of the body of Christ.

The implications of this close relationship between the universal and local aspects of the church are far reaching. The fact that each local assembly is (or ought to be) a visible expression of the body of Christ has practical implications affecting the overall ministry of each local church.

Implications

First, this relationship demands that only the *regenerate* comprise the membership of the local church (2 Cor. 5:17; John 3:3-7). The local church is not only to include *only* the regenerate but it should include *all* regenerate. (Compare Acts 2:47 and Hebrews 10:24-25.) The New Testament recognized no Christian "hitchhikers" who claim to belong only to the universal church and have not united with the local body. Every Christian is to assume his part and exercise his gift in a local assembly.

Second, the local church is not subject to any other body, either secular or religious, though it cooperates with both.

Third, the church has an ordered and a purposeful membership (1 Cor. 14:33; 14:40; Eph. 4:7-16; Titus 1:5).

Fourth, the church has a unified membership (Heb. 13:17; Rom. 16:17).

Finally, the church has a growing membership, both quantitatively and qualitatively (Eph. 4:12-15; Matt. 28:19).

The Body of Christ

The major figure in the New Testament relating to both aspects of the church—local and invisible—is the *body* of which Christ is the head. The Apostle John says, "The Word was made flesh, and dwelt [literally 'tabernacled'] among us, and we beheld His glory, the glory as of the only begotten of the Father, full of grace and truth" (John 1:14, KJV).

Our Lord's incarnate body served the same function as the tabernacle in the Old Testament—that of making visible the invisible God as His glory indwelt it. God designed His church as a dwelling place for Him, the place of meeting between God and men, and the place of sacrifice. Our Lord's incarnate humanity fulfilled all of these functions.

The church today is to be for each generation what the body of our Lord was for His—that is, the visible expression of the invisible triune God; the place where God can meet with people; where He dwells; and where the sacrifice of our Lord is preached.

If the church is to be an expression of the glory of God for a lost world, then there ought to be some visible expression of that glory. The New Testament indicates only four characteristics the church can have that the world may see and thereby know it is truly the body of Christ. These visible evidences are:

1. Love. Our Lord tells us that the badge of our discipleship is love (John 13:35).

2. Unity. Some have called this evidence the "ultimate apologetic." Our Lord speaks of *unity* as that which

> *"Every Christian is to assume his part and exercise his gift in a local assembly."*

will make the world know that the Father has sent the Son (John 17:21, 23).

3. *Good works* (Matt. 5:16). Ideally, when the world sees our good works, it will be brought to glorify the Father who is in heaven.

4. *Hope.* Peter speaks of being able to give an answer to those who ask concerning "the hope that is in us" (1 Peter 3:15). The world must see something in our lives which expresses that hope.

Implications for Ministry

An understanding of the church as the visible incarnation of Jesus for this generation has important implications for youth ministry. In the Incarnation, God took on Himself human flesh. He involved Himself in our lives. He got into "our skins." That means if we are to be effective in ministry, we have to be willing to incarnate ourselves into the lives of other people.

Merely running programs is not enough. We must "get inside their skins" to feel what young people feel, to think what they think, to hurt when they hurt, and to spend the time and energy needed to bring healing and reconciliation.

The Purpose of the Church

The local church has three primary functions. The first is to teach effectiveness in and provide an environment for *worship* (1 Peter 2:5). Worship is the acknowledgement of the presence of the infinite, triune God and the accompanying response of praise, thanksgiving, service, and obedience.

Second, God designed the church for *evangelism* (Matt 28:19). Evangelism, in its strictest sense, is sharing Jesus Christ by the power of the Holy Spirit and leaving the results to God.

Third, God designed the church for the *edification* of its members (Eph. 4:11-16). Discipleship may be defined as a time investment between two or more believers using the Word of God and their spiritual gifts for the purpose of mutual encouragement and spiritual growth.

The Church Gathered and Going

At this point a distinction should be made between the local church assembled and dispersed. The church assembled is primarily for the purpose of edification and worship. The church dispersed is primarily for the purpose of evangelism.

Not an Option

Believers—not buildings, or programs, or anything else—are the church. As believers, we don't have a choice as to whether or not we are a part of it. This is true for at least four reasons:

1. *The church is ordained of God.* Originally, Christians regarded both aspects of the church in the New Testament as one. The local church is the church in miniature, a replica of the whole, giving, visible, and temporal expression to the invisible and eternal body of Christ.

2. *The church is united to Jesus Christ.* Four figures of speech graphically express that unity. Just as the Lord told the Apostle Paul that Paul was persecuting Him (Acts 9:5) when the preceding chapter showed that Paul was persecuting the church; so you cannot persecute or, for that matter, neglect the local church without persecuting or neglecting our Lord Himself.

3. *God commands faithful church attendance* (Heb. 10:25).

4. *You can't live a good Christian life without the church* (Heb. 10:25; Acts 2:42). By definition, *a good Christian* is one who obeys God's Word. Since in His word, God tells us the importance of the church and commands our attendance, no one can claim that he can live an acceptable Christian lifestyle without the church. A person who is loyal to Jesus Christ, who supports His work and wants it to go forward, will find that the best way to support that cause is through the local church. He cannot slight the local body without slighting the invisible body and ultimately the Head of that body Himself.

The church then is that fellowship of men and women who have come into a personal relationship with God through Jesus Christ. It is to the world the visible expression of our now invisible Lord. Until the day He returns to earth, the church is to worship, evangelize, and edify. □

Youth Ministry and Christian Education

31

by George Hreha

"If you aim at nothing, you'll hit it every time" is a maxim which points out the need for setting and carrying out clearly defined goals and objectives. It's true of any endeavor, but the old saying may be particularly relevant to youth ministry. Why? Because youth ministries have traditionally emphasized exciting activities and programs without determining how they advance the goals of the youth ministry or the overall direction of the local church.

Youth ministries tend to *exist unto themselves*; yet the church's youth ministry should be a vital part of the church's Christian education program. The following Christian education designations suggest an interdependence and continuity that should exist between programs in the local church: (1) Babies and toddlers (birth—2), (2) Early childhood (2—5), (3) Children (Grades 1—6), (4) Youth (Grades 7—12), (5) Adults (College—Senior Citizens). Youth ministry should be a part of a *chain of ministries* in the local church, ministries that share the same overall philosophy and purpose.

Another problem which often surfaces is that once youth workers state their purpose, they tend to ignore it, and rarely take time to evaluate activities based on stated goals and objectives. The purpose of this article is to intoduce briefly a philosophy of Christian education that includes an *interdependence* between youth ministry and the Christian education program of the local church.

Interdependent Ministries

Simply stated, *Christian education* is one-half of the local church's personality. The other half, consisting mainly of pastoral preaching and counseling, might be termed the *pulpit ministry*.

These two ministries (or two parts of the church's ministry) are interdependent. One cannot fully succeed unless the other has some measure of success. Success in one area and not the other makes for isolated ministries, not healthy "body life."

What's It to You?

The pastor is a key to the success of the youth ministry and, therefore, the pastor and the youth worker should develop a good working relationship.

1. *The youth worker should seek shepherding and direction from the pastor.*

2. *The pastor should share in the vision and direction of the youth ministry.* He should know the youth ministry's purpose and be concerned about its growth. The youth worker should take the initiative to involve the pastor in setting direction for youth ministry.

3. *The youth leader and pastor should publicly support each other.*

4. *The youth leader and pastor should mutually edify each other.* The "unity of the Spirit in the bond of peace"

George Hreha is associate pastor of Christian education at Grace Baptist Church in Glendora, California. His responsibilities include coordinating the educational programs for all ages, developing and directing the intern program, and assisting in pastoral ministries. For three years, George was minister of youth at the Glendora church. During that time he developed and coordinated the junior high, high school, and college programs. George holds a master's degree in religious education from Talbot Theological Seminary.

"*Christian education is one-half of the local church's personality.*"

(Eph. 4:3) must be seen among the church staff before it will be successfully developed in other parts of the body.

"So then, those who had received His word were baptized; and there were added that day about three thousand souls. And they were continually devoting themselves to the apostles' teaching and to fellowship, to the breaking of bread and to prayer" (Acts 2:41-42). These verses suggest at least four characteristics that should be incorporated into the overall purpose statement of the Christian education program and into the goals and objectives of the youth ministry: (1) an atmosphere of warmth and acceptance (fellowship), (2) solid biblical instruction (the apostle's teaching), (3) application of Scripture to life (breaking bread and praying), (4) evangelistic outreach (3,000 souls were added).

Warmth and Acceptance

Research indicates that the most important factor affecting people's choice of a church is its "warmth."[1] Before doctrine or teaching or music, people want to be received and cared for. Youth ministry should take place in a nonthreatening environment that makes young people feel accepted no matter what they know or do not know.

Biblical Instruction

Traditionally, the Sunday School has played a significant role in providing biblical instruction to teens. A midweek youth Bible study can also be utilized effectively in youth ministry. Whenever possible this should be scheduled during the same time the family comes to church for midweek services.

Application to Life

Scripture lessons taught to teenagers must be life-related. A major goal of youth ministry should be to develop changed lives. The following activities might be used to accomplish this goal:

1. *Discipleship groups*
   - Youth pastor with sponsors
   - Sponsors with leaders
   - Leaders with students
   - Students with other students
2. *Care groups*
   - Students with students
3. *Parents' meetings*—to inform parents of youth ministry goals and programs and to encourage the parents' ministry to teens in the home.
4. *Churchmanship*. Youth should be involved in beneficial church activities. This is necessary to teach them that they are a vital part of the church and its future direction and ministry. Teens can serve the church through projects that minister to the physical facilities or special needs of age groups (i.e. church work days, dinners for senior citizens, etc.).
5. *Leadership development* is the ultimate in the life-application process. Involvement in ministry allows leaders to rise to the occasion and serve because of the abilities God has already given them. Youth workers must cooperate with emerging leaders by

providing channels of expression for their God-given abilities.

Outreach

Young people must understand they are *ministers* in their own right who have the responsibility to reach out and eventually reproduce other believers. This involves learning to reach church kids who are not involved in the youth ministry, as well as reaching those students outside the church sphere.

Training opportunities must be provided for learning to communicate their faith.

Programs and activities must be specifically designed to reach teens for Christ, not just care for those who are already Christians.

Examples of successful youth outreach activities include:
1. Concerts
2. Campus clubs
3. Campus Life meetings
4. Camps
5. Media programs such as "Son City"
(See chapter 18.)

Summary

- Youth ministry should be an integral part of the total Christian education program of the local church.
- Youth ministry should be directed toward clearly defined goals and objectives which are compatible with the basic directions of the Christian education department and the church as a whole.
- A basic philosophy of Christian education and of an interdependent youth ministry should express the following characteristics: (1) an atmosphere of warmth and acceptance, (2) solid biblical instruction, (3) application of Scripture to life, and (4) evangelistic outreach. □

[1]Lowell Brown, *Sunday School Standards* (ICL Leadership Resource, Regal Books, 1980).

> "Before doctrine or teaching or music, people want to be cared for."

The Interdenominational Youth Organization

A Resource for Reaching the World's Youth

32

by Paul Fleischmann

Today's youth are the world's most fruitful mission field. Surveys confirm that 95 percent of all persons who receive Christ do so before age 21.[1] The urgency of evangelizing and discipling youth is obvious. But, in most churches, budgets and manpower for youth ministry are limited. Because of these limitations, church youth workers often continue their ministries primarily to the youth who are already involved in their churches.

Yet Christ's commission to the church remains. His last recorded words on earth were, "And you shall be My witnesses both in Jerusalem, and in all Judea and Samaria, and even to the remotest part of the earth" (Acts 1:8). Obviously, Christ wants the church to reach out beyond its own walls. And youth must be a prime target for the church's outreach efforts.

History of Interdenominational Youth Ministry

What efforts have been made to reach youth? Though youth have always been ministered to through the church, it wasn't till the 18th century that the church formed special groups for young people. Beginning with the first English Sunday School class for youth in 1798, the youth movement spread rapidly across the world so that, "at the opening of the 20th century, organized youth groups in local churches were the rule rather than the exception."[2]

Part of the reason for this rapid expansion was the formation of a variety of independent youth organizations. Hundreds of temperance groups for youth sprang up in the early 1800s. The Protestant missionary awakening spawned the Baptist Youth Missionary Society of New York City in 1806. The YMCA, founded in 1844, had a primarily religious purpose; it has been said that this organization is the forerunner of the modern youth movement in Protestant churches.[3]

In this century, the formation of several independent youth organizations has contributed greatly to church youth ministry. *Young Life* was born in 1941, through the burden of Jim Rayburn, a church youth minister who was committed to seeing unchurched youth reached for Christ. His "revolutionary approach" involved going on campuses and relating to student body leaders and athletes in an informal, yet effective manner.

Youth for Christ was founded in 1944 under the leadership of Chicago pastor Torrey Johnson and young Billy Graham, YFC's first full-time staff member. Large "rallies," Bible clubs, and quizzing and talent contests, characterized those early days of YFC.

Campus Crusade for Christ was founded in 1951 by Bill Bright who, while leading a church evangelism program, received a clear call from God to begin a worldwide ministry through college students. God blessed Bright's efforts through the use of evangelistic "team meetings" to fraternities, sororities, and athletes; 24-hour "chains" of prayer; the development of materials for personal evangelism; and the training of students via conferences and retreats.

Paul Fleischmann has been involved with Campus Crusade for Christ, International for the past 13 years. He is now the national director of youth worker development. He is also an adjunct professor at Western Baptist Seminary in Portland, Oregon.

Largely as a result of these major interdenominational youth organizations, church youth ministries achieved an unparalleled era of innovative philosophies and programming. The impact which began a generation ago still resounds today.

Basis for Cooperation

Such results have come about through a delicate balance between local churches and interdenominational organizations. In recent years some people have implied that the only legitimate structure for evangelism and discipleship is "the church on the corner." But a closer examination of biblical and historical patterns suggests the need for a broader perspective. Such an examination also suggests the need for continuing cooperation between local churches and interdenominational youth organizations.

1. Cooperation is consistent with the biblical picture of the church as a living body. "The body is one, and yet has many members. . . . There should be no division in the body, but the members should have the same care for one another" (1 Cor. 12:12, 25). The body of Christ has room for a wide diversity of gifts, offices, and abilities. But the body is not meant to center all of its attention on itself. Its chief purpose is to glorify God through the fulfillment of the Great Commission.

To accomplish this, the body has been given leaders, such as those who hold the offices of evangelist and pastor/teacher (Eph. 4:11). The purposes of these equally important offices are the same: "the equipping of the saints for the work of service" (Eph. 4:12). Yet their ministries look very different. The Apostle Paul's ministry as an evangelist was to "preach to the Gentiles" (unbelievers) and equip others to do the same (Eph. 3:6-11). Obviously, this task could not have been accomplished within the walls of "the

church on the corner." Though Paul was absent from a local church much of the time, he was still as much a part of the body as the pastor/teacher.

2. Cooperation is consistent with the Apostle Paul's ministry. Paul's function as a part of the body of Christ at Antioch helps demonstrate the broader

> ## "There has been a growing skepticism about the validity of any movement or organization outside of 'the church on the corner.' "

scope of the local church. Dr. Ralph D. Winter, president of the U.S. Center for World Mission suggests that Paul, while on his missionary journeys, operated a structure similar to some of today's interdenominational organizations:

"He was, true enough, sent out by the church in Antioch. But once away from Antioch, he seemed very much on his own. The little team he formed was economically self-sufficient when occasion demanded. It was also dependent, from time to time, not alone upon the Antioch church, but upon other churches that had risen as a result of evangelistic labors."[4] Winter concludes that two structures exist within the church and that these structures are intended to work together:

"Thus on the one hand, the structure we call the *New Testament church* is a prototype of all subsequent Christian fellowships where old and young, male and female are gathered together as normal biological families in aggregate. On the other hand, *Paul's missionary band* can be considered a prototype of all subsequent missionary endeavors. . . . Note that the structure that resulted was something definitely more than the extended outreach of the Antioch church. . . . It was something else, something different."[5] The distinctions were evident, yet cooperation between local churches and Paul's

missionary band was both natural and effective. This cooperation was a pivotal factor in promoting the expansion of the early church.

3. Cooperation is consistent with church history. These two functional dimensions of the church have intertwined throughout history to fulfill

God's plan of the ages. Their cooperation has been compared to the warp and woof of a piece of cloth. The stationary threads (the warp) resemble *local churches*. The threads (the woof) woven back and forth across these stationary threads resemble the various interdenominational *movements* which affect local churches. Together they weave the strong tapestry of God's church.[6]

As one looks at the history of youth ministry already mentioned, he can see a piece of this tapestry in the making. But this pattern of God dates back much farther than 200 years.

"Even in the Old Testament . . . these two dimensions are seen," says author, Carl Wilson. "There the Law was represented in the temple and the priestly teaching throughout the land, and the prophets raised up and went about rebuking the people for departure from the Law."[7]

As mentioned before, "Paul's missionary band" was a distinct entity which specifically nourished the churches. Then, in the fourth century, the monastic movement sprang up alongside the local church diocese. When the diocesan pattern began to break down, the monastic pattern provided stability for almost 1,000 years and contributed significantly to the rebuilding of the diocese and to the perpetuation of Christianity itself. "At many points there was rivalry between the two structures," says

Winter, "but the great achievement of the medieval period is the ultimate synthesis delicately achieved."[8]

Through involvement in the monastic movement, Martin Luther rediscovered "justification by faith," which ushered in the Reformation. Later, the Pietistic movement nourished the church through men like John Wesley, who united Christians of various churches.

William Carey established the Baptist Missionary Society which set off a proliferation of similar mission societies. The missions movement that resulted caused the 19th century to be called "The Great Century" because the first Protestant attempt at missions rapidly brought Protestantism into world prominence. It is also interesting to note that most local churches and their denominations—such as Presbyterians, Lutherans, Baptists, and Methodists—were products of past movements.[9]

Over the last several decades, there has been a growing skepticism about the validity of any movement or organization outside of "the church on the corner." Granted, a proper relationship between the two structures is important. But history demonstrates that local churches have suffered when the interwoven "parachurch" movements have not been present or healthy.

The biblical and historical pattern is one of unity amid diversity. We must allow the uniqueness of the two structures to be a healthy stimulus to both structures as we work together toward common goals.

Important Attitudes for Cooperation

Fruitful cooperation is not possible unless certain attitudes are present. The above analysis of past cooperation between the two structures of the church should provide a broader perspective on which to base present and future cooperation. Some conclusions seem to follow:

1. *We must try to reach all the youth within our potential sphere of influence.* That sounds like a tall order—and it is. Seminary president Earl Radmacher says, "Evangelistic outreach . . . this is the reason for the existence of the local church. Unless they (the local churches) experience this growth, they are failing."[10]

It is so tempting to focus only on "our kids." Parents and church bodies expect it—and it is the right place to start. We need to be united and growing in Christ. But unless we reach out from this base, we are not fulfilling Christ's purpose for us: "That they may all be one . . . that the world may believe that Thou didst send Me" (John 17:21). Since youth make the vast majority of salvation decisions, we need to trust God to help us reach entire schools for Him.

2. *We must cooperate like the members of a smoothly functioning body.* When we realize the scope of Christ's commission, it somehow seems easier to cooperate with anyone who can help us fulfill that goal. Interdenominational movements and local churches must realize that they are on the same team. They need each other. The Apostle Paul said: "So we, who are many, are one body in Christ, and individually members one of another" (Rom. 12:5).

church and is denied as a part of the church by some."[11]

The dual role of "servants" and "change agent" is difficult to balance. But as we saw in the developing history of youth ministry, the stimulus provided by this role has been historically significant.

In light of the tremendous need to reach youth and the tremendous shortage of manpower and other resources, any lack of cooperation or pride which keeps us from maximizing our efforts is tragic. Yet many today do not want to use any material or method that does not have their organizational label on it. As a result, valuable time and money are wasted in duplicating efforts.

Youth For Christ/Campus Life states in its staff manual: "If we or the local church in any way regard each other as a competitor, then we don't understand the nature of the body of Christ. We are *not* out to steal the allegiance or the attendance of church kids. We are not out to criticize and spotlight the shortcomings of the institutional church. We are a special task force to aid in one particular aspect of the church's mission."[12]

It is not consistent with human nature to admit that we need help from one another. Yet *interdependence* is a basic concept in the body of Christ. Paul exhorts us on this subject: "Be

---

"We must not allow rivalry to stifle the potential impact of our combined ministries."

---

3. *We must not allow rivalry to stifle the potential impact of our combined ministries.* Carl Wilson, author and longtime pastor who trains people to disciple through local churches, states: "The movement is raised up to effect changes in local churches and should lose itself as a servant of the local churches. Because the movement is called to change the local church, it is often seen as a threat to the local

of the same mind toward one another; do not be haughty in mind, but associate with the lowly. Do not be wise in your own estimation" (Rom. 12:16). As people in both structures have this attitude, they will be open to one another—to listen and to learn. And they will be free to change as God uses the relationship for their individual growth and for a mutual ministry with results that reach beyond what each could do separately.

4. *We must "think the best" of each other—no matter what.* Some youth pastors have been "burned" by people in interdenominational organizations, and vice versa. But God would not have us be at odds with one another. "If possible, so far is it depends on you, be at peace with all men" (Rom. 12:18). So often our conflicts are "vain imaginations" or little things which get blown out of proportion. That is why the Apostle Paul instructs, "Do not let the sun go down on your anger" (Eph. 4:26). Applying this verse sometimes requires taking the courageous first step toward reconciliation.

5. *We must both take the initiative to work together.* Dr. Earl Radmacher states: "No one would want to deny the good being done by the various agencies of Christian service outside of the local church but—these organizations should work hand in hand with the local church."[13]

In order to work "hand in hand," the staff of interdenominational organizations must be willing to join a church and become as actively involved as possible. They may have to patiently work through the structure of the church to *adapt* the use of their gifts in a way that will serve the church most effectively.

The youth worker also must remain teachable. He may need to ask the interdenominational staff to share ministry insights with him. Even if the interdenominational staff are not members of his church, the youth worker should make an effort to get acquainted. Most cities have so few salaried youth workers, that it is not difficult to find each other. And at the very least, occasional meetings are a source of great encouragement.

Practical Steps to Cooperation

1. *Locate the interdenominational organizations in your area.* If you do not know who they are, try your phone book, a veteran minister, or a local Sunday School convention. Even if you live in a small town, you may be surprised at what organizations operate nearby. Do not limit yourself to those organizations that relate only to youth. Others may have a lot to offer your ministry as well.

2. *Pray that God will bless their work.* Thank God for the good things that you see and trust Him to meet areas of need.

3. *Establish regular times of communication.* Get to know organization members. Share prayer requests and pray together. Maintain an attitude of humility (Phil. 2:3-5). Be as positive and supportive as possible; interdenominational staff members are much like you—they need encouragement. Share your schedules of major future events.

4. *Place one another on your mailing lists.* This is an easy way to keep each other informed and aware of what's happening in your ministries. Let the mail remind you to pray for each other.

5. *Determine the extent to which interdenominational organizations can be a resource to you.* Seek to understand their backgrounds, philosophies, methods, materials, and local programs. If, as church history suggests, God uses these movements to effect change in local churches, it might be wise to ask, "What can I learn from this organization? How can it benefit me?"

6. *Invite the staff of interdenominational organizations to get together socially with you.* Spending an evening together, dining together, or exercising together often provides mutual encouragement.

7. *Ask for advice.* Don't be afraid to share a problem or a weakness. Often the interdenominational staff member can provide unbiased insight and counsel. And there's nothing that brings people as close as praying together through a hard time.

Church Involvement

1. *Invite staff of interdenominational organizations to join your church.* Since new staff frequently transfer from one part of the country to another, they may be looking for a church home that has a youth program where they can serve.

2. *Challenge them to minister within your local church.* Granted, the bulk of their ministry may be away from the "church on the corner," but help them to see how "equipping the saints" in the local church can multiply their ministry. Don't wait for them to volunteer. When you know their gifts and abilities, challenge them specifically.

3. *Clarify that you would welcome any student the staff members discover is without a church home.* As a rule, most new teen believers will not come to your church unless they know other young people are there. So let staff members know if you have youth group members in the schools where interdenominational staff are working. Call interdenominational organization staff members after their major evangelistic thrusts to see if there are any new believers you might invite to your youth group.

4. *Support the staff of interdenominational organizations financially through your church.* As a part of your church missions budget, this support will give the whole congregation a greater vision for reaching the youth of your area. You might even consider supporting a staff member through your youth group alone. This will unite your group around a tangible means of reaching their generation for Christ.

Combined Ministry

1. *Feature staff of interdenominational youth organizations at your meetings or*

events. Ask them to speak or become involved in some other appropriate way. Volunteer to return the favor if they so desire.

2. Combine efforts on major evangelistic events. Occasionally, top-level Christian talent can be brought in. Often a city-wide outreach which you actively support can provide real momentum for your own group.

3. Capitalize on conferences and outings sponsored by interdenominational organizations. For example, Campus Crusade for Christ sponsors an outstanding national high school conference called "Rocky Mountain Get-A-Way," which draws over 1,000 students every summer. Other organizations sponsor many such events held regionally and locally during student vacations and breaks. It may not be worthwhile to try to duplicate conferences like these since there is so much money, time, and effort involved. By planning an effective follow-up effort, and by sending adult leadership, you can make the event work for the benefit of your church's youth ministry.

4. Gather all those who work with youth from across your city or area. Cooperate with interdenominational organizations in formulating the program. Let the emphasis of the meeting be on sharing and praying for the youth of your area. Revivals of the past have been known to start at gatherings such as these.

5. Gain the support of the senior pastor for combined ministry efforts like the above. Give him a good presentation of what you want to do and why. An informed pastor can do as much for a church youth ministry as any one other human element.

Difficulties in Cooperation

By way of summary, it might be helpful to interpret these suggestions in light of the difficulties some youth workers face as they relate to inter-

"Interdenominational organizations need to place a greater emphasis on encouraging students to join local churches."

denominational organizations.

"There's a tension between us, but for no apparent reason." As I pointed out, throughout church history there has always been a kind of creative tension between the two structures of the church. The "warp and woof" example illustrates the weaving of threads in two different directions which makes the fabric strong. This kind of tension is constructive, though at times a bit uncomfortable. Solomon reminds us: "Iron sharpens iron, so one man sharpens another" (Prov. 27:17).

But all tension is *not* good. It could be that Satan has just hit you with one of his "flaming missles" (Eph. 6:16) by sowing "vain imaginations." One of the most common temptations regarding interdenominational organizations is the tendency to stereotype each other. This can often be the source of a condescending, critical spirit. Another of Satan's "darts" is getting you to compare ministries. The Apostle Paul says that you are not to think more highly of yourself than you

tions it certainly is a valid objection. (In my own 12 years of experience, it is fair to estimate that 90—95 percent of all Christian students I worked with were involved in local churches— most, quite actively so.)

As a rule, however, interdenominational organizations need to place a greater emphasis on encouraging students to join local churches. But doing so is often not as easy as some church leaders assume. Many young people are suspicious of the institutional church. Their prejudices have led them to believe that the church is old-fashioned and irrelevant. So when some young people come to Christ, mere "salesmanship" alone will not always cause them to become active in local churches. Even the adult staff person has little influence. In the overwhelming majority of cases, his peers will help him decide. That's why it is so important to be in communication with the staff of the interdenominational organization. If they tell you of a new believer in a high school or college where you have young

"Ultimately, church youth workers need to begin working on campuses themselves."

ought to think; but to regard yourself with *sound judgment* (Rom. 12:3).

If necessary communicate directly with the source of the tension, since love for one another should characterize the body of Christ (1 John 4:7). Usually, regular times of communication can keep this kind of tension to a minimum.

"Interdenominational youth organizations win a lot of young people to Christ, but I don't see them joining churches." This generalization isn't true in all cases—but in many situa-

church members, encourage those members to invite him to church.

Ultimately, church youth workers need to begin working on campuses themselves. As they develop sensitivity to the students' world, they will be able to encourage this kind of transition more naturally.

"They are taking away my student leader." Once again this is not a black and white issue. Interdenominational organizations which gear their meetings specifically to the secular student often appear more attractive than

some of the local church meetings which by nature must appeal to a broad spectrum of Christians. The issue should not be, in most cases, to make students choose between the two groups, but rather to *balance* their involvement in a healthy way. Outreach on the campus is essential and a mark of biblical Christianity, but it should not be at the expense of nurturing the body of Christ through the church.

This lesson of balance is crucial. If either structure of the church gives up on the other, the likely result will be young people whose concept of the church is lopsided.

This whole process of cooperation calls for maturity on behalf of the adult leadership. The Apostle Paul characterized carnal Christians as dividing their allegiance between two ministers of the Gospel (Paul and Apollos). It is no less carnal for the *ministers* to be dividing the people's allegiance. "I planted, Apollos watered, but God was causing the growth. . . . For we are God's fellow-workers" (1 Cor. 3:6, 9). If we are serious about reaching the youth of our cities, this kind of maturity must be commonplace.

"A staff member of an interdenominational organization is a member of our church but he's irregular in attendance and not involved." Before judging too quickly, find out why he appears inconsistent. It could be that he is using his office of evangelist as a cop-out for church involvement when he really does have opportunity to do more. If this is the case, he needs to be confronted.

On the other hand, it could be that his ministry to the unchurched is so all-consuming that significant involvement at the home base is hard. This was certainly the Apostle Paul's situation most of the time. I belong to a church in which a number of staff from the national offices of Campus Crusade for Christ also belong. Though some of us hold responsibilities such as deacon in the church, due to travel schedules and other ministry involvements, we some-

times think it is more important to spend a Wednesday evening with the family than to attend the weekly church prayer meeting. Admittedly this is a delicate balance, one which is easily misunderstood and one which requires sensitivity to the Spirit's individual leading.

Take some initiative to help the staff member become involved. When you have a feel for his schedule, challenge him with some appropriate involvement. Graciously express your concerns about the extent of his participation in the life of the body, and trust the Holy Spirit to give him direction.

"I'd like to work with the interdenominational organizations in our city, but I often disagree with their philosophy, doctrine, or methods." First, be sure of your basis for disagreement. Is it hearsay? Is it a personality conflict? Is it a stereotype? Or have you seen concrete evidence?

If you have seen evidence, then determine whether the disagreement is worth making an issue. Though the disagreement may be real, it may make little difference from an eternal perspective. And be sure *you* are above reproach. It could be that his incorrect way of doing it is superior to your way of *not* doing it!

If the issue is important, don't compromise; but at the same time don't stop communicating either. Recognize the things you share in common (e.g. desire to reach students, need for prayer, etc.). Cooperate wherever you feel you can. Avoid being a hindrance to his ministry through your attitudes or your actions.

Paul made the statement about those preaching from wrong motives: "What then? Only that in every way, whether in pretense or in truth, Christ is proclaimed, and in this I rejoice, yes, and I will rejoice" (Phil. 1:18).

"Interdenominational organizations have ministries on campuses where I would like to work." Be sure you can explain why you feel God is calling you to work on that campus. If the students from your church are en-

couraging you and you sense God is in it, fine! But if you can establish yourself on one of the many campuses without a Christian ministry, then that is something to prayerfully consider.

However, if you find yourself on the same campus with an interdenominational organization, count it all joy! Many hands make light work! Set up regular meetings with the staff for communication and prayer. Meet as soon as possible to share what you would like to do on the campus. Get the staff's reactions to your plans and determine any areas of potential conflict. Discuss how to handle students who may want to become involved in both ministries. Determine if meetings or events can be jointly utilized. (In one situation, a local church and an interdenominational organization cooperate at every level. As a result they are seeing a rapidly developing movement for Christ on the campus.)

Respect each other's position and commitment. The organization that was on the campus first may know valuable things about the campus. Ask advice and be willing to accept suggestions and even criticism with humility. Above all, avoid a competitive spirit, which students and faculty are quick to pick up. If a problem arises, go directly to the staff leader, believing the best and believing that God will work out the solution. As you continue to "weave the tapestry" in unconditional love, God can use you to reach entire campuses for Him.

Conclusion

The close cooperation of local churches with interdenominational organizations might not be so imperative if Christ's command to win and disciple people did not encompass the whole world. But it does. With Jesus as our source of unity, we must make every effort to work together effectively.

This urgency is not yet felt by all. A national leader of youth in a large denomination made this statement recently: "I am not saying this is right, but most youth pastors in our churches have the attitude: 'We'll take care of our youth groups. Let Youth for Christ, Young Life, and Campus Crusade for Christ take care of the high schools. And for the most part, let's go our own separate ways.' " This kind of thinking is not only unbiblical but counterproductive in light of the church's objectives.

Cooperation is essential! Ralph Winter summarizes it well: "Historical patterns make clear that God, through His Holy Spirit, has clearly and consistently used another structure other than the modality (local church) structure. It is our attempt here to help church leaders and others to understand the legitimacy of *both* structures, and the necessity for both structures not only to exist but to work together harmoniously for the fulfillment of the Great Commission, and for the fulfillment of all that God desires for our time."[14]   □

[1]William Benke and Milt Bryan, "The World's Most Fruitful Field," *Evangelizing Today's Child*, IV, 6, 1977, p. 4.
[2]Roy G. Irving and Roy B. Zuck (eds.) *Youth and the Church* (Chicago, Moody, Press, 1968), pp. 60-63.
[3]Ibid., p. 61.
[4]Ralph D. Winter, "The Two Structures of God's Redemptive Mission," *Missiology: An International Review*, 1973, p. 122.
[5]Ibid., pp. 122-123.
[6]Ralph D. Winter and R. Pierce Beaver, *The Warp and the Woof* (South Pasadena: William Carey Library, 1970), p. 63.
[7]Carl Wilson, *With Christ in the School of Disciple Building* (Grand Rapids: Zondervan, 1976), p. 45.
[8]Ralph D. Winter, "The Two Structures of God's Redemptive Mission," *Missiology: An International Review*, 1973, p. 128.
[9]Wilson, op. cit., p. 39.
[10]Earl Radmacher, *The Nature of the Church* (Portland, Oregon: Western Baptist Press, 1972), p. 381.
[11]Wilson, op. cit., p. 45.
[12]*Campus Life's Operations Manual* (Wheaton, Illinois: Youth for Christ International, 1973), chapter 3, p. 2.
[13]Radmacher, op. cit., p. 357.
[14]Ralph D. Winter, "The Two Structures of God's Redemptive Mission," *Missiology: An International Review* 1973, p. 136.

33 The Youth Worker and the Christian College

by Catherine J. Foote

Dr. Catherine J. Foote is a professor of Christian education at San Jose Bible College in San Jose, California. Previously she was minister of education at Jefferson Street Baptist Chapel in Louisville, Kentucky where she was involved in inner city children's and youth ministries. Catherine holds degrees from Pacific Christian College and Southern Baptist Theological Seminary.

When I was in grade school I used to go with my parents to a large park in our city. Across the street from this park was a small Christian college, called at that time a "Bible seminary." I remember asking my parents about the place, and though I don't remember their exact reply, whatever they said gave me the impression that the school was something like a monastery. I pictured quiet, somber people walking with heads bowed, carrying large Bibles, and speaking in hushed tones. I used to stand and stare at the building, waiting for someone to come out so I could see what a "seminarian" looked like. I knew I would never have the courage to go over there and see for myself.

After graduating from high school, I came into contact with the college again. Having made a decision to prepare myself for a vocational ministry, I chose to attend the school that I had wondered about as a child. As a student of a Christian college, I had to revise those childhood impressions to conform with reality.

I not only attended a Christian college and a seminary, but now I'm teaching at a Bible college. And I've concluded that the average person's impressions of those institutions are not much more accurate than my childhood speculations. These misconceptions can obscure the nature of education and life at a Christian college. As a result, students form unrealistic expectations which can cause problems when they are ready to make decisions about their educational future.

The youth worker, who is often in a position to counsel young people regarding educational decisions, should be aware of some of the myths and realities concerning the Christian college. The purpose of this chapter then is to examine the Christian college in terms of both the myths and the realities that exist.

Types of Christian Colleges

Many types of schools fall under the classification of "Christian colleges." These schools can, however, be divided into two broad categories. The first is often called a *Christian liberal arts college*, and is designed to provide a broad range of course offerings and majors. The purpose of this type of college is to integrate a Christian perspective with a variety of disciplines. These colleges tend to be the larger of the two types of schools, and prepare individuals for a number of different vocations.

The second type of Christian college trains individuals for professional ministries, usually in a local church. These colleges tend to be more limited in scope, offering majors in biblical studies as well as practical ministries such as preaching or Christian education. Often these schools are called *Bible colleges* or *Bible institutes*.

When choosing a college the student should be aware of the college's purpose. This will help him realistically evaluate strengths and weaknesses of the school, and help prevent frustration later as he tries to fit personal goals into the college curriculum.

Myths

The following myths represent common misconceptions regarding Christian colleges. A variety of sources, including adult church members, youth workers, and pastors, perpetuate these myths. Visits to campuses, particularly on days specifically set aside for that purpose, do little to dispel these myths. In fact such visits, when students, faculty, and administration all tend to be on their best behavior, can even contribute to the misconceptions.

The Summer Camp Myth

Myth #1: *"Oh boy, camp fire every night, just like summer camp!"*

Many Christians have had positive, growing experiences in summer camps. The combination of Christian fellowship, studies in God's Word, and an environment conducive to meditation and worship creates a mountaintop experience. Naturally, individuals want to continue this experience when the week of camp is over.

Often, young people assume the best place for this to happen is at a Christian college. After all, so the reasoning goes, the three camping ingredients—24-hour fellowship, intensive Bible study, and a controlled Christian environment—are also present on the Christian college campus. And college isn't just for a week, but for months at a time!

Often, the high school graduate wishes to extend this camp "high" and so attends a Christian college. He soon becomes disillusioned. Living with other Christians on a long-term basis involves coping with each other's problems and personality flaws. Learning to live with one another and love one another over the course of a semester, a school year, or even longer isn't easy. A college freshman who expects relationships to be as natural as they were in a camp setting will be disappointed.

Along with discovering the work involved in Christian relationships, the freshman finds that college Bible courses are hard work. In summer camp he never had to do homework, the staff taught the material on a less demanding level, and when the study was over, the pool or ball field awaited him. Now at college, things have changed. A student who approaches college studies in the way he approached camp studies soon falls behind.

Finally, the college freshman learns that the expected spiritual atmosphere is not always present on the Christian college campus. This discovery and the accompanying disillusionment are dealt with in another section of this chapter.

The shattering of this summer camp myth does not have to be a negative experience. It can be a positive experience of growing up in Christ, of becoming more aware of the demanding nature of the Christian life. The problem comes when the new student is not able to make the adjustment in terms of expectations and perceptions. In that case, one of two things is likely to happen.

First, the student may change schools, thinking that the problem is the college—he hasn't found one that is "truly spiritual." Second, the student may drop out completely, concluding that he or she is not "Christian" enough. A student needs to realize from the beginning that the Christian college experience will not be four blissful years of summer camp.

The Holy Huddle Myth

Myth #2: *"Everyone here is holy."*

Some students come to a Christian college expecting that all the students will be "spiritual." A student with this expectation will be disappointed for at least two reasons:

First, each person has his own ideas of the characteristics and behavior that merit the label "spiritual." As one person's ideas of proper Christian behavior conflict with another's, one or both individuals assume that the other is lacking in spiritual maturity. This confrontation causes frustration for all concerned.

Second, and perhaps more significant, is the fact that students on a Christian college campus are generally like Christians anywhere else. They are not "super Christians." They are in the process of becoming Christlike. Included in that process are times of victory as well as times of stumbling. The new student who is not prepared for the fact that classmates will have times of weakness, impatience, and sin can be disillusioned.

The Protection Myth

Myth #3: *"At last, I'm safe; it will protect my faith."*

Closely tied to the assumption that Christian colleges are populated by "super Christians" is the belief that attending such a school will automatically protect and nurture a student's faith. This myth causes three incorrect perspectives. The first of these is illustrated by a student who attends a Christian college because he is afraid of "losing his faith" at a secular university. This becomes a problem as the young person begins to depend on the college to protect his faith rather than seeking personal answers from God.

Jane Struck points out that, "attending a Christian college, seminary, or Bible institute will not produce a cure-all to problems some students struggle with at any school—whether secular or Christian."[1] This is not to say that a student's faith will not be strengthened in a Christian college setting. The point is that the strengthening comes through a careful examination and exploration of his faith. Ultimately, the student must develop a personal faith that can deal with difficult issues.

College years are times for asking and answering questions concerning basic assumptions about life. Though a Christian college can be a good place to formulate answers, it should not protect anyone from the difficult questions.

A second problem is the despair students feel as they realize that they don't measure up to the "super Christian" image. As they consider their own shortcomings in relation to the assumed strengths of others, they feel lonely and frustrated. They ask, "What is wrong with me? I came to this college to become more spiritual, and I'm still struggling with the same old problems."

This feeling of not measuring up leads many students to drop out of school. Young people need to realize that attending a Christian college will not be an instant cure-all for every spiritual problem.

Third, the protection myth may lead young people to choose a Christian college because of personal problems. Some students attend a Christian college because they are having serious struggles with their faith, or perhaps are facing problems in other areas of their lives. Such students expect one of two things. Either the pure spiritual atmosphere of the college will solve the problems, or the other Christians at the school will solve the problems. In either situation the students are not facing the problems themselves, but expecting someone else to handle them.

A Christian college can be a convenient place to hide for a while, but ultimately hiding makes the problems worse. Youth workers be warned: A Christian college is not a place to send a problem young person whom no one else has the energy or time to deal with.

The Easy Out Myth

Myth #4: *"It's easier than 'real college.'"*

The belief that a Christian college is academically less demanding than other colleges creates difficulties for both the student and the school. After failing the first college test he took, one freshman put it this way, "No one told me that I was going to have to study as hard *here* as at other colleges."

At times students who are unprepared for college-level academics choose a Christian college with the assumption that the work will not be too demanding. Such students do not apply themselves to learning and become frustrated with the intellectual demands of their professors. By the end of the first semester, many of these students drop out, feeling discouraged and perhaps a little bitter toward the school. The Christian college is not Sunday School five days a week. It is an institution that specializes in college-level instruction from a Christian perspective.

The College Church Myth

Myth #5: *"It's like church and school combined."*

A Christian college is not a church. Some students attempt to make the college fill the function of the body of Christ in their lives. This is an impossible role for the school to fulfill. Students must find a place in a local church to minister and to be ministered to. Those who don't, usually experience dryness in their Christian lives.

In the college setting, the approach

> *"Students must find a place in a local church to minister and to be ministered to."*

to Scripture can be on a rather scholarly level, with little attention to day-by-day, personal application. Yet some students assume since they are studying the Bible for classes, that they don't need to maintain personal devotions or participate in Sunday School classes.

In addition, students may not realize that they must be involved in ministry in order to grow. These students assume that since they are at a Christian college they are growing. They may view their time in college as a preparation for ministry without seeing that ministry must take place where they are right now. These mistakes can be quite harmful to the students' faith. Many students with this attitude graduate from college feeling farther from God than when they started school.

The Matchmaking Myth

Myth #6: *"It's the perfect place to find a mate."*

One final myth is that Christian

colleges are matchmaking institutions. This attitude creates pressure on male-female relationships. Students who go on a date or merely study together regularly may discover that their friends have labeled them a "couple" and perhaps even have them engaged. A Christian college can be a good place to meet fellow Christians and even future spouses, but that is not its primary purpose.

Realities

As important as it is to help young people overcome the myths surrounding Christian colleges, it is also important to acquaint youth with some of the significant realities. First, in a Christian college, students, professors, administrators, and staff share some important basic assumptions. John Mostart, in writing of the distinctive characteristics of Christian college education, points out that one of these is: "extensive concentration on biblical and closely related studies, a well-conceived program of practical Christian service, curricular opportunities that enhance skills in specific ministries, and general educational content that is well oriented to divine revelation."[2]

Second, great personal involvement and deep relationships can develop between faculty and students. These realities produce recognizable benefits:

A Christian college can be an effective place for dealing with personal and intellectual questions. A student doesn't have to be concerned about a hidden agenda aimed at destroying his faith. The faculty builds up and strengthens faith, as well as helping the student learn to express and share his faith. The significance of this is not that the faculty can keep the student "safe" from making mistakes or falling down. The point is that when the falls come, there is someone to help the student back on his feet. This process of learning can be very positive.

A Christian college can provide positive Christian models. This is one of the most important aspects of life at a Christian college. One reality in education is that a student learns as much from the kind of person a teacher is as he does from the classroom sessions. During college years many young people are looking for individuals whom they can pattern their lives after. On a Christian college campus many persons, in varieties of ministries, can provide these models. Often the comparatively small size of a Christian college can enhance this modeling process. The small size allows students and faculty to get to know each other well. It is much more difficult for a student to get lost in the shuffle.

The Christian college education is a viable academic alternative. The quality of education at any school depends on the quality of its personnel. Christian colleges attract many dedicated, scholarly individuals who have much to offer. Studying under these men and women can be intellectually challenging as well as enjoyable. The Christian perspective they add to higher education is valuable, and students have much to gain.

Suggestions

Here are some suggestions for youth workers who are helping young people choose colleges: First, be realistic. Help youth find out what a specific college can offer, what are its unique benefits, as well as what that college cannot offer. Students must be aware of what a Christian college is and what it is designed to offer. Expecting something else means facing frustration and disappointment.

Second, good vocational counseling must go hand in hand with the college choice. As mentioned above, some Christian colleges have limited curriculum, particularly if the major focus of the college is to train vocational ministers. Students become disenchanted when they discover they are not being prepared for their chosen vocation.

Third, help youth realize that a Christian college is not a substitute youth ministry. In terms of being ministered to, students in a Christian college can become the most neglected group in the church. Often the leaders of the church assume that ministering is being taken care of at school. All Christian college students, as well as faculty, administration, and others, need to be involved in and cared for by a local body of believers.

Finally, be aware that a Christian college is not for everyone in the youth group. The choice of a college should be based on careful, prayerful consideration of all options. A Christian college has much to offer, but there are also good reasons for attending other types of schools. Youth leaders should avoid the tendency to create a hierarchy within the group on the basis of college or vocational choice.

Christian colleges are important, needed institutions. When viewed properly they have much to contribute to individuals and to the church.

[1]Jane Struck, "Where Else?" *Christian Life*, August, 1977, p. 48.
[2]John Mostart, "Preparing for Future Shock," *United Evangelical Action*, Fall, 1978, p. 18.

Notes

Section 6

"We should never be satisfied until we see the believers come to maturity."
—J. MacArthur

34 The Imperative of Bible Study

by John MacArthur

Dr. John MacArthur *is pastor of Grace Community Church in Sun Valley, California. He is also an adjunct professor on the faculty of Talbot Theological Seminary. John is a popular conference and radio speaker as well as speaker on the "Voice of Calvary" television program. A graduate of Talbot Theological Seminary, Dr. MacArthur has authored several books including* Keys to Spiritual Growth, Focus on Fact: Why You Can Trust the Bible, *and* Why I Believe the Bible.

No book is more important or more widely read than the Bible. And yet no book is more misinterpreted and generally misunderstood. This fact is particularly sad when it applies to God's people.

Jesus said, "Therefore, you are to be perfect, as your heavenly Father is perfect" (Matt. 5:48). God wants us to be perfect, complete, whole, and mature. Paul gave a similar command: "Finally, brethren, rejoice, *be made complete*" (2 Cor. 13:11).

If perfection, or maturity, is the goal, then what is the tool? "All Scripture is given by inspiration of God, and is profitable for doctrine, for reproof, for correction, for instruction in righteousness: that the man of God may be perfect, thoroughly furnished unto all good works" (2 Tim. 3:16-17, KJV). With perfection as the goal and the Bible as the tool, youth ministry should be built on a strong commitment to and emphasis on the Word of God.

The Place of Bible Study

Why place such a strong emphasis on Bible study?

1. Bible study is necessary for growth and maturity. The church suffers greatly from biblical illiteracy. The Prophet Hosea said, "My people are destroyed for lack of knowledge" (Hosea 4:6). The Apostle Paul pleads for a renewing of our minds (Rom. 12:2). Clearly, spiritual maturity depends to a great extent on the ministry of God's Word.

2. Bible study is a deterrent to sin. What are we to do with spiritual babes? *Nurse* them with the milk of the Word so they won't be tossed to and fro by every wind of doctrine. Biblical truth is a tremendous deterrent to sin, regardless of what form the temptation takes.

3. Bible study builds for service. The most mature, equipped, and responsible people are the *most effective* servants of Christ.

4. Bible study is necessary for effective witness. Ultimately, witnessing depends on knowing God's Word. We need to remain abreast of the world we live in, to understand prevailing thought and culture. But man is not saved by reason, rather by revelation. For young people to be effective witnesses of Jesus Christ, they must know His Word.

The Equipping Ministry

"And He gave some as apostles, and some as prophets, and some as evangelists, and some as pastors and teachers, for the equipping of the saints for the work of service, to the building up of the body of Christ; until we all attain to the unity of the faith, and of the knowledge of the Son of God, to a mature man, to the measure of the stature which belongs to the fulness of Christ" (Eph. 4:11-13).

In the Sermon on the Mount, the goal is perfection, the perfect equipping of believers. Now that really puts the standard high. Sufferings, trials, the Word, the ministry of the Spirit—all these work in a believer's life to make him mature, grown up, and fully equipped. But God also gives gifted leaders to the church "for the equip-

> ## "The pastor-teachers and the evangelists are the catalysts who set in motion the equipping of the believers."

ping of the saints" (Eph. 4:12). The pastor-teachers and the evangelists are the catalysts who set in motion the *equipping* of the believers.

People have asked me time and time again, "What is your goal in the ministry?" And I always say simply, "My goal is to bring the saints that God has given me to maturity." I'm not interested in getting more people in my building than somebody else has in his building. I'm not trapped in some success psychosis which says success is based on how many people I have. That just isn't biblical. My purpose is *not* to fill a building.

I am not responsible for how many,

wisdom, that we may present every man complete in Christ" (Col. 1:28). Paul's goal for his ministry was to *perfect the saints*; to build them, that they might become mature.

As workers in the church, we should never be satisfied until we see the believers come to maturity. That's our calling. That's the reason we teach the Word of God. We are not so much called to a profession, but to a passion. We belong to the church, not to entertain it, not to just program it, not to simply organize it, but to bring it to perfection, to full spiritual maturity.

The Apostle Paul said, "Put on the new self who is being renewed to a

> ## "I am not responsible for how many, but for what kind."

but for what kind. The early apostles understood this. Listen to Paul: "And we proclaim Him, admonishing every man and teaching every man with all

true knowledge" (Col. 3:10)—the facts, the truths of the Word of God. People will never be able to function on principles they do not know. Teaching the

Word of God brings growth. *Revival* in Nehemiah's day began with, "Bring the Book!" (Neh. 8:1)

Our task is never complete as long as people linger in spiritual infancy. We need to be careful about asking God to send more people to us, when we haven't made disciples out of the ones we already have. Giving young people "pabulum" all the time, directing kids into all kinds of activities, and never teaching them the Word of God is wrong. I think church workers will be held accountable, because anything less than a total commitment to teaching the Word of God in order to bring believers to maturity is a misuse of the ministry.

If we are going to mature the saints, we're going to have to be on the apostolic wavelength. We're going to have to feel the passion that Paul felt. This was his burden when he wrote to the Thessalonians, "Night and day keep praying most earnestly that we may see your face, and may complete what is lacking in your faith" (1 Thes. 3:10).

Youth workers, we can never be satisfied with just keeping kids "active." Our satisfaction will come with *winning* them to Jesus and *maturing* them. Our job is to equip the saints so that they can take the Water of Life to thirsty people. This should be the heartbeat of our work. □

35 Informal Youth Bible Study

by Larry Richards

Dr. Lawrence O. Richards *is a well-known convention speaker, curriculum developer, youth worker and Christian educator. He has written many books including* Creative Bible Teaching, Youth Ministry, Theology of Christian Education, *and the* Answers for Youth *series.*

The minute the first group of teens walked through the back door, talking and laughing, you could sense the enthusiasm. Some dropped school books in the hall. Two guys tossed baseball gloves in one corner. All of them clustered in shifting groups, chatting energetically.

By a quarter after, some 40 high schoolers had gathered, eager for what had become the high point of their church's ministry with youth: the Thursday Bible study at Dean and Alene's house.

Let's watch what happened that evening, and then go back and see the principles of youth Bible study which Dean and Alene had learned to apply so effectively.

Setting the Stage

About five minutes before the planned starting time, students begin crowding into the living room. Tonight all the furniture has been moved, except for a sheet-draped table at one end of the room and a pad of newsprint on an easel near the table. Dean sits casually on the table, and the students gather in a semicircle, sitting on the floor.

"Tonight," Dean announces, "we're going to start with a medical feature. We've got a patient here who I want you to observe closely. Then we're going to make a diagnosis."

Dean points dramatically to the far door, and the room fills with laughter as Floyd, a high school senior, stumbles into the room and falls flat. He struggles to his feet mugging, and drags himself around the room,

blinking his eyes, making weird grunting sounds as he twists his jaw grotesquely to one side. Finally he reaches out, pawing for Dean. Dean helps Floyd up on the table and covers him with the sheet.

Under Dean's direction, the group quickly diagnoses the "patient":
- "paralyzed leg"
- "dumb"
- "half-blind"
- "terminally ugly"

Dean writes the group's suggestions on the newsprint pad with a felt-tipped pen. Then he asks dramatically, "And who is our patient for tonight?" Pulling back the sheet he reveals Floyd, flat on his back, but now holding up an identifying sign: TYPICAL TEEN.

Mixed laughs and moans come from the group, but are quickly replaced by hisses and boos.

Dean plays out the skit to the end. "You mean the typical teen's problem isn't a paralyzed leg?" (Nos and more hisses.) "It's not being dumb?" "It's not being half-blind?" When he finishes reading the list, accompanied by a rising crescendo of "nos," Dean tears the sheet off the pad and says, "OK, how *would* you diagnose the biggest problems of a typical teen? I'll give you and the person next to you just 45 seconds. See if you can come up with three things that are real problems for most teenagers."

The students are used to Dean's fast-paced changes, and each immediately jumps into conversation with a neighbor. When Dean calls time, each pair has several ideas.

Before Dean asks for their ideas, he explains more precisely what he is looking for. "We're talking about problems *inside us*. Parents aren't a problem, but negative feelings *about* a parent, that's a problem. Just like being paralyzed is a problem inside a sick person, we're looking for problem's inside high schoolers. So let's pick out just the 'inside' problems you thought of. OK, let's list 'em."

The ideas come slowly at first, but each suggestion seems to stimulate a fresh idea as the kids sort through their first thoughts and focus on their inner problems:

- self-discipline at school
- getting upset with a sister
- resenting chores
- wrong thoughts

When a sheet of newsprint is filled, Dean explains the focus of that evening's Bible study.

Discovering Truth

"We all know that Jesus can help us with these problems," says Dean. "He can cure what's wrong inside anyone. But one thing bothers me even more than having problems like these. It's when sometimes I don't even *want* Jesus to help me with my problems. That's what we're going to look at tonight. And we're going to see if we can get past that place of resistance and really let Jesus work in our lives to heal the inner problems you and I have."

Dean passes out the study guides and Alene explains them. (See the sample study guide on page 128.)

"This is a passage from John 5," says Alene, "about a paralyzed man Jesus healed. Most of you know the story. A man who'd been paralyzed for 38 years is approached by Jesus. Now, the Bible tells many stories of Jesus healing. But this is the only one in which Jesus asks the sick person, 'Do you want to be healed?'

"Get in groups of five or six and study the passage. Your study guide gives several possible reasons why Jesus might have asked that question. See if you can build a case to support

one of those reasons, or think of some other possible reason why Jesus asked the question. You've got about 20 minutes to study together and talk over what you discover."

The students quickly break into smaller circles. Dean and Alene join two of the study teams. Three groups leave the living room for the kitchen and hall. The next 20 minutes are noisy as the students look at the passage and discuss the options suggested on their study sheets. It's a little more than 20 minutes later when Alene leaves her group and calls to everybody: "Just two more minutes, gang."

When time is up, the whole group gathers as Alene guides them through the next step of the Bible study process.

"What's exciting to me is that the Bible's not just a book of history. Jesus is alive today just as He was 2,000 years ago. He's just as much here with us as He was there with the man at the pool of Bethesda. And Jesus can still heal the hurting places in our lives and make us whole.

"Think about it for a minute. If Jesus were to walk in here now and look right at you, and ask you if you wanted to be healed—what problem would He be referring to? One of those on our list here? Something else?

"Just think for a minute. I won't ask you to share your answer. But ask yourself, what problem in my life would Jesus want to cleanse and heal and make whole tonight?"

Alene pauses and turns to look with the kids at the list they'd made earlier on the newsprint.

After a few moments she turns back to the kids. "Just suppose Jesus did ask you that question, 'Do you want to be healed?' We've talked about how the invalid might have reacted to that question. How do you think you'd react?

"How many of you would feel kind of afraid—afraid of the new responsibility healing might bring?" (Alene raises her hand to show the response she wants, and several of the kids raise

their hands too.)

"OK. How many would be afraid to hope. You've tried and tried to overcome the problem, and it's just too painful to think of more failure?" (More teens raise their hands now than on the previous question.)

"How many of you would feel too *alone* to hope—afraid that no one else would really understand or support you?

"OK. And how many would be really *excited* at the idea of being healed; so that if you knew you could be made well, you'd jump at the chance?"

Sharing in Groups

Dean walks up front to join Alene. "We're going to go back into groups to talk again. But this time we're forming special groups. We're each going to get together with others who feel as we do at the thought of Jesus working in our lives.

"If you raised your hand to indicate that you were most likely to be afraid of responsibility that change might make, then you'll go into the kitchen. If your response was fear you'd just fail again, you meet with me in the dining room. I know that lots of times I've held back and not let Jesus work in my life because I was afraid I'd fail again and couldn't stand the thought of more guilt. . . ."

Dean continues arranging groups, suggesting that anyone who isn't sure where he or she fits should pick a group that is closest to his or her reactions. Then Dean gives these final instructions:

"We're going to try and help each other understand why we're likely to respond the way we do. So see if you can describe some incident when you felt afraid, or alone, or excited by something Jesus was doing in your life. If there's anything that's helped you open your life to God in spite of your feelings, share that too. And then let's take time to pray for each other in our groups. Jesus wants to heal us inside and make us whole people. He's got the desire and the power. And whenever we're ready, He'll work in our lives."

Now the students divide into four groups, and Dean writes down a simple discussion guide on another sheet of newsprint:

- Share personal experiences.
- Why do you feel as you do?
- What has helped you be open to God?
- Pray for each other.

The groups break up and quickly begin their sharing. After about 30 minutes, Dean goes to each group and suggests they take 10 minutes or so to pray.

About an hour and 45 minutes after the study began, two of the groups break up and Alene gets out pop and potato chips. Some of the teens leave, and others sit around the living room talking in small groups or one on one. The group in the kitchen is too involved in their sharing to break up at all. Alene brings them pop and their own bag of chips. It's 30 more minutes before that group dissolves.

At 10:30 the last two girls stand on the steps outside the back door, talking with Alene. It's 11:00 when they finally get into their car and go home.

Evaluating What Happened

Informal Bible studies like Dean and Alene's start with a small group and are often held in a youth sponsor's or teacher's home. They're marked by warmth and sharing and enthusiasm.

Of course, these qualities are closely linked with having adult leaders who care and who are warm, friendly people. Over time, trust and personal relationships grow when this kind of adult takes the time to build relationships with young people. But in addition to these personal characteristics, several structural principles for de-

veloping informal Bible studies can make the difference between dry, intellectual Bible studies that fail to touch the lives of teens, and Bible studies that are motivating and personally meaningful. Let's go back and focus on several of these principles that make informal Bible studies with teens so exciting and enriching.

Framing a Bible Study

The word *frame* introduces an important concept. We can understand it by noting that if one were to take pictures of any of our lives, there would be a number of *settings* and a number of *relationships* involved.

For instance, one frame might be breakfast time, with the setting our

"Youth must see how the study will focus on a personal need."

kids, *this Bible study is important to you because we're going to focus on how Jesus can work in your life to bring healing to a place where you hurt.*

The first great mistake many Bible study leaders make is to ignore or try to shortcut this *framing* step. For enthusiastic, motivated Bible study, youth must see how the study will focus on a personal need—a need which is clearly placed in his or her own frame of reference.

Studying the Bible Inductively

By adolescence, most teens in our churches are familiar with major Bible stories and doctrines. Now they are capable of moving from the "what" of Bible content to the meaning of

"The critical issue for adolescents is, 'How does what the Bible says apply to my life?'"

home, and the relationships with our family. Teen frames include home, school, friendships, sports, work, etc.

The first few activities that Dean introduced in his Bible study were designed to establish the frame in which teens could place the Bible passage they would be studying.

The elements of that particular frame?

- typical teen
- problem area
- inside (within the person)
- any of many locations and/or relationships

The whole introductory process, from Floyd's staggering entry and the initial brainstorming, to the shift from joking to listing teens' inner problems, was planned to be fun. But it was more than fun. It was a carefully designed process meant to say to the

Scripture for their own lives.

The critical issue for adolescents is, "How does what the Bible says apply to my life?" Thus, the informal youth Bible study should be (1) *inductive*, meaning that it lets teens make their own discoveries, and (2) *"how"-focused*, meaning that it helps teens apply truth to their lives.

How does one structure such a study?

- First, establish the life "frame" which shows the need for the study.
- Second, explain what the teens are to look for in the passage to be studied.
- Third, set up a method which will help teens find the answer to the question(s) raised.

In the Bible study described earlier, Dean first explained what the students were to look for; then Alene restated that explanation: *Jesus can cure what's wrong inside us. But why do we hesitate to let Him work in our lives?*

The study guide (page 128) is the method that gives the teens a structure for their study. They are to read the passage. Then they are to study the passage for evidence as to which of the statements suggested on the guide best explains Jesus' question, "Do you want to be healed?"

Personal Sharing

The third process that is vital in informal Bible study moves toward *application* through *personal sharing.*

Several things encourage personal sharing. First is a climate in which adults model openness and honesty about their own lives ("Lots of times I've held back and not let Jesus work in my life because I was afraid" [Dean]).

Second is *gradual* encouragement to share. Note that Dean and Alene's students did not move toward personal sharing till near the end of the study, and that each student was placed with a group of other teens who indicated beforehand that they tended to respond in the same way. Thus the structure of the study helped the teens feel "like" the others with whom they were grouped before they began to share.

Freedom in personal sharing grows gradually as a trust level develops in a group of young people who come to know and care for each other. As trust grows and Bible studies encourage personal sharing, and as discovered Bible truths are applied to real life, the informal Bible study becomes a powerful motivating force for living out God's Word. And it also becomes a context in which young people can minister significantly to each other.

In a brief chapter like this one, we can't explore informal Bible study in depth. But remember these points:

- The *location* should be a home or other informal setting.
- The *time* allowed for the kind of study described here should be a minimum of 90 minutes.
- The *role* of adult leaders is to be warm, loving guides who treat teens as friends.

Also remember these three vital elements in the structure of an informal Bible study with youth:

"The role of adult leaders is to be warm, loving guides who treat teens as friends."

- There must be a *framing* step, which defines what area of teens' lives will be touched by the study.
- There must be an *inductive study* step in which teens explore God's Word to discern ways in which often-familiar passages show them *how* to live.
- There must be *personal sharing*, in which participants can share with others the meaning of the truths they've discovered. Out of such sharing, mutual encouragement to obey God can develop.

Informal Bible studies with these features can be one of the youth worker's most important tools for helping young people grow. □

See study guide on page 128.

John 5:2-9, NIV

²Now there is in Jerusalem near the Sheep Gate a pool, which in Aramaic is called Bethesda and which is surrounded by five covered colonnades. ³Here a great number of disabled people used to lie—the blind, the lame, the paralyzed. ⁵One who was there had been an invalid for thirty-eight years. ⁶When Jesus saw him lying there and learned that he had been in this condition a long time, He asked him, "Do you want to get well?" ⁷"Sir," the invalid replied, "I have no one to help me into the pool when the water is stirred. While I am trying to get in, someone else goes down ahead of me." ⁸Then Jesus said to him, "Get up! Pick up your mat and walk." ⁹At once the man was cured; he picked up his mat and walked.

"Do You Want to Get Well?"

1. Jesus probably asked this question because the man *didn't* want to get well. He'd lived off others for 38 years and it would be too hard to accept responsibility for himself.

2. Jesus probably asked this question because the man was afraid to hope. He'd probably hoped at first, but 38 years of failure makes it too painful for a person to think of changing.

3. Jesus probably asked this question because the man felt so abandoned and alone. It's hard to have hope when you feel no one is there to give you support and help.

4. Jesus probably asked this question to get the man's attention. Of course he wanted to be well; he just needed to have his attention turned to Jesus.

Sample Study Guide

Preparing Messages That Meet Needs | 36

by Bill Perkins

Young people are looking for answers. The Bible has those answers. Unfortunately, Bible truth is too often packaged and delivered in ways that don't affect teens where they really live. The acid test of any message to young people is, "Does it meet needs?" A message that meets needs is one that skillfully handles the following elements.

Bible Context

A message that meets needs must be derived from the Word of God, not read into the Word of God. Practically speaking, that means that no good communicator of divine revelation bends the Bible to support some pet illustration. Instead, he studies the Bible and, on understanding the text, finds illustrations to support its meaning. That's not as simple as it sounds. Often it's easier to lift a verse out of context than it is to study the background of the passage and teach its true meaning.

But ultimately, the question is, "Who knows how best to meet the needs of people—God or man?" God knows best, of course, and He dispenses His cures in His Word. The speaker merely administers God's prescriptions in the proper doses.

Paul wrote Timothy, "All Scripture is inspired by God and profitable for teaching, for reproof, for correction, for training in righteousness; that the man of God may be adequate, equipped for every good work" (2 Tim. 3:16-17). A message which meets the needs of youth must be a message derived from God's Word.

Introduction

A message that meets needs has a strong introduction.

Consider the introduction of a message as the bait on a hook. It should have listeners sitting on the edges of their seats, eager to hear what follows. What ingredients go into such an introduction? Every good introduction should:

1. Introduce the subject.
2. Get attention.
3. Focus on a need.

Of those three goals, perhaps focusing on a need is hardest to do. How does one expose a real need in the life of a listener? One method involves developing the introduction around one of three questions that the Bible topic might naturally raise in a listener's mind: "Do I believe it?" "Do I understand it?" "What difference does it make?" For example:

● A passage on the Resurrection will probably trigger a doubting listener to wonder, *"Do I believe it?"* So an introduction might question the credibility of the Resurrection and cause the listener to realize his need to know that the Resurrection is biblically and historically documented.

● A verse which speaks about the benefits of adversity might raise the question, *"Do I understand it?"* A good introduction, then, would motivate the listener to understand God's purposes for allowing adversity, but learn to trust God in difficult situations.

● A verse on being filled with the Spirit might cause the listener to ask, *"What difference does it make?"* The listener's need is to realize that every Christian is weak and ineffective without the Spirit of Christ controlling his life. An introduction might

Bill Perkins is pastor of Southwest Bible Church in Houston, Texas. Before coming to Southwest, Bill worked with Campus Crusade for Christ, International and Young Life. He has traveled throughout the United States as a speaker at youth conferences, camps, and evangelistic meetings. Bill is a graduate of the University of Texas and Dallas Theological Seminary.

focus on that need by illustrating the impotence and frustration of self-effort.

Following is an introduction to a message that's based on John 3:16. It combines the three purposes of an introduction—to get attention, introduce the subject, and focus on a need.

"Suicide has become the number two killer of teenagers, second only to accidents. A Gallup poll indicates that 40 percent of America's teenagers regularly use alcoholic beverages and that almost 30 percent smoke marijuana. The *Dallas Times Herald* reports that there are so many teenagers running away from home that police are unable even to keep up with all of the reports.

"Why are so many of your peers turning to drugs, or leaving home, or taking their own lives? Though I'm sure there are many reasons, I'm convinced that the single greatest reason is that they feel nobody cares. Someone once wrote, 'The supreme happiness of life is the conviction that we are loved.'

"Perhaps there is no more important question for a person to answer than the question, 'How do I know God loves me?' In the Gospel of John, we find a very clear answer: 'For God so loved the world, that He gave His only begotten Son. . . .' "

A clear understanding of a passage and the functional question which it answers can lead to a pertinent, attention-getting introduction.

Body

The body of a message that meets needs should be biblically sound and zero in on the topic.

The body of a message on John 3:16, for example, might concentrate on two points which teach how we know God loves us:

1. We know God loves us because He gave His Son.
2. We know God loves us because

He gives eternal life.

Regardless of the number of points, the body should develop the theme of the message, as presented in the introduction.

Transitions

A message that meets needs contains smooth transitions. Transitions facilitate movement. They are the hinges which allow the message to move smoothly from point to point. Good transitions accomplish objectives similar to those of good introductions:

1. They review preceding material.
2. They maintain attention.
3. They establish springboards for new information to be presented.

Not all transitions can accomplish all three objectives, but they should at least furnish an effective bridge between major points.

Illustrations— Gateways to Understanding

A message that meets needs should effectively use illustrations.

An illustration should span the gap between the abstract and the concrete, while maintaining interest.

The biggest problem most speakers have with using illustrations is finding those which best clarify the point to be made. A key guideline to remember is: Never use an illustration just because it's funny or moving. Use only those illustrations which truly clarify the point being made. Used indiscriminately, illustrations confuse, because they sidetrack the listener to a thought other than the one which the speaker wishes to communicate.

Because good illustrations, jokes, and anecdotes are so valuable, be on the lookout for them. Collect and index them for ready availability, using a 3" × 5" card file.

Though you can find excellent illustration anthologies in Christian bookstores, go beyond them. Read newspapers and magazines, and listen to newscasters—always alert for good illustrations. Use your own life experiences as a source of illustrations. And remember: Suitable illustrations become gateways, leading your audience to higher roads of understanding.

Conclusion

The conclusion of a message should package the main points in capsule form so they may be easily remembered and applied.

> *"The effective use of illustrations rests primarily on a speaker's ability to understand his audience."*

The effective use of illustrations rests primarily on a speaker's ability to understand his audience. For example, an illustration which communicates to businessmen is likely to cause high school students to tune out. To prepare messages which meet teenagers' needs, a speaker must understand the world of teens. Illustrations must be geared to the hearers.

Many speakers feel that the conclusion is the hardest portion of a message to compose. Some speakers deliver a superior introduction and body, then "tire out" and settle for an inferior conclusion. But the conclusion deserves careful thought and preparation. It can be the *coup de grace* that dramatically drives home the truth of God's Word.

Prayer

A message that meets needs should be bathed in prayer.

Prayer is essential before, during, and after the development of a message. Prayer for spiritual insight into God's Word is essential. The psalmist prayed, "Open my eyes, that I may behold wonderful things from Thy law" (Ps. 119:18).

When you first sit down to study, ask God to show you the purpose for which He intends to use the passage. Ask Him to enable you to accurately handle the Word of truth (2 Tim. 2:15). Pray that the Spirit of God will enable you to deliver the message in such a way that it pierces the hearts of your listeners. (See Heb. 4:12; Eph. 4:18.)

Internalization

Finally, a message that meets needs should be internalized.

"God's Word must first be allowed to have an impact on the messenger."

God's Word must first be allowed to have an impact on the messenger. Only then can it effectively make an impression on others.

If your life does not bear out your message, your words will have a hollow ring. If you seek to teach others, you must be taught yourself (Rom. 2:21). But if you allow God's Word to work in your own life, you will be in a position to prepare messages that meet needs and bear fruit. □

37 | Discouragement and the Youth Worker

by Alan Hlavka

Alan Hlavka worked with high school students at the Church of the Saviour, Wayne, Pennsylvania where he developed a discipleship-oriented ministry that had wide evangelistic outreach in the community. He has spent seven months touring the United States researching outstanding church ministries.

Frustration and discouragement—if you haven't experienced them yet, then you haven't been involved with youth work very long. If you have felt discouraged about your ministry to youth, it doesn't mean that you have a bad attitude or lack spirituality. We all experience times in our ministry when we wonder what has gone wrong.

Sources of Discouragement

1. *Students let you down.* You build relationships with key students, train, and equip them. Just when you feel that you are making some headway, they "drop out." They get involved with something at school that neutralizes their commitment to your ministry. Or their walk with God falls apart. Or they meet "him" or "her," and their attendance at youth group activities becomes erratic. For any number of reasons, teens you had been counting on fade out. Few things are as discouraging.

2. *The church leadership and congregation don't understand what you are trying to accomplish.* You feel deeply convicted about what you ought to be doing with your students, but those around you have some distinctly different ideas. If they are not entirely opposed to the way you do things, they definitely desire to make some alterations. Their responses can range from mild nagging to pointed opposition. Either way, such lack of respect can quench your spirit.

3. *Parents spoil your plans.* You finally have a student coming regularly and beginning to grow spiritually. Then Mom and Dad decide they must move to another city, or simply pull their teenager out of the youth ministry, or use detention from your group as punishment. Any of these actions is, of course, the parents' prerogative, but that fact doesn't help you.

4. *Your budget is deficient.* The congregation wants you to "reach those kids," but they may not be providing the finances needed to accomplish the task. You may be experiencing financial pressures in your personal life too. Inadequate funds in either area can make you feel as if your hands are tied.

In addition to the sources of discouragement just cited, practical restraints such as building facility problems, leadership shortages, time constraints, lack of resources and tools, etc. can also be frustrating.

As if all of these discouraging situations aren't bad enough, the youth worker often struggles with some devastating self-image problems—attitudes that downgrade and demoralize.

Successful Ministry= Successful Self?

Perhaps, like many of us, you have a tendency to link your self-worth and identity to your "success" in the ministry. If your ministry falters or lacks significance, it is easy to begin seriously questioning your self-worth. Conversely, if your youth group flourishes, then you feel good about yourself solely on the basis of your performance.

As a youth worker, you might not have the titles, degrees, or recognition that accompany other positions. So you wonder, "What right do I have

"Linking 'who you are' with 'how you perform' breeds insecurity and discouragement."

to think well of myself, having neither 'success' nor a 'full education?'" Linking "who you are" with "how you perform" breeds insecurity and discouragement.

Lack of Self-confidence

People don't follow you because you lack confidence, but you lack confidence because people don't follow you. It's a vicious cycle. Obviously, the initiative for leading rests with you, but the soul-searching process of finding the faith and confidence to take that initiative can be hard.

"Why don't I have the confidence that inspires the loyalty of others?" you ask yourself. And the answer is, "You are afraid that if you try to lead, you'll fall flat on your face." Fear of failure keeps you from "leading the charge." So, you don't develop the personal character that is demanded to be a person worth following.

All in all, it's not difficult to see that discouragement can be an all too common experience for a youth worker. How do you deal with it? Obviously, if you have walked with the Lord for any length of time, and have taken the Word of God seriously, you already know a number of biblical solutions to discouragement. These solutions center around one foundational truth: you need to focus on the person, character, and acts of God as opposed to your current circumstances. In addition, the following two principles can help you in the

battle against discouragement: (1) View the events of life and ministry as coming from the sovereign hand of God. (2) Become a "plodder" in the ministry, and eliminate quitting as an alternative.

1. View the events of life and ministry as coming from the sovereign hand of God. First, recognize that God runs this world, and thus is in control of your life (Prov. 21:1; Isa. 4:5-6). Since *God* designs the circumstances, people, and events surrounding your life, why are you so easily discouraged? Isn't your loving, grace-filled God the One that has set your path before you? Of course!

So instead of seeing the detours in your ministry as bad "breaks," settle down and acknowledge that your circumstances have been wisely ordained by God. Since He is the controller of all things, you are not being "burned" by your circumstances; you are being nurtured and developed by God. What a difference in perspective!

One qualification—if your ministry is suffering because of your own

"You may not be the fastest or the best, but you can keep running."

laziness, lack of preparation, lack of discipline, etc., then you *ought* to be discouraged and frustrated. Allow your condition to lead you to repentance and change. Don't attempt to pin your sinfulness on the "sovereignty of God." Repent, and let God change you.

Countless things outside of your control can cause severe discouragement. If you view them as intrusions, you are in trouble. But if you see the

circumstances of life and ministry as coming from God's hand, then you can view temporary setbacks and adversities as instruments of God's purpose.

2. Become a "plodder" in the ministry and refuse to quit. Many of us look at others in youth work and wonder why we are not equally gifted. We go to youth conventions and listen to impressive professional speakers. We drool when we see the size and substance of other ministries, or the charisma of other youth workers. And most of us are faced with the indisputable facts: We're not youth ministry "superstars."

Few youth workers can walk into a ministry, make a few decisions, and suddenly begin reaching kids right and left. For most of us, our ministry to young people is a long, and sometimes painful process.

Here's the good news: You may not be a "superstar" or the most gifted person to enter the ministry, but you can be a plodder. You can stick with it and tough it out. You may not run the fastest or the best, but you *can* keep running (Acts 20:24; 2 Tim. 4:7).

You see, only the finishers count. Jesus faced an impossibly difficult task—paying the sin debt for you and me. He faced excruciating physical pain and even worse, total separation from His heavenly Father. Christ had never been out of intimate union with His Father, but on the cross the Father turned from the Son, and the Son cried out in pain—pain that you and I will never know.

What if Jesus had quit? What if He had said, "I can't take it anymore, get Me out of here!" What would have happened then? Jesus knew He had to face the Cross with all of its pain and rejection, but He didn't quit. He completed the task.

I remember when I first started

working with high school students. Nothing seemed to work with that youth group. I shared Christ with kids and some even trusted Christ, but they rarely stuck with it. I had a Bible study, but not that many kids showed up. And so there I was, month after month, struggling away with little success, little fruit. I became so discouraged that I really didn't know if I could take it anymore.

One day I called a friend who had been working quite successfully with students for years to tell him how tough things were. He asked, "Alan, do you think that you're cut out for working with students?"

Suddenly, I knew the right answer.

"I don't know, but I'm not going to find out by quitting. I believe God is going to put this thing together. Though I'm discouraged and frustrated, I know God has put me here, and I'm not going to let the circumstances overwhelm me."

Within 12 months of that decision, my ministry blossomed. We began reaching hundreds of kids and had a far greater impact on their lives than before. What would have happened if I had quit?

You need to know that God has called you to the youth ministry. If God has called you, He will give the strength to overcome discouragement and do His will. If God has called you,

don't entertain the thought of quitting.

If you are tenacious, you will eventually find people turning to you for ministry, because people are drawn to a leader who refuses to quit—someone relentlessly convicted and holding fast. You *can* finish the race. You *can* keep going. Ask God to take any enticement to quit out of your mind. Decide that quitting is not an option.

You are serving the God of the universe. He has ordained you to do what you must. Because you are willing to trust Him, He will do tremendous things through you. □

Prayer and the Youth Worker 38

by Curtis Mitchell

Jesus Christ, in one of His last recorded discourses, assured His followers that if they would *ask*, He would *do* (John 14:13-14). Christ implied that divine action, in some mysterious manner, is conditioned on believing prayer. It's a believer's responsibility to ask. It's God's responsibility to do.

James voiced much the same truth when he said, "Ye have not, because ye ask not" (James 4:2, KJV). When the believer does not ask, God is not responsible to do, and so the believer "has not."

This two-sided division of responsibility (i.e., a believer's asking and God's doing) worked effectively in the early church. Study of the Book of Acts reveals that the believers fervently and persistently asked, and God consistently did. To be sure, God worked through humanity, but it was nevertheless His power at work. In light of the priority Scripture places on prayer, it's difficult to envision the successful functioning of a youth ministry apart from the consistent and proper practice of prayer. For you, the youth worker, principles of effective prayer

Teach Us to Pray

Instruction in how to pray is of highest important to a young disciple. This is true not only because a believer must "ask," but also because he must be careful not to ask "amiss," or in the wrong way (James 4:3). Our Lord's disciples evidently realized this fact, because in the only instance in which Scripture records their asking the Lord to teach them anything, they asked for prayer instruction (Luke 11:1). They urged, "Lord, teach us to pray." Evidently the disciples had noted that, with Jesus, prayer was a force rather than a mere form. Indeed they seemed to recognize prayer as the secret of Jesus' spiritual success.

The disciples' request prompted the longest and most significant single instruction on prayer found anywhere in God's Word (Luke 11:1-13). Perhaps no lesson is more desperately needed today among believers than this practical lesson on how to pray.

The most startling thing about Christ's lesson on prayer is what was

Dr. Curtis C. Mitchell has been a professor in the Biblical Studies and Theology Department of Biola College in La Mirada, California for the past 13 years. Before coming to Biola he was in the pastorate for 15 years. Dr. Mitchell has an extensive speaking ministry in West Coast churches and conferences. He has authored two books, Let's Live and Praying Jesus' Way. He has degrees from Biola College, Western Conservative Seminary, and Grace Seminary.

"The quality of your personal prayer life will directly influence your effectiveness in working with students."

---

must be applied in two areas:

(1) *Your* prayer life. The quality of your personal prayer life will directly influence your effectiveness in working with students.

(2) *Students'* prayer life. You must teach students how to pray so they can experience open communication with God their Father.

left out—the things the Lord didn't say about prayer. For example, He said nothing about any "correct" physical position for prayer. Nor did He give His disciples formal prayer lines to be recited in rote fashion. (Most conservative Bible scholars agree that this so-called "Lord's Prayer" was never intended to be recited in a ritualistic manner.)

The Lord said nothing about assuming a pious tone of voice when praying, or using some special "prayer vocabulary," i.e., King James English. On the contrary, Jesus always addressed the Father in the same vocabulary used in ordinary speech.

Christ began His prayer instruction with the words, "When you pray, say. . . ." At the very outset, it's evident that prayer is a precise *act* rather than a nebulous *attitude* as prayer is often construed to be today. It is an act, not performed in cold ritualism, but in intimate fellowship with the heavenly Father.

The word "Father," as uttered by Christ, implies close filial intimacy. The most startling aspect of New Testament prayer is its direct, intimate address to one's own loving Father. That's how Christ prayed and how He taught us to pray. We are to address a deeply concerned Father who is vitally interested in every aspect of our lives and who desires to give us "good things" (Matt. 7:11). Our young people need to experience this open relationship as they communicate with the Lord.

It's also evident from Christ's instruction that prayer is essentially petition. It is not primarily praise, adoration, or thanksgiving; though such activities can legitimately be included in prayer. It is *asking* the Father for things! The model prayer which Christ gave His disciples ("the Lord's Prayer") consists almost entirely of petitions.

After a brief word of address to the Father, Christ launched into six model petitions, six specific requests. In fact the whole lesson is on how to effectively ask God for things. The pious sounding notion that petitionary praying is selfish is not supported by the New Testament.

So many times in the hurried, activity-oriented youth worker's life, we *have* not because we *ask* not. We need to simply ask.

Six Model Petitions

Jesus' six model petitions fall into two obvious groups: *The first three petitions center around the outworking of God's program.* Likewise, much of our prayer effort should be in this area. This might include petitions on behalf of our local church, our pastor, missionaries, evangelistic endeavors, youth ministry, etc.

The most amazing thing about these first three petitions is that they all are petitions for things that are providential certainties: (1) God's name will be hallowed; (2) God's kingdom will most certainly come; and ultimately, (3) God's will most surely will be done on earth as well as in heaven (Luke 11:2, KJV). Why then pray for such things? Yet study of the prayers of both Paul and Christ reveals that such praying was unquestionably their practice. In following their examples, we too should pray for such matters.

The final three petitions center around a believer's own personal needs. A study of the Lord's teachings reveals that no personal need is too great or too insignificant to be brought before God in petition. This fact needs to be clearly communicated to youth. We are addressing a heavenly Father whose concern for us reaches even to the numeric quantity of our head hairs! (Matt. 10:30) Dare we think anything too trivial? We are addressing the God who upholds the universe. Dare we assume anything is beyond His power?

Yet having said this, it becomes evident—both from the model prayer and from the practices of the New Testament—that prayers were voiced for significant issues as well.

To pray for only obvious trivialities is in a sense like approaching the President of the United States with an assurance from him that any legitimate request would be granted, and then asking him for postage stamps.

Praying Spiritually

It also becomes clear that biblical praying should be essentially for spiritual issues. This is not because prayer for material needs is wrong. That such prayer is not wrong is evidenced by the fourth petition, "Give us this day our daily bread." But people's real problems are in the realm of the spiritual. The Lord knew this when He said, "Seek ye first the kingdom of God . . . and all these things shall be added unto you" (Matt. 6:33, KJV).

Today's student must understand that his spiritual relationship with God will directly affect his physical life. Five of the six petitions are for spiritual needs. Virtually all of Christ's prayers in the New Testament center on the spiritual.

Paul, when praying for believers, always prayed for their spiritual needs. For example, when praying for the saints at Colossae, the apostle voiced seven petitions (Col. 1:9-12), and all were for spiritual needs. No doubt there were financial problems in that church. No doubt there were physical needs in that church. But Paul saw their real needs as spiritual.

How different is this emphasis from much current prayer practice. If we were to closely evaluate the prayer requests at our weekly prayer meetings, we'd likely find that 75 to 95 percent are for material needs. When we pray for our church, it's for the mortgage payment. When we pray for our missionaries, it is for a new truck needed on the field. When we pray for our brothers and sisters, it's that they may be delivered from gall stones, varicose veins, or some other physical ailment. And when we pray for our youth group, it's for more students.

It isn't wrong to pray for mortgages, trucks, gall stones, varicose veins, or more kids; but such praying, on an exclusive basis, reflects an insensitivity to the real problems. As youth workers we must meet the needs of our students; and nothing runs deeper or is of more ultimate value than their spiritual relationships with the One who can supply their every physical need.

We are engaged in a titanic spiritual struggle with "principalities and powers" under subtle satanic direction (Eph. 6:12). We need to ask the Father to open our eyes. We need to be made aware of our real problems. We need spiritual knowledge and discernment. We need spiritual strength. We need to grow in love.

Praying Persistently

After instructing the disciples regarding the types of needs for which they were to petition the Father, Christ immediately gave the Parable of the Persistent Friend (Luke 11:5-8). In this parable we discover the *manner* in which petitions should be voiced: The man in the parable needed help. So desperate was his situation that the objections from the neighbor within did not stop the persistent cry for assistance. Christ taught us to voice petitions to the Father with this same urgency and persistence.

In another parable (Luke 18:1-8), the Lord pictured prayer through the analogy of a desperate widow pleading before an unjust judge. Though rebuffed repeatedly in her petition, she kept hounding the judge till, overwhelmed by the sheer weight of her persistence, the judge was persuaded to grant her request.

To be effective youth workers, we should develop a "consistent persistency" in our prayer lives. We must teach our young people this manner of prayer as well. But persistent asking must never be confused with vain repetition. Christ taught persistence but condemned vain repetition. His criticism was never against repeating petitions as such, but against *vain*

repetitions. Indeed, in the Garden of Gethsemane, Christ Himself twice repeated the same petition in almost identical language.

Vain repetitions involve the false idea that we'll gain a hearing with God by much speaking—that the very act of repeating a request is itself worthwhile.

On the other hand, persistent petition is quite different. It is prompted by the burden of the heart. It is driven by the force of an almost overpowering sense of urgency to cry out repeatedly day after day. Thus it was with the man petitioning his neighbor at midnight. Thus it was with the widow before the judge. So, Christ illustrated prayer in terms of driving, earnest, persistent petition.

Many Christians would be wise to tear up their prayer lists, take a fresh piece of paper, and write four words on it: "Lord, burden my heart!" In addition, they might write: "Lord, open my eyes to significant needs." Then let those believers keep crying out to God for a burdened heart till they can really get concerned about significant issues.

The New Testament records nothing of simply mouthing insincere and unconcerned petitions. Real prayer comes from a sense of burden which produces specific, sincere, and earnest petitions. A pray-er who is prompted by such a burdened heart persists—keeps asking, keeps knocking day after day. What greater, more desperate need can burden our hearts than the millions of lost young people across America—the millions who statistically become harder to reach for Christ every year they grow older.

To those who urgently persist, the Lord promises: "For every one that asketh receiveth; and he that seeketh findeth; and to him the knocketh it shall be opened" (Luke 11:10, KJV). To further strengthen this promise, the Lord used the analogy of a human father. Just as a good earthly father can be trusted not to give his children

stones for bread or serpents for fish (Luke 11:11-12), so our heavenly Father can be trusted (even more so) to give "good things" to those who fervently and persistently petition Him (Matt. 7:11).

Praying Submissively

How does the Father answer persistent petition. It might be construed from certain statements of Christ that any and all petitions will be granted if one is simply persistent. After all, doesn't Christ promise that everyone who asks will receive? (Luke 11:10, KJV) But the seemingly unqualified nature of this promise must not be isolated from its context.

In this case the promise is limited by the statement: "How much more shall your Father which is in heaven give good things to them that ask Him?" (Matthew 7:11, KJV) The giver is "your heavenly Father," the One who *knows what is best*. He will not respond to the fervent petition by giving harmful things, but by giving "good" things. He doesn't give just anything; He gives "good things" to those who ask Him. Typical youth group members often struggle with these seemingly conflicting promises. They must realize that God always does the "good thing."

Implied also in this concept of asking and expecting our Father to supply "good things" is the idea of petitioning with childlike submissive *trust*. When a child petitions a father, it is in complete confidence in the parent's character. This involves trust, not only in the father's ability to meet the need, but also in his love and wisdom to give only those things which are in the trusting child's best interests.

Childlike submissive faith says in effect, "Father, from my limited vantage point it looks as though I need this particular thing, and I haven't the slightest doubt as to your ability to supply it. But, Father, I also have confidence that You are all wise and loving. The final decision rests with You."

This is the same kind of faith that caused Christ to say, "Father, if it be possible, let this cup pass from Me; nevertheless, not as I will, but as Thou wilt" (Matt. 26:39, KJV).

That's always the primary condition for effective prayer. It's referred to at times as "abiding in Christ," at other times as "asking in faith"; but both are ways of saying, "Thy will be done."

Praying in His Name

Added to all of these promises are the fantastic prayer possibilities unveiled by Christ to His followers in the Upper Room shortly before His death. In that final, intimate discussion with His followers, the Lord told them that from that point on they had the privilege of petitioning the Father in His name. He made it clear that this was a privilege previously unknown to any disciple. At least six times in the Upper Room, Jesus urged His followers, "ask in My name."

To pray in His name means far more than simply adding those words as a sort of good luck charm to the end of our prayers. It means that because we are united with Christ in salvation and are positionally and vitally "in Christ," we can actually pray in His person. In spite of our personal unworthiness, we need not hesitate to ask because we are in Christ and can petition in His name.

It also means that we petition by His authority and with His power. Think of that! We can now petition the Father with all the authority of Christ! What a privilege! What an opportunity! It's like placing a draft on the bank of heaven with the check actually signed by Jesus Christ! That's what it means to pray in His name and on the basis of who He is.

Are you beginning to see the astounding possibilities of prayer? Are you beginning to fathom the direct connection between your prayer life and the success of your youth group? How about between your students' prayer lives and their growth in the Lord? Can you see why Christ spent so much time teaching His disciples the fine art of prayer?

Prayer is the divinely ordained means whereby God moves to accomplish His operations on this planet. "If you ask . . . I will do!" This is the pattern that worked in the first century church, and for 2,000 years it has never failed to function whenever God's people have dared to apply it.

Your first and foremost responsibility is to *ask* . . . fervently, submissively, and persistently. And if you ask, God will act. □

"Prayer is the divinely ordained means whereby God moves to accomplish His operations on this planet."

Trusting God for the Impossible

39

by Bill Perkins

Anyone who has ever been involved in youth work has probably spent some time dreaming about a truly dynamic youth ministry. Such a vision might involve hundreds of dedicated students turning their campuses upside down for the Lord. Such a dream ministry might include a huge youth meeting, complete with quality music and a powerful Gospel message, as well as small-group discipleship. This dream ministry might involve the training of youth workers who would have an impact on the world.

The "Impossible" Ministry

If you've ever dreamed along these lines, you've probably also discovered that reality has a way of popping such inflated hopes. Instead of directing a vibrant ministry to teens, maybe you're given the task of resuscitating the corpse of a dead youth group. Instead of turning out in droves to your meetings, the youth in your area may seem too far gone for you to even see, let alone reach. Instead of equipping legions of new youth workers, perhaps your church seems bent on tying your hands and feet and throwing you into an ocean of teenagers whom you're supposed to rescue all alone. In short, your vision of a dynamic, growing youth ministry seems an impossible dream.

The good news is, God delights in doing the impossible. The Bible is filled with accounts of believers who were told by their contemporaries, "It can't be done!" Though the sidelines were crowded with doubters, men and women stepped out in faith and saw God make their impossible dreams a reality. Moses lived to see the Promised Land. Young David saw Goliath fall. Esther saw God deliver the Hebrews from a Persian massacre. The disciples witnessed the miracle of Jesus feeding the 5,000 with only five loaves and two fish.

What qualities characterized those people who saw God accomplish the impossible? What principles can we draw from their lives to help us see our impossible dreams become realities for God's glory? One incident in the life of Peter can help answer those questions.

Daring to Dream

Matthew 14:22-23 sets the scene: Jesus was alone on a hilltop, praying. His disciples were in a boat, rowing across the Sea of Galilee. The wind swept gently over the barren hills and across the water.

Then it happened! The wind turned and rushed down the ravines to churn the lake into a tempestuous foam. The disciples strained at the oars (Mark 6:48). In the stormy darkness, the waves rose like shadowy sea monsters.

From His vantage point, Jesus saw the disciples struggling against overwhelming odds. Aware of their fatigue and discouragement, He set out toward them, walking on the water. The disciples could scarcely believe their eyes. What was that gleam in the darkness, that awesome figure with the fluttering robe? That One on the waves drew near them, and then

Bill Perkins

seemed to pass them by. Thinking they were seeing a ghost, they cried out in fear. During that moment of fear when their boat seemed so small and the sea so great, they heard a familiar voice. Jesus called out, "It is I, do not be afraid" (Mark 6:50).

Peter was in that boat. Exhausted from rowing, and discouraged by the slow progress, he too was frightened by what he saw. But in a fraction of a moment, he glimpsed a unique vision. He saw an opportunity to be a part of something so impossible that only Jesus Christ could make it a reality.

Peter cried out over the wind and waves, "Lord, if it is You, command me to come to You on the water"! (Matt. 14:28) Now you must admit that it took imagination to devise such a dream. Quickly and clearly, Christ gave the order, "Come!" (Matt. 14:29) Without a moment's hesitation, Peter leaped over the side of the vessel. Fixing his eyes on the Lord, Peter walked on the waters—while the wind tossed his hair and the waves drenched his robe.

Then his faith wavered. He glanced from the Lord to the furious black waves and began to sink. Despairingly, he cried out, "Lord, save me!" (Matt. 14:30) Instantly, Jesus stretched out His hand to His drowning disciple, and they both climbed unhurt into the boat. The wind became calm and the lake smooth. In adoration and amazement, the disciples proclaimed, "You are certainly God's Son!" (Matt. 14:33)

Ways Peter Trusted Christ

Peter trusted Christ to do the impossible through him. In the face of exhaustion, fear, and discouragement, Peter allowed Christ to make his impossible dream come true. How did he do it?

1. He recognized the presence of Christ. The loftiest hopes and the most extravagant plans are all possible in the presence of the One who makes the waters a path under His feet.

Gideon defeated a numerically superior enemy with only 300 men. Moses challenged the power of Pharaoh. David faced the strength of Goliath. How? All had a keen awareness of the Lord's presence.

The God of Gideon, Moses, and David is also with us today. The Lord Himself said, "I will never desert you, nor will I ever forsake you" (Heb. 13:5). To trust God for the impossible, we must recognize His presence even in the face of seemingly insurmountable obstacles. But there is more to it than the mere realization of the presence of Christ.

2. Peter requested the impossible of Christ. Peter ignored the potential ridicule of his peers which could have resulted from his request to walk on water. The fact that no one else had ever asked for such an experience did not quench his eagerness to step out on the waves. Peter boldly asked Jesus Christ to enable him to do something which no mortal had ever done before.

To trust God to do the impossible, we must first *ask* Him to do the impossible. Jesus told His disciples, "If you ask Me anything in My name, I will do it" (John 14:14). God's will is also involved, but the truth remains that God does the impossible for those who dare to ask.

3. Peter relied on the power of Christ. Peter knew he was unable to do the supernatural without the approval and power of the Lord. Only when Peter allowed himself to be distracted by the howling wind and turbulent waters did he begin to sink. But even when he found he was in danger of drowning, Peter acknowledged the power of Christ by calling on Him for help (Matt. 14:30).

Today, many distractions would cause you to shift your eyes from the power of Christ to your own weaknesses. Such distractions tend to magnify your past failures and disappointments, causing you to sink into a sea of unbelief. When that happens, everything about your youth ministry becomes very expected, very possible, and very mundane. What must you do to be pulled from such dangerous waters? Peter called out to the Lord and relied on His power.

The psalmist said that God stretched the heavens out like a curtain or tent (Ps. 104:2). God's mighty hand controls all of the power generated throughout the universe. So the angel could say to Mary, "For nothing will be impossible with God" (Luke 1:37).

All the problems which could hinder the development of a dynamic youth ministry are opportunities for God to demonstrate His power. In order to trust God for the impossible,

"All the problems which could hinder the development of a dynamic youth ministry are opportunities for God to demonstrate His power."

"God does the impossible for those who dare to ask."

you must fix your eyes on Him and not look at the waves that surround you. God has the power to do the miraculous if you have the courage to tap His infinite resources.

"Impossible" dreams are well within your grasp if you will

(1) recognize the presence of Christ, (2) request the impossible of Christ, and (3) rely on the power of Christ.

How to Trust God for the Impossible

Four practical steps toward trusting God for the impossible in your youth ministry are:

1. Go to a quiet place where you can be alone with God. In a spirit of prayer, ask God to fill you with the knowledge of His desires for your youth ministry. Ask him to expand your imagination so you can envision a ministry which only He could pull off. Write down what you expect that ministry to be. Be as specific as you can.

2. Write out every reason why you think such a ministry could never happen. Read Judges 6—7 and note how the presence of the Lord affected Gideon's military strategy. Next to each obstacle you anticipated, write Hebrews 13:5: "I will never desert you, nor will I ever forsake you." Contemplate how the presence of Christ can affect your ministry.

3. Recognize that God is willing and able to answer prayer. List the ingredients you feel are essential to the realization of "impossible" goals. Begin to pray daily and encourage others to pray with you. Remember John 14:14.

4. Memorize Luke 1:37: "For nothing will be impossible with God." Ask God for the faith you need to draw on His infinite power. The next time you are sinking into a state of discouragement, read Matthew 14:22-33 and rely on Christ's power to accomplish the impossible in and through you. □

OTHER YOUTH SOURCES
FROM SONPOWER

YOUNG TEEN SHORT STUDIES

COOL WHEN THE HEAT'S ON by Linda Stafford. How young teens can handle the pressures they face. 6-2444; Leader's Guide 6-2039

HOMEGROWN by Linda Stafford. Biblical principles for strengthening family relationships. 6-2442; Leader's Guide 6-2037

LIKES ME, LIKES ME NOT by Linda Stafford. A short study on friendships for junior highs. 6-2440; Leader's Guide 6-2012

SHAPING UP by Linda Stafford. Based on the life of David, this course on Christian character building challenges young teens to make godly choices. 6-2445; Leader's Guide 6-2040

WHO'S NUMBER ONE? by Linda Stafford. What is God's idea of success? A thought-provoking study for junior highs. 6-2443; Leader's Guide 6-2038

YOUR MOVE! by Linda Stafford. Based on the life of Abraham, this study helps junior highs focus on the decision-making process. 6-2441; Leader's Guide 6-2035

SONPOWER HIGH SCHOOL ELECTIVES

ANYBODY HERE KNOW RIGHT FROM WRONG? by Bill Stearns. A practical how-to book on Christian ethics. Biblical guidelines for choosing between right and wrong in any situation. 6-2724; Leader's Guide with MTMs 6-2662; Rip-Offs Student Booklet 6-2679

CAUTION: CHRISTIANS UNDER CONSTRUCTION by Bill Hybels with Jay Caress. A nuts-and-bolts look at making progress in the Christian life. Deals with universal, everyday problems. 6-2759; Leader's Guide with MTMs 6-2861; Rip-Offs Student Booklet 6-2675

DR. LUKE EXAMINES JESUS by Bill Myers. Teens can learn to live without fear, guilt, and feeling like spiritual klutzes. 6-2768; Leader's Guide with MTMs 6-2664; Rip-Offs Student Booklet 6-2682

FROM ROCK BOTTOM TO MOUNTAINTOP by Bill Stearns. Making sense out of life's ups and downs. Stearns analyzes real-life teen situations and emotions and matches them up with what the Bible says. 6-2580; Leader's Guide with MTMs 6-2667; Rip-Offs Student Booklet 6-2685

HOME SWEET BATTLEGROUND? by Pamela Heim. Trouble with parents? With God's help, teens can learn to communicate with them honestly, openly, and lovingly. 6-2586; Leader's Guide with MTMs 6-2674; Rip-Offs Student Booklet 6-2692

HOW DO I LOOK FROM UP THERE? by Lois Dodds. Takes a new and different look at what the Bible says about self-worth. Helps teens learn to love themselves God's way so they can risk loving other people. 6-2584; Leader's Guide with MTMs 6-2671; Rip-Offs Student Booklet 6-2689

IF THE WORLD FITS, YOU'RE THE WRONG SIZE by Bill Stearns. Is it possible for teens to live a committed Christian life in today's non-Christian world? Stearns shows teens how to overcome the world system through the biblical concept of discernment. 6-2588; Leader's Guide with MTMs 6-2659; Rip-Offs Student Booklet 6-2694

LIFE IN A FISHBOWL by Tom S. Coke. Have hang-ups? So did the Corinthians. This book gives teens workable guidelines for problems that bug everyday Christians. 6-2764; Leader's Guide with MTMs 6-2862; Rip-Offs Student Booklet 6-2677

LIFE: JESUS-STYLE by James Long. This study of the Sermon on the Mount sheds light on the "impossibly Christian" standards Jesus establishes for life. 6-2575; Leader's Guide with MTMs 6-2661; Rip-Offs Student Booklet 6-2680

LIGHT ON THE HEAVY by Jerry Jenkins. A not-too-heavy, not-too-light look at basic Bible doctrines for everyday Christians. 6-2769; Leader's Guide with MTMs 6-2983; Rip-Offs Student Booklet 6-2678

LIVING IN SONSHINE by James Long. The message of Hebrews take teens beyond the warm glow and into the Sonshine itself. 6-2576; Leader's Guide with MTMs 6-2666; Rip-Offs Student Booklet 6-2684

THE NEW YOU by Harold Myra. Straight answers to some of the tough questions new Christians ask. 6-2581; Leader's Guide with MTMs 6-2669; Rip-Offs Student Booklet 6-2687

NOBODY'S PERFECT by Terry Powell. The attitudes of nine non-perfect New Testament people can help teens lead a more Christlike life. 6-2577; Leader's Guide with MTMs 6-2663; Rip-Offs Student Booklet 6-2681

PREPARING FOR WORK by John William Zehring. How work can be a real ministry, not just a job. Practical advice on how to find—and prepare for—the right career. 6-2582; Leader's Guide with MTMs 6-2670; Rip-Offs Student Booklet 6-2688

REPRODUCED BY PERMISSION OF THE AUTHOR by Sammy Tippit and Jerry Jenkins. Today's teens need heroes—people they can copy. This book shows teens how they can become more like Jesus Christ, the only good model for anyone's life. 6-2579; Leader's Guide with MTMs 6-2668; Rip-Offs Student Booklet 6-2686

MORE THAN JUST YOU by Tom S. Coke. Teens learn how the Holy Spirit can make them *more* than just themselves. 6-2578; Leader's Guide with MTMs 6-2665; Rip-Offs Student Booklet 6-2683

YOU ME HE by Sammy Tippit and Jerry Jenkins. Uncompromising biblical guidelines for dating, love, and sex, in a world with no standards. 6-2766; Leader's Guide with MTMs 6-2986; Rip-Offs Student Booklet 6-2676

POWER PAKS FOR YOUTH LEADERS

ARE JUNIOR HIGHS MISSING PERSONS FROM YOUR YOUTH MINISTRY? by Mike Frans. Step-by-step help for building a ministry to the important young teen age-group. 6-2186

FROM SWAMP TO SOLID GROUND by Dave McCasland. Proven principles to help teachers of junior highs prevent and solve problems. 6-2189

THE MAGIC BUBBLE by Pat Hurley. A critical examination of young and older teens and the worldly philosophies that affect them. 6-2181

OOPS! HANDLING PEOPLE WITH CARE by Bill Ameiss. For anyone who is serious about entering into an honest Christian relationship with another person. 6-2185

PENETRATING THE MAGIC BUBBLE by Pat Hurley. A practical guide to developing a person-oriented youth ministry. 6-2183

THE PENETRATORS by Pat Hurley. How to develop into a more effective youth worker without changing your own personality or losing your identity. 6-2184

ROUGHING IT by Dave McCasland. Ten proven steps toward successful junior high camps and retreats. 6-2190

WHERE'S IT AT? by Gary Richardson. A simple-to-use on-target tool to help you evaluate and shape a youth ministry tailored to your youth. 6-2182

Buy these titles at your local Christian bookstore or order from
SP Publications, Inc., Wheaton, Illinois 60187